294

1919

A Land Fit for Heroes
Britain at Peace

Praise for Mike Hutton's previous books:

The Vice Captain
'Fascinating details of Soho from a completely different angle. It made me nostalgic to visit the watering holes of my youth... I can thoroughly recommend this book on London's naughty square mile. It's beautifully written.' (George Melly)

The Story of Soho: The Windmill Years 1932–64
'Hutton has an engaging style and the story races along.' (*Theatre Magazine*)
'This is a lively memoir, uncovering tales of villains and tarts and the birth of the sex industry... fascinating stories, well told.' (*Books Monthly*)

Life in 1940s London
'Well researched and well paced, this scrupulous account is occasionally hilarious, often touching and all the better for the author's recollections.' (Brian Sewell)
'Hutton transports you through a period of difficulty and triumph. His personal recollections bring the city to life.' (*BBC History Magazine*)

1919

A Land Fit for Heroes
Britain at Peace

Mike Hutton

AMBERLEY

Front of jacket, top: 'Gassed' *by John Singer Sargent (1918).*
Front of jacket, bottom: *A celebration by W. Heath Robinson. (Both © Mary Evans Picture Library)*
Back of jacket: 'The Greatest Mother in the World' *by A. E. Foringer. (Courtesy of Library of Congress)*

Half title page: *Ship building on the Clyde.*
Title page: *Idyllic scenes such as this masked the hardship of rural life.*

First published 2019

Amberley Publishing
The Hill, Stroud
Gloucestershire, GL5 4EP

www.amberley-books.com

Copyright © Mike Hutton, 2019

The right of Mike Hutton to be identified as the Author of this work has been asserted in accordance with the Copyrights, Designs and Patents Act 1988.

ISBN 978 1 4456 7911 2 (hardback)
ISBN 978 1 4456 7912 9 (ebook)

British Library Cataloguing in Publication Data. A catalogue record for this book is available from the British Library.

Typesetting and Origination by Amberley Publishing Printed in the UK.

CONTENTS

ACKNOWLEDGEMENTS

Recollections passed down by my parents and others of that generation created a basis for this book. My particular thanks to Bertha Russell, Jack O'Brien, Bob Foskett, Percy Walker, Elizabeth Davies, Sally Fry and Charlie Gilbert.

I would also like to thank:
Helen Anderson, at the Fine Art Society
Katie Cameron, archivist, Marks & Spencers
Archivist for the Sainsbury Archive at the Museum of London
Archivist for the John Lewis Partnership
Philip Clifford, Brooklands Museum
Bob Marriot, archivist for Weatherbys
Susan Scott, archivist for the Savoy Hotel
Sophie Grounds, Director of Communications, Browns Hotel
Staff at the Ritz Hotel
Staff at the Jewish Museum, London
Staff at the Victoria and Albert Museum Reading Room
The Arthur Lloyd Website

Additional thanks are due to Jeanne Rae for transcribing my illegible writing and for her interest in and knowledge of the period.

Photographic Acknowledgements

Contained within are illustrations from the author's own private archive. The author is grateful to the following for permission to reproduce other illustrations:

Mary Evans Picture Library
The Imperial War Museum
The Fine Art Society
Marks & Spencers plc
Sainsbury's plc
Leicestershire County Council
The John Lewis Partnership
The Savoy Hotel
Toby Savage Photography
Joan Beretta
Elizabeth Davies

Part I

AFTERMATH

I

A BLEAK BACKGROUND

She was defined by the Great War, but was this old lady self-obsessed and selfish, or a reminder of a period when undying love and romance still flourished? She certainly belonged to another age. Tall and slender, her tailored black skirt extended almost to her ankles. The crisp white blouse she wore was patterned in lace, and rose high to settle just below her jaw line. Her frizzy grey hair would have been unruly had it not been drawn back in a severe bun. Her manner was serious, her face seldom breaking into a smile. To a young teenager she appeared to come from a distant past and was somehow rather intimidating. She spoke slowly, as if giving consideration to each word. Her Yorkshire accent was refined, but more by Leeds than Lancaster Gate.

Despite her rather aloof manner my Aunt Mattie increasingly fascinated me. She wasn't a real aunt but a distant cousin of my father's, and we were her only remaining relatives. A retired librarian, she spent much of her time with us reading. She made it clear she didn't think much of 1960s Britain, and certainly not my taste for rock'n'roll. She even censored Fats Waller's *The Sheik of*

Araby, declaring the lyrics obscene. I was beginning to resent her intrusions into my life, but I sensed an air of mystery. One day I innocently asked Mattie why she had never married. Her response was unexpected. For what seemed an age she stared at me, not answering, although I noticed tears welling up. Without a word she stood and went to her bedroom, leaving me confused and embarrassed. Some days later, without prompting, she suddenly said 'I was in love once.' She paused and then, with greater emphasis, 'I suppose I still am.' Now she was in full flow, but speaking as if alone, denying my presence. It transpired she had been engaged to her childhood sweetheart, Ronald, a schoolteacher. Plans had been made for them to marry on his next leave, but fate intervened and, tragically, he was killed on the Somme in 1916. Not unattractive as a young woman, she deflected the interest of a number of suitors, including some of her fiancé's best friends, but she remained faithful to Ronald's memory. In her mind death had in no way ended their engagement. By today's standards this reaction might seem odd, even ghoulish. For a time I thought how noble and romantic she was.

A few months after this last visit we learned that Mattie had died. Following the funeral I went with my parents to clear her flat, which was part of a rambling, ugly Victorian house in Headingley. I found it rather unnerving, going into the home of someone who had only recently died. It seemed like an intrusion, as if I'd entered uninvited. The flat mirrored Mattie herself: neat and tidy, yet in something of a time warp. No television or modern appliances. An ancient carpet sweeper rather than a Hoover. Kitchen equipment more suited to a museum than a modern home, and a tattered copy of Mrs. Beeton's *Book of Household Management*. The sitting room had an old settee with a faded loose cover and a couple of button-backed chairs set alongside a small, gate-legged dining table, on which was an unopened copy of *The Guardian*. Her modest collection of clothes spilled out from an open wardrobe in her bedroom. The air was musty with the cloying smell of mothballs. On her bedside table were two sepia photographs of young men in army uniform. Was Ronald the good-looking one? He stares straight at the camera, buttons shining, swagger stick under his left arm. Or was her sweetheart the other man with a stronger, less sensitive face and the wary look of someone uncomfortable in the glare of the camera? There was no indication on the back of the photos as to who either of the men was. Mattie's only brother had also been killed in the war, though it was impossible to discern any family likeness in either man.

There were other family photograph albums featuring unknown friends and relatives, pictured under grand porticos and in more modest parlours: babies and children, bewhiskered old men and Victorian ladies – but no sign of a potential Ronald. Then, tucked away in a beautifully illustrated book on *The English Year*, my mother found a sepia photograph. It showed a handsome young man with wavy hair, dressed in a smart suit. Was he the same man holding the swagger stick? Doubts began to form. The photo had been taken by a studio in London's Holloway Road. Lying next to the photograph was a pressed flower, probably sent from the front, still delicately nestled in tissue paper. At the bottom of the photograph someone had written, in the smallest handwriting 'With love from Gus.' Who was Gus? Was it a nickname for Ronald or some other admirer? Was my romantic vision of a woman faithful to her fiancé forever to be ruined? Which of the three men was her suitor? Or perhaps there were two? Maybe he was one of her fiancé's friends, showing his concern. We shall never know. Whatever the truth, Mattie was still a victim of the war, along with thousands of other families whose albums feature unknown faces, staring out from across the years, relics of a bygone age.

Our fascination with the Great War endures. Schoolchildren are taken to visit graves in France and Belgium. Endless rows of white gravestones record the death of a generation: from the vastness of Tyne Cot, to tiny cemeteries tucked amidst cornfields in rolling countryside, all immaculately kept by the War Graves Commission. The horror and sacrifice of those killed and maimed a hundred years ago was kept alive for my generation by our parents. They had witnessed the devastation and ongoing effects of the conflict. It gripped them and refused to let go. This was crystallised for me in an act that still has me cringing in shame. As an unthinking and rowdy form of 12-year olds, we mocked and laughed at our French language teacher as he started coughing uncontrollably. He was a small, meek little man who always had trouble controlling his students. We nicknamed him 'Mouse'. His normally pallid skin turned puce. A class, which only moments before had been imitating his frantic arm movements, fell silent as the attack overwhelmed him. Frightening yellow mucus flooded from his nose. Bent forward, it gushed from his mouth, splattering onto the exercise books piled in front of him. Realising something was dreadfully wrong I ran forward with another boy. He fought us off with an almost demonic strength. Wide-eyed and demented with rage, he vented a volley of abuse. I remember my blazer being flecked with his phlegm. As he staggered to the doors he shouted "Gas, you morons, bloody mustard gas." We never saw him again. No explanation was given and, strangely, we were never punished for our appalling behaviour. The guilt of that day still clings to me like glue. Whilst the Allies were the victors in the Great War, it was achieved at a huge cost. Vast swathes of British youth from all social backgrounds were lost. Death did not discriminate by class. The sons of aristocrats and the landed gentry were not spared. Junior officers were the most vulnerable in battle. Thousands of potential leaders were lost, along with skilled tradesmen, teachers and office workers. Farm workers, directors, ship-builders, all were culled, together with huge numbers who were never able to fulfil their potential. At the outbreak of hostilities thousands of young men volunteered. In those early days it all seemed like a huge adventure, an opportunity to leave a humdrum life behind. Across the country Pals Units from the local area were formed. Friends, workmates, members of sports clubs all flocked to join up. Percy Walker was only 17 when he enlisted with the Bradford Pals in August 1914. It was probably Percy's full Christian name that led to him being co-opted into the Royal Horse Artillery rather than the West Yorkshire Regiment. Perhaps it was a recruiting officer with a love of racing who came across the young recruit rejoicing in the name of Persimmon Walker. How many parents name their first son after a horse, no matter how famous? Percy's dad was a bookie and presumably, as his son was born in the same year, he thought naming the boy after the first Royal Derby winner was a grand idea. In his mind 1896 provided a great double, and one he didn't have to pay out on either! He was convinced that, with such a name, his son was destined for a life of wealth and good fortune. The wealth was never achieved but there was good fortune aplenty as Percy survived after serving for four years at the front – and this despite his having had no dealings whatsoever with horses before joining up.

The Royal Horse Artillery was the senior arm of the Royal Artillery. They manned mobile guns, giving cover to the cavalry and infantry. A battery contained six 13-pounder field guns, and consisted of around 200 gunners and NCOs, serving under the command of five officers. Over 200 horses supplied mobility for the units. The British countryside had been stripped of most of its horsepower: hunters, hacks and thoroughbreds were all recruited. Even after the abortive cavalry charge at Mons in August 1914 horses continued to be used extensively. They supported the soldiers, pulling the field guns through the mud and fields rutted with frost. They were more reliable than motor transport in getting supplies to the front. Despite the setting up of many Veterinary Centres their losses were awful, with an estimated two million horses perishing across both sides of the conflict.

Although living well into his nineties, it was only in his final years that Percy began to talk of his wartime experiences. This, it seems, was common amongst those who survived the horrors of the war. Percy had a charmed life, living through the Battle of the Somme, Passchendaele and Vimy Ridge. Despite being gassed and with increasing deafness, he was still standing come Armistice Day. On July 1 each year he would appear at breakfast wearing his best suit and medals, in memory of the first day of the Battle of the Somme in 1916 and the friends and comrades he lost during the war. On November 11 he would walk proudly, medals jangling, to his local Remembrance Day service. Here was a man typical of thousands, who gave up so much for his country and returned to the prospect of unemployment and little thanks: a promising education interrupted and a future blighted by his four years of service. Some returning home were completely shattered by the effects of shell shock and most continued to be haunted by their experiences. At least the war had given those serving the opportunity to meet and mix with people outside their normal social background. For some this led to a greater shared understanding, whilst others had long-held prejudices confirmed. Even in the heat of battle the British class divide was upheld.

In the spring of 1918 there still appeared to be no end in sight. Neither side seemed capable of a decisive breakthrough. The daily list of deaths and casualties was numbing, each bringing devastation with the delivery of an impersonal telegram. It was the Germans who finally launched what they believed would be the most telling offensive of the conflict. This was to be the final surge to bring them victory. Lined up against each other, the two sides were like two exhausted heavyweight boxers. General Erich Ludendorff sought a final knockout punch so, on March 21, more than 1 million shells were directed at the British Fifth Army. By the end of that day,\ more than 20,000 British troops had been captured by storm troops who broke through their lines. The Germans were jubilant, even declaring March 24 to be a national holiday. Surely this was the vital final blow?

Despite winning back control of Passchendaele and launching long-range rocket attacks on Paris, they were wrong, but their confidence was understandable. With Passchendaele won at such a cost to the Allies in 1916, they assumed British morale would falter. There was panic in Paris as it was pounded by 'Big Berthas', huge cannons with a 75-mile range, manufactured by Krupp. This underlined the march of technology in modern warfare. Combat was now totally impersonal and lethal. Although the German gains in territory were significant, it was at great cost in casualties and equipment and the advance proved impossible to sustain. With the arrival of additional

American troops the balance of power shifted. On July 15 Ludendorff played his last card and ordered a massive offensive, but a counter attack by the French found the Germans cut off and exposed. August 8 turned out to be one of the blackest days in German military history. With the enemy demoralised and exhausted, the Allies mustered over 100 tanks to rip into the German lines. As they retreated it became obvious that they were a spent force. They were demotivated. Huge numbers of their comrades had been killed since March. To go on was madness. Still in two minds, Ludendorff suggested an armistice. The Kaiser was furious and dismissed his Quartermaster General of the German army. Troops were refusing to take orders and there was a mutiny by naval crews in Kiev. Despite calls from the High Command to 'Fight to the finish' the end was in sight. The Allies refused to negotiate. Humiliated, the Kaiser slunk away, driven to the Dutch border, never to return to his homeland.

Allied troops at the front could not believe that the carnage was over. Just one week earlier the poet, Wilfred Owen, had been killed by a sniper. His poems *Anthem for Doomed Youth* and *Futility* (published posthumously) captured the feelings, now widely acknowledged, of those who fought, but these were not reflected by British High Command. The orders issued to the troops signalling the end of the conflict lacked any understanding of those who had given so much. No sentiment, no rejoicing, just the good old British stiff upper lip: 'Hostilities cease 1100 hours, November 11. Defensive precautions will be maintained. There will be no intercourse, of any description, with the enemy.' Earlier in the day, in a train parked in a siding in the forest of Compiègne about 40 miles north of Paris, and in a carriage used regularly by the French military commander,

Ferdinand Foch, the stipulations of surrender were set out. The punitive terms designed to humiliate the Germans were to sow the seeds for the emergence of the Nazis, ultimately leading to World War II. They included the surrender of all German military hardware and equipment and the removal of all troops from foreign territory, together with the surrender of their fleet, submarines and aircraft and the release of all allied prisoners of war. Additionally, Germany had to accept the blame for the war and pay huge sums in reparations for the damage caused.

As the guns fell silent there was little celebration at the front. Across Britain the reaction was also muted. In the small town of Market Harborough the local paper reported that the end of hostilities was greeted with 'sober self-restraint'. People were worn down by years of worry and shortages. Not so in London. Crowds poured onto the streets, deserting their shops and offices. Patriotic songs were sung and complete strangers embraced and danced. The older generation was scandalised by some of the wanton behaviour. Bells rang out and bunting appeared as if by magic. Flags were waved from open-top buses. The King and Queen Mary took to the balcony of Buckingham Palace. Never at ease under the gaze of the public, the King bowed stiffly in acknowledgement of the huge crowds stretching down the Mall. Parties were hastily arranged at London's swankiest hotels. Champagne corks popped at the Ritz. The wealthy and well connected let their hair down. Paper hats were worn askew and the tables and floor were littered with discarded crackers, whilst the tail-coated waiters looked on impassively. At the Savoy all inhibitions were lost as 2,700 glasses were smashed in a night of wild excess, led by a group of Australian soldiers. As the evening wore on they stripped off the tablecloths, fixed them to chandeliers and swung from them like trapeze artists. At Claridge's, however, decorum was maintained. Here there was a nod to Edwardian opulence and grandeur, rather than to the vulgar trend for novelty and excitement.

Duff Cooper, soon to be a diplomat and leading politician, recorded in his diary whilst awaiting his demob, 'We had a motor meet us at Liverpool Street. All London was in uproar – singing, cheering, and waving flags. In spite of real delight I couldn't resist a feeling of profound melancholy, looking at the crowds of silly cheering people and thinking of the dead.' He had served with honour, winning the Distinguished Service Order in 1918. No matter, he was a terrible snob. He was far from being alone. Later that day former Prime Minister, H. H. Asquith, was driven to the House of Commons, where he was greeted with cheers. A man of high intellect and many political achievements, he was ill suited to being a wartime leader, resulting in his resignation in 1916. Much of his time and attention during the early years of the conflict had been given over to his infatuation with his daughter's best friend, Venetia Stanley. He wrote to her daily when they were apart, often revealing the discussions of the cabinet, and even military secrets. Although still leader of the Liberal party he now had to listen to his successor, David Lloyd George, as he laid out the terms of the armistice before the house. Lunching at Buckingham Palace later that day, it was obvious the King still admired Asquith. He told Margot Asquith, 'No man ever had a better or wiser friend than I had or have in your husband.' Lloyd George was the polar opposite to his predecessor: Asquith, mannered and cerebral, Lloyd George, instinctive and garrulous. Yet a contemporary politician, meeting him for the first time, suggested, 'There is something very remarkable about him.

He creates the impression of a great man, and he does it without seeming theatrical and without seeming insincere.'

Once the armistice had been signed Lloyd George wasted little time in calling a general election. Parliament was dissolved on November 14 and the election scheduled for a month later, on December 14. The result was to be declared on December 28, to allow time for the votes of the troops serving abroad to be counted. Lloyd George's coalition was supported by most of his Liberal colleagues and the Conservatives. Former Prime Minister Asquith led the opposition. A number of important factors affected the outcome. With the split in the Liberal Party, chosen candidates who supported the Prime Minister and the Leader of the Conservatives were issued with a coalition coupon, indicating that the government endorsed their candidacy. The result was a landslide victory for the coalition, and even Asquith was defeated in his East Fife constituency. The Conservatives were the real winners in the election, although they continued to serve under Lloyd George, who many thought of as an Independent. The Labour Party increased its share of the vote, particularly in Wales, which had previously been a liberal stronghold. This was not reflected in the number of seats won. Real problems loomed for the government in Ireland as Sinn Fein made considerable gains but refused to take their seats in parliament.

Two factors had a significant influence on the outcome of the election. It was the first time that virtually all men over the age of 21 (and those over 19 who had seen active service) were entitled to vote. Also, importantly, women over 30 were entitled to vote provided they met a property qualification. These changes led to an increase in the electorate to 21 million. Although around 8 million women met the voting criteria this still only represented around 40 per cent of the female population of Great Britain. The Conservatives and Unionists had been worried that the increase in voting rights would lead to a dangerous shift towards socialism, but the age and property requirements for women worked in the coalition's favour. During the campaign women had been the most vocal in demanding that Germany should be made to pay the full costs of the war. There was widespread support for the demand for revenge, though Lloyd George was concerned that pressing Germany too hard would have long-term repercussions. He was right. The harshness of the peace terms led to huge resentment in Germany, and eventually to the rise of Adolf Hitler.

Before the outcome of the election was known, Britain celebrated its first peacetime Christmas in five years. Generally, it seems to have been a gloomy, rather introspective affair. Churches were packed but the colour black dominated, as grieving parents, wives and sweethearts, dressed in mourning, tried to come to terms with the savage effects of the war. Alongside them stood pale-faced young men, some with missing limbs or unsightly facial wounds, injuries that continued to serve as a reminder to the rest of the population of the lasting consequences of war. Thirty per cent of young boys and men aged between 13 and 34 in 1914 had been killed, with a further two million wounded in action. It is estimated that the worldwide death toll was in the region of 9 to 15 million.

With hundreds of thousands of servicemen due to be demobbed, unemployment and lack of housing took centre stage. Lloyd George was particularly good at creating memorable slogans. Unfortunately, his catchy promise to build 'Homes fit for heroes' was to haunt him as in the short-term it proved impossible to fulfil. Wealthy landowners were welcomed back to their ancestral homes or London mansions, the worthy middle-class to their comfortable villas. But what awaited the ordinary working man? Modest cottages or crowded slum dwellings for those who had a home, but for many their reward for serving their country was meagre or non-existent, and this was destined to cause trouble in the months ahead.

2

SOME HOMECOMING!

Having survived the misery of the trenches, expectations on returning home were heightened. Back to wives, sweethearts and family. Suddenly even a modest and humdrum life had huge appeal. However, the realities of homecoming often ended in misunderstanding and resentment, with the initial joy dashed or slowly eroded. The vast majority of returning men had changed. Separation and the horrors encountered left their mark and, with most unwilling or unable to talk about their experiences, a barrier formed. Those at home couldn't appreciate the long-term effects of seeing so many friends killed or maimed. Some young lovers, who had married in haste at the outbreak of war or on a precious leave from the front, now doubted their youthful rashness. Others happily worked through their problems, but rumours or admissions of infidelity soured marriages and divorce was not an option for any but the wealthiest. Children often resented the grumpy, strange man who arrived in their home. Wives found their menfolk changed, distant and irritable, seemingly in a different world. Some reported that their husbands suffered frightening nightmares.

Those offered an early release into civvy street were the lucky ones. It was a massive logistical problem to arrange the demobilisation of over 3 million servicemen. An early plan proposed by Winston Churchill soon ran into trouble. As Minister of State for War his idea was to arrange the release of 'key workers' in industry. As these were often amongst the last recruited many resented this and thought it totally unfair. Trouble erupted in Southampton. About 500 troops were told they were to be returned to France, having previously been advised that they were in Southampton for their demob. Emotions ran high and the troops refused to obey orders. This was mutiny. For a time there was absolute chaos. General Sir Hugh Trenchard attempted to address the men but was heckled and manhandled. He sent for more than 200 crack troops, including military police. They surrounded the mutineers, threatening punitive force unless they surrendered. Most did but the ringleaders had to be subdued by water cannons.

This was a foretaste of problems to come. In January there was a mass mutiny in Folkestone. In protest at a plan to send them back to France, 10,000 men ignored orders and refused to attend reveille. They were also protesting about the additional privileges awarded to officers and the dreadful food they were being served. This was serious. A soldiers' union was proposed and senior officers were unable to stop a march through the town by the troops, where generally they were given a sympathetic reception. Soon there were uprisings in southern Britain and crowded lorries were driven up to London with troops shouting, 'We won the war, give us our tickets.' Trouble spread to Kempton Park, Felixstowe and Aldershot. Events were in danger of getting out of hand. The authorities were genuinely worried that general discontent would spread, leading to outright revolution. Churchill's initial plan was revised, with those having served the longest getting the earliest discharge. Food and overall conditions for the troops were also improved, which, for a time, had a calming effect.

By March militant Canadian troops were causing trouble, underlining the sense of bloody-mindedness sweeping the country. Kinmel Park Camp in North Wales was a holding facility for 15,000 men waiting to be transported home. The conditions in the camp were dreadful. Barracks designed to take fewer than thirty men were housing over fifty. This was bound to cause tension. Worse, their departure was being delayed by a supposed lack of fuel, caused by a series of strikes blighting the country that had also led to a severe shortage of food. Months of waiting and reduced rations provided the spark needed for a major uprising. As trouble spread through the camp about 20 of the ringleaders were locked in the guardroom. Hot-headed friends of those detained charged the wooden building and the prisoners were released. By now a full-scale mutiny was underway. Rifles were seized and shots fired. By the time the authorities won back control five men lay dead and about thirty were injured. Some had been shot, others bayoneted. Whilst endless parades and drilling added to resentment, the news that the Americans had been given preference in shipping their troops home enraged the waiting Canadians. Eventually, around fifty mutineers were court-martialled. During the hearing the court was told that canteens and the YMCA had been raided, with booze and cigarettes amongst the items stolen. Roughly half of those charged were found guilty, with sentences ranging from 3 months to 10 years. Their offences were judged to be of mutiny rather than murder.

By June the Canadians were at it again, understandably, as those stationed in Epsom were still waiting to go home seven months after the end of hostilities. This time the trouble was sparked by a Derby Day punch-up in The Rifleman pub in Epsom. Two Canadians were arrested and detained in the local police station. On 17 June about twenty of their mates, stationed at Westcote Camp on Epsom Downs, went to the police station, demanding that the prisoners be released. On being refused, they returned to camp and recruited several hundred supporters. Frustrated, and generally fed up with life, they rampaged through the town, eventually attacking the police station. The police defended themselves with their wooden truncheons but the fighting was vicious, and a dozen policemen were injured. A middle-aged constable died later in hospital. High command was worried that publicity would further inflame troops still awaiting demobilisation. Given that the crimes were so serious it seems strange that the prosecution presented such a weak case. The accused were found guilty of rioting but not guilty of manslaughter and only received a lenient one-year jail sentence. There was a sense that matters relating to mutinies and rioting by servicemen were being swept under the carpet.

Civil violence was adding to general alarm that the situation could escalate out of control. The mood throughout the country was surly and truculent. Suspicion of all foreigners was a common denominator throughout society and in January Britain's colour prejudice surfaced. Despite black and Chinese seamen having served throughout the war, they became the target for outright discrimination in Glasgow. Increased competition for jobs led to white workers attacking their former shipmates. Backed by the union, they extended their attacks to lodging houses and cafes used by the colonial sailors. Unemployment and the lack of housing led to further civil unrest. By the end of January Glasgow was in turmoil. Strikes broke out across the city, with huge crowds gathering in George Square. What prompted a genuine riot is uncertain. It was possibly an over-enthusiastic baton charge by the police as they attempted to control the crowds who had commandeered the trams that were trying to cross the square. Bottles and rocks were hurled at the policemen and iron railings uprooted. Many were injured as the violence continued, the police unable to restore order. It was feared that this was a full-scale Bolshevik uprising. The government opted for extreme measures, deploying 10,000 (mainly English) troops with machine guns and backed up by tanks. Troops were posted on rooftops in an attempt to identify the ringleaders, who included the future Labour minister, Manny Shinwell. It was only after the Riot Act was read out that the disturbances started to decline. Despite the leaders (including Shinwell) being jailed, concessions were won in the form of reduced working hours. Strikes and unrest also rocked Belfast and Liverpool, but the shock of seeing tanks on the streets of Britain, together with the agreed reduced working hours, restored an outward sense of calm.

A simmering sense of discontent still bubbled away beneath the surface and in June the police went on strike. Prime Minister Lloyd George talked of 'an anarchist conspiracy'. There had been a police strike earlier in 1918, prompting suffragette Sylvia Pankhurst to comment 'The London police on strike. After that, anything can happen.' That thought worried the government. The police had genuine grievances. The cost of living had doubled since the outbreak of war and a policeman's wages were only the same as an unskilled farm labourer whilst, with so many colleagues serving abroad with the armed forces, their workload had increased. They were working longer hours and rarely received overtime payments. Despite their genuine case, the strike of 1919 descended into farce. Only 1200 men out of a total of 7,000 obeyed the strike call. Retribution was swift and brutal. All the strikers were instantly dismissed. However, their action led to the formation of the Police Federation, designed to protect police interests and address any further grievances. In return it became illegal for police or prison officers to strike or belong to a trade union. The Liverpool police also came out on strike, with a far greater level of support. For four days Liverpool was a lawless city. The *Liverpool Daily Post* reported 'an orgy of looting and rioting'. Troops opened fire in an attempt to restore order. One man was killed and hundreds arrested. Once again the strikers were dismissed, losing their pension rights. Justice at all levels in Britain remained harsh.

Nonetheless, the country had received a severe jolt to its confidence. It had flirted with complete social breakdown but eventually stepped back from the brink. It was not just the government feeling uneasy. Was this really the world envisaged so soon after victory? Perhaps expectations of a better life had been unrealistic. The twin problems of unemployment and lack of housing were obvious, even to the casual observer. Despite a temporary mini boom it was difficult for industry to assimilate the 10,000 men now being discharged each day. Many of their old jobs had been filled, and soon crowds of the unemployed were to be seen huddled in despondent groups on street corners. Some were reduced to selling matches whilst those able to play a musical instrument formed street bands. Wandering along the gutters of our leading cities, busking for coppers, with service medals pinned to their demob suits, their presence jarred. It was embarrassing for them to have sunk so low and many looked away. Lloyd George boasted of the government's intention to build 500,000 homes for the returning troops but it was a promise that proved impossible to keep. Only 50,000 houses had been built since 1915. The war left the country short of builders, and there were few apprentices to fill the gap. Raw materials were in short supply and expensive, due in part to the falling value of the pound. In 1919 the Housing and Town Planning Bill was ratified to address the problem. Subsidies were set up to enable costs to be shared between tenants and local authorities, an early example of affordable housing. Although initially slow to take off, over the next few years council estates began appearing on the outskirts of towns and cities. Bathrooms and indoor toilets were a revelation to people born in slums. Despite all the good intentions the housing shortage remained a major source of discontent. The problems facing the country appeared never-ending. These were underscored by a natural disaster that, worldwide, brought death on an even greater scale than the Great War, prompting fears that the country was cursed.

'Spanish Flu' first arrived in Britain in the spring of 1916. It was believed to have originated in Spain, but the American Midwest and China were subsequently thought to have been the source. Starting with chickens, the virus apparently mutated to pigs before transferring to humans, and the rat-infested trenches proved an ideal breeding ground. Newspapers were discouraged from reporting the extent of the illness for fear of causing public alarm. The virus was spread across Britain by troops returning from the front as, crushed into crowded trains, they travelled to the major cities, the suburbs and the countryside. The young were the most vulnerable, and what initially appeared to be mild symptoms often accelerated alarmingly. Famously, it was recorded that someone who was feeling perfectly healthy at breakfast could be dead by teatime. Aching limbs and a high temperature were quickly accompanied by mild headaches and sore throats. Coughing led to breathing problems and damage to the lungs. Some had dark spots appearing on their faces whilst others turned blue as they suffocated due to lack of oxygen. The outbreak in Britain reached its peak in 1919. Worldwide, the effects of the pandemic were devastating. It is calculated that in excess of 50 million died whilst about 20 per cent of Britons were affected, with a death toll of 228,000. All sorts of weird remedies were touted. Most revolved around alcohol; a nip of whisky or perhaps a glass of port were thought to do the trick. Hundreds of quack cures were advertised and coffins, stockpiled for the war dead, had to be utilised. Carpenters worked flat out to meet the demand. There were heartrending cases of men who had survived the ravages of battle falling to the virus. War weariness was added to the list of reasons given for the cruel cull. Lloyd George fell victim but survived, as did Clementine Churchill, although her personal maid was not so lucky. The barman at The Savoy came up with a cocktail, insensitively called the 'Corpse Reviver'.

In addition to the riots, strikes and illness stalking the country, problems in Ireland returned. With the outbreak of war it had been agreed to suspend the introduction of Home Rule. Thousands of Irish volunteered to join the British Army and served with honour. The initial reaction to the Easter Rising in 1916 had been muted. Many Irish viewed the rebels as hot-headed troublemakers. This changed with the heavy-handed response of the British to the rebel leaders and the execution of 15 men changed the mood in the country. By 1919 the call for an independent Ireland had grown. Britain's relations with Ireland and the Irish had always been complex, driven in part by religious differences but also by the British sense of superiority, a characteristic that infuriated many other nations. Prior to the war Britain had been the greatest world power and, with imperial red dominating the world atlas, this feeling of superiority was shared across all the social classes. The Irish were not alone in their sense of resentment. Over the centuries the Irish population had been stripped of much of their own land. The deaths and starvation caused by the potato famine and the callous disregard of the landowners were still raw in the memory of the elderly. Stories were handed down of mass emigration, caused by people being treated like third-class citizens in their own country.

Many of the great estates, with their grand Georgian mansions, belonged to the largely Protestant Anglo-Irish. Some of these landowners could trace their roots back to Norman times. The Ulster Protestants were descendants of Lowland Scots, who were allowed to occupy land confiscated from the Catholics in the 17th century. They were generally hard-working and successful. They became known as Unionists, with a fierce loyalty to a united Britain. They dominated the local economy and viewed the Irish Catholics with a certain contempt. Whilst it is impossible to attribute characteristics to a whole ethnic or religious group, in Ireland differences were often noticeable. The native Irish were sometimes accused of 'kissing the Blarney Stone' or having 'the gift of the gab.' This equated to being insincere and unreliable. This perceived lucidity was perhaps a consequence of being denied a formal education over centuries. Often unable to read or write, they learned to paint visual pictures in their conversation. This was frustrating to a plain-speaking Ulsterman and distrust found a fertile breeding ground.

In the 1918 general election the Irish Nationalists, led by John Redmond, won just six seats. Sinn Fein seized the nationalist baton, winning a sizeable 73 seats (although they refused to take them up at Westminster). In an attempt to find a solution to this increasingly difficult and dangerous situation, the government proposed a new Home Rule Bill that set out a plan for Ireland to rule itself within the confines of the empire. The south and the six counties of the north were each to have their own parliament – one in Dublin and one in Belfast – and MPs representing them in Westminster. The north accepted these terms but not the south. In defiance of the British government, in 1919 they established their own parliament (The Dáil) in Dublin and declared independence. This was to lead to civil war, and troubles that still rumble on 100 years later.

The first skirmish that marked the start of the Anglo-Irish war took place in the Tipperary Village of Soloheadbeg. As Christmas 1918 approached, members of the Third Tipperary Brigade of Irish volunteers received reports that a large consignment of gelignite was going to be delivered to the local quarry. Led by Séamus Robinson (who had recently been involved with the 1916 uprising), together with Sean Treacy, Dan Breen and other members of the Tipperary Brigade, it was decided to capture the explosives. Acting on their own initiative, and without clearance from HQ in Dublin, they formulated their plan. A look-out in Tipperary alerted them when the cart loaded with explosives was heading their way. The horse was led by a couple of workmen, and two policemen with rifles slung over their shoulders followed. The plan was to stop the cart as it passed the gates of the field where they lay in wait, order the policemen to surrender their weapons, seize the cart and make off with it. When challenged, and alarmed at the sight of masked men, the policemen ducked behind the cart reaching for their weapons. Sean Treacy opened fire with his Mauser automatic rifle, whilst

Robinson and Breen fired their revolvers. It was all over in a matter of seconds. The two policemen lay dead on the road, though the workmen were unharmed. There was general shock and outrage at the killings. Even the nationalist newspaper described it as deplorable. *The Times* in London devoted two columns to the ambush.

A security clampdown was introduced, and the authorities banned all markets and regional fairs. Police cars tore around the country roads looking for clues, whilst an aircraft was used for the first time in the manhunt. Huge rewards were offered for information, but none was forthcoming. The event was of particular importance as the ambush had not been sanctioned by volunteer headquarters. Following a meeting between Robinson and Michael Collins, Sinn Fein reluctantly agreed to accept that the Irish War of Independence had begun.

In the 1921 general election Robinson was elected to Dáil Eireann, the revolutionary Dáil, as a Sinn Féin TD.

In April 1919 the British over-reacted savagely to another civil disturbance. Owing to relatively minor unrest in the Amritsar area of the Punjab, Brigadier General Ronald Dyer declared martial law, banning all public meetings and gatherings. April 13 was the date for the Sikh Baisakhi Festival and, seemingly unaware there was a ban in place, tens of thousands gathered to celebrate. A huge section of the crowd funnelled into a walled enclosure known as the Jallianwala Bagh, situated close to the Golden Temple. Infuriated, Dyer led a force of Indian and Gurkha troops to confront the crowd. Without prior warning he gave the order to fire and continued until all ammunition was exhausted, leaving 379 officially dead whilst over 1000 were left lying injured and untended. Dyer followed up the shootings with a series of floggings. Others caught were forced to submit to a number of appalling and demeaning acts, including crawling on their hands and knees along the street where the initial disturbance had started.

Despite support from Sir Michael O'Dwyer, the governor of the Punjab, Dyer was called back to Britain to face an enquiry. He said his decision to open fire was taken for 'The moral effect on the people of the region'. This attitude even rankled with high command. He was censured and forced to resign from the Indian Army. Although it was to be a further 30 years until India obtained its independence, like the executions in Dublin, Amritsar resulted in a distrust of the British and weakened existing bonds. There was a footnote to that tragic April day. Twenty-one years later the former Punjab governor, Sir Michael O'Dwyer, was shot dead in Caxton Hall in London. His killer was Udham Singh, who had been injured in Amritsar that day. Whilst revenge is best served cold, it also cost the assassin his life. Singh was hanged in Pentonville Jail in July 1940.

Despite other great empires falling, by the end of the war Britain had further extended its imperial possessions. These were to prove increasingly difficult to control. The country was constrained by debt and its resources severely stretched. The year 1919 was to witness the first signs of decline from a pinnacle of imperial power. Overseeing Britain's increasing problems was the controversial and unconventional Prime Minister, David Lloyd George. A lifelong womaniser, he managed to have his wife and mistress live with him at 10 Downing Street. Admittedly his mistress, Frances Stevenson, was also his secretary, but the arrangement caused much gossip and not a few ribald jokes. A larger-than-life character, controversy was a constant companion throughout his career; perhaps the greatest of which was the 'cash for honours' crisis. He described the House of Lords as '500 men, chosen at random from the ranks of the unemployed' and had long been irritated by their ability to frustrate legislation proposed by the Commons. The appointment of honours had long been considered a murky process; past favours repaid, albeit in a relatively subtle way. Any pretence of worthiness was now discarded by granting honours (at a price) to often totally unsuitable people. Between 1916 and 1922 over 1,500 knighthoods were bestowed to help swell party funds for the Prime Minister. More than 90 peerages were granted over the same period. It was an expensive business for those who craved public recognition. A knighthood would set you back a cool £10,000, a baronetcy was a snip at £30,000, whilst a peerage would cost in excess of £50,000. The Order of the British Empire (OBE) was created by King George V in 1917 and proved a more affordable option that many were prepared to pay for. Unlike his predecessor, Henry Asquith, Lloyd George understood the power of the press and so the leading newspaper proprietors were duly ennobled. Step forward Lord Beaverbrook and Viscounts Northcliffe, Harmsworth and Rothermere. Despite his initial distaste for hereditary honours, Lloyd George eventually joined the club, becoming Earl Lloyd George of Dwyfor in 1945.

The government felt it was now time for the people to express some patriotic fervour to offset the recent riots and strikes. A committee, under the chairmanship of the Foreign Secretary, Lord Halifax, suggested a Peace Day public holiday on July 19. The centrepiece was to be a massive victory parade. Thousands gathered overnight from all over the country. At the head of some 15,000 allied troops were Field Marshal Douglas Haig and General Ferdinand Foch, the allied supreme commander, with General John Pershing representing the United States.

The crowds cheered and waved Union Jacks as troops from around the world marched by. No sooner had one military band passed than another could be heard in the distance. Khaki dominated, but there were sailors too and representatives of the Royal Flying Corps (now merged with the Royal Naval Air Service to form the Royal Air Force). Commonwealth troops provided flashes of vivid colour, to be followed by stirring bagpipes and tartan kilts. Given it was arranged at such short notice the parade was a huge success. It ended in Whitehall, where a monument to the fallen and wounded was unveiled. Typically, Lloyd George came up with the idea of a monument at the last minute, allowing only two weeks for the architect, Edwin Lutyens, to complete his initial design, to be known as the Cenotaph (meaning 'empty tomb' in Greek). Cobbled together in wood and plastic, it did at least create a focal point for the huge parade. By the following year the permanent structure was completed in Portland Stone and inscribed simply to 'The Glorious Dead'. Subsequently, a two-minute silence was observed across the country on 11 November, Armistice Day. King George V, capturing the mood in most of the country, issued a message: 'To these, the sick and wounded who cannot take part in the festival of victory, I send out greetings and bid them good cheer, assuring them that the wounds and scars so honourable in themselves, inspire in the hearts of their fellow countrymen the warmest feelings of gratitude and respect.'

Unfortunately, in this turbulent year, nobody seemed to have informed the angry crowds in Luton. Disgruntled servicemen booed as patronising speeches were made by the mayor and councillors gathered outside the Town Hall to celebrate Peace Day. They were infuriated by lavish plans for a banquet that night for the great and the good of the town. Many unemployed, along with troops still awaiting discharge, surged forward, scattering the mayor's entourage. Inside the building rioters smashed windows and tore down doors. As police arrived there was a vicious pitched battle. By now the crowd had swelled to several thousand. Police reinforcements were summoned from London but struggled to regain control. To an ironic rendering of *Keep the Home Fires Burning* the Town Hall was torched and shops were looted. By the following morning Luton looked like a war zone.

Perhaps it was the sense of entitlement assumed by the wealthy and influential that stoked this profound feeling of unfairness. The working class resented a return to the old order. Their children sang the hymn *All Things Bright and Beautiful* at school that included this verse:

The rich man in his castle
The poor man at his gate
God made them high or lowly
And ordered their estate.

Children still do sing the hymn, though that verse is usually left out. How convenient for the rich to have God on their side, rubber-stamping the vast social divide. This chasm would be stubbornly slow to close.

3

LIFE ABOVE STAIRS

In 1919, long before the arrival of Russian oligarchs and oil-rich Arabs, the super rich in the UK were mostly the aristocracy. The leading families tended to divide their time between London and their country estates. Both still had much to offer in keeping this cosseted group occupied, yet was this to be the last hurrah of the idle rich? The vast social divide in Britain was most noticeable in rural areas where there was an inbuilt deference that had filtered down through the centuries, and there remained much tugging of forelocks, raising of caps and curtsying.

Owning land equated to power and influence. Not just a few acres but vast tracts, extending miles and covering farms and villages and including mineral rights. Just a few thousand aristocrats owned three quarters of all the land in Britain before the outbreak of war, with 25 per cent of England and Wales controlled by just 700 individuals. The scale of ownership was staggering. The Duke of Sutherland weighed in with over a million acres. Increased taxation and death duties led him to sell off a few acres in Scotland – 250,000 actually, still leaving him top of the pile in land ownership. The Duke of Rutland also off-loaded half of his Belvoir Estate for a useful £1.5 million. The Duke of Buccleuch hung on to his vast acreage, split between Northamptonshire and the Scottish Borders. There were another 40 estates with land in excess of 400,000 acres. Urban land was considerably more valuable and the Duke of Westminster inherited an estate estimated at £14 million at the turn of the century, including much of Mayfair and Belgravia. The eye-watering wealth of the Earl of Derby was in the form of an annual income reckoned to be about £300,000, partly derived from coalmines handily situated within his modest 70,000 acres.

Next in the pecking order came the landed gentry, who were able to claim estates stretching to over 10,000 acres. More than a thousand of the 'squirearchy' owned land in excess of 1000 acres. So it was that over 90 per cent of all British farmland was owned by the upper classes. These great estates were still run on what we would now consider to be feudal lines. The landowner ruled supreme. Tenanted farmers were answerable to their masters for their rent, a proportion of their produce and any game killed on their land. The landowner's power often extended to controlling whole villages, including shops and pubs that also paid rent, so often money earned locally was filtered back to the landowner. Even the clergy had to be mindful of the wishes of the local lord to ensure his continued 'living' within the parish. No controversial sermons, thank you! There were few signs that the age of subservience was over.

A brief boom after the war fizzled out as the pound lost half of its value and the national debt ballooned to £8 billion. With surtax at over 70 per cent for top earners and death duties also increased, landowners joined the growing chorus of those disillusioned by the outcomes of victory. The 'new rich' were now the perceived villains, described by Stanley Baldwin as 'Hard-faced men who looked as though they had done well out of the war.' A popular song in 1919 referred to a recruiting poster that asked 'What did YOU do in the war daddy?'

> And all the profiteers who'd lived so long in clover,
> fell a'sighing and a'sobbing when the hated war was over,
> for they made their bit in the Great War daddy!

Many businessmen had adapted their production to meet the needs of the war effort and made fortunes in the process: a corset factory making webbing belts and gaiters, or garment manufacturers churning out endless lengths of khaki material. These wealthy men were buying up the land and huge country houses that some of those with inherited wealth could no longer afford. As is often the British tradition, those making vast profits could not wait to ape the lifestyle of the 'old money'. Soon they were able to buy titles to complete their transformation. Money and titles could be acquired, maybe, but this still did not get you accepted in high society. These businessmen had, of course, helped in the war effort but their newly acquired wealth was resented, though they were now a force to be reckoned with. Losing your land and country pile was bad enough but when key staff, like butlers and housekeepers, were enticed away from their former employers with inflated wages, prejudice against the 'new rich' hardened. Such problems do not seem to have affected the 6th Duke of Portland, living at Welbeck Abbey in Nottinghamshire. Although the staff had been reduced from their pre-war levels they still formed a sizeable army. One man was employed full time just to clean windows, a task not unlike painting the Forth Bridge. As a keen breeder of racehorses (winning the Derby in succeeding years) the duke employed a retinue of able assistants to support his stud groom. Despite his lordship's love of horses he was also keen to embrace the latest technology. He quickly replaced coachmen with a team of chauffeurs to ferry guests from the railway station to his house for the frequent house parties, where they would marvel at the electric lighting he had installed.

House parties were resumed in earnest after the war. Slightly less lavish than previously, they still represented an age of self-indulgence. Local railway platforms would become clogged with baggage as servants scrabbled to identify their employer's trunks and valises. Many gatherings would attract up to 50 guests, with a similar number of visiting servants to attend to their needs. The guest lists for these exclusive weekends were strictly monitored. Bankers and financiers had gained access to this magic circle following the approval of the late King Edward VII. The wealth and influence of these men had to be acknowledged in such difficult times. For the more conservative landowners this was a bitter pill to swallow, particularly as some of the most influential financiers were Jewish. Anti-Semitism was common. Generally the guest list was drawn from a small group who met regularly. The doctor or chaplain would receive occasional invitations to lunch at the great house, but had to enter through the servants' quarters. Only the most famous artists, musicians or authors were likely to pass muster. Those employed in the theatre or, worse still, in trade, were absolutely persona non grata.

A house party had to be arranged with military precision. The right mix of guests for an enjoyable weekend was essential. The allocation of bedrooms required particular thought and understanding in a society where many marriages were arranged for financial reasons rather than love. Extra-marital affairs were commonplace and tacitly accepted, provided discretion was exercised. A couple of children (including, hopefully, a son and heir) were required to cement a union. Once this was achieved many conducted what today would be called an 'open marriage'. There were happily married couples that stayed loyal to each other but, with so many having had to compromise on true love, many looked for the exhilaration of a new romance. A well-connected girl was expected to be a virgin on her wedding night so 'wild oats' tended to be sown rather later in life. The corridors of our leading stately homes were witness to numerous nocturnal expeditions.

Another major concern for the house party hostess was how to keep the guests suitably occupied during their stay. Good food, country sports and the odd assignation guaranteed contented guests. The morning started with a massive breakfast, and tables groaning with food confronted those who arrived early. An array of cold meats, ham, game and poached fish or – for the more traditionally minded – kedgeree, nestled under silver domed dishes. Fancy some eggs? Freshly fried or boiled, coddled or scrambled, all were available. China or Indian tea was served in delicate porcelain cups, or strong coffee was available to aid the recovery from the previous evening's excesses.

With the first meal of the day out of the way and the morning papers scanned, it was time for a little gentle exercise. A set or two of sedate lawn tennis was enjoyed during the summer and golf was popular though rather time-consuming. It was hunting and shooting that was central to the guests' enjoyment. Often the meet was held at the host's own grand house. Most attending would have learned to ride almost before they could walk. This was the heyday of fox hunting in Britain, supported as much by the country followers as the riders galloping across the countryside. Their pink coats, shiny boots and baggy jodhpurs added a splash of colour, whilst the ladies riding side-saddle contributed a dash of glamour. Servants served whisky and port from silver trays before the sound of the horn sent the riders on their way.

For many men the shooting season was the highlight of their year. Beaters, wearing light-coloured coats, drove the game towards the guns. Behind each gun, loaders were ready with second and third guns to ensure no break in the barrage. Previously, gamekeepers had been involved in a year-long struggle to fight vermin and rear the thousands of pheasant chicks so vital to the estate. Poaching was considered to be the most serious rural crime and those caught could expect the harshest of sentences.

For anyone not taking part in strenuous activities a full formal lunch was served. Later, those returning from hunting or a shoot would expect tea. Sandwiches, scones and cakes did the trick. Then it was time for a short stroll in the garden before contemplating what to wear for dinner. Any lady invited to one of Britain's great houses had to bring several trunks of clothes as she was expected to change several times a day. A simple frock for breakfast, hunting gear, tweeds for walking, something more formal for luncheon, then a change for tea before the serious business of dressing up for dinner. The young replaced flared skirts, popular during the war, with long, tubular skirts. Older ladies were less inclined to be influenced by the latest fashion trends and still wore buttoned gloves. Hair was worn shorter, so a tiara looked rather fetching, whilst a long silk scarf and an oriental fan provided an exotic touch. The whole effect might be set off with a glorious sprinkling of the family jewels. Men also needed a full wardrobe. White flannels for tennis, country-wear, shooting jackets, hunting gear and not forgetting a blazer and a couple of cravats. A dinner jacket and a tailed suit were both essential. Dressed to the nines the guests sat at a long table, glistening with an array of glasses, cutlery and candelabra. The seating at the table revealed much about your social status and importance as a guest. The nearer you sat to the host, the better. To be stuck at the end of the table next to some old bore or the youngsters could cause considerable soul searching and distress. Even at the top end of society such things mattered and were the cause of unwelcome gossip.

As food was central to successful house parties, cooks and chefs were much prized. A French chef carried a certain kudos. A good English cook was, however, capable of turning out huge quantities of plainer fare for hungry guests. The menu on offer had been reduced since the Edwardian era, but guests were still offered seven or eight courses, including soup, fish, meat and game, each served with an appropriate wine. There were flans, tarts, gateaux, and a selection of homemade ice creams and sorbets. Fresh fruit and a cheese board followed, accompanied by a fine vintage port. At this point the ladies retired, leaving the men to talk about their day and tell dirty jokes. Time then, for a few hands of bridge, along with a cognac or a good malt whisky. Feeling at peace with the world, sleep beckoned, or perhaps another amorous trip along the corridor. For a chap who still felt peckish, a round of sandwiches could be sent up to his room. Then, before you know it, you'd be woken by your valet and it was time to start all over again.

For children growing up in these grand houses, life could be lonely and confusing. Frequently only seeing their parents at bedtime, they spent their early lives with a nanny or governess.

The sheer size of the building was often quite bewildering to a child. There were grand halls, dining rooms, drawing rooms and musty libraries. There were smaller parlours and a billiards room, not forgetting the massive ballroom leading off the impressive staircase. Some children never discovered the full extent of their parents' country home. The inviting smells coming from the kitchen drew children to its warmth. There were sculleries, storerooms and the servants' dining hall. Upstairs it was possible to get completely lost along darkened corridors. There were countless bedrooms, with their doors stretching into the distance. The servants' quarters, nestling just beneath the roof, were out of bounds. Freezing in winter and airless in the summer, these small rooms had mean little beds, often lined up like dormitories. Given the scale of the houses the youngsters were probably pleased to be confined to the familiarity of the nursery and even the dreaded schoolroom, and possibly preferred the bustle of the London mansion.

After time in the country London offered the gentry a wide range of social events to keep them busy throughout the summer months. 'The Season' started with the summer exhibition at the Royal Academy, which in 1919 ran from May 5 to August 9. It was good to be seen showing an interest in the arts. The odd purchase aimed to lighten the feel of their London homes, which tended to be dominated by dull oil paintings and rows of long-forgotten ancestors staring down from dining room walls. Prominently displayed at the Academy was a portrait of the Marquess of Londonderry by Sir John Lavery. Also on display by the same artist was a fine depiction of the grand ballroom at Londonderry House on Park Lane. It was comforting to see their class represented, better than some of the more modernist daubs. There was comfort for the traditionalists in the works of artists like Lamorna Birch and Alfred Munnings. Stanhope Forbes was another favourite, even though that year's offerings veered off piste with two works of munition workers. Of the almost 1,600 works displayed, only 245 were by members of the Royal Academy. This provided the more adventurous of the upper crust with a chance to spot the next soaring star of the art world. Following a preview for the privileged few, 200,000 attended the exhibition.

Having enjoyed a spot of culture, afterwards came a visit to the Chelsea Flower Show, which had been cancelled during the last two years of the war. Many aristocrats had a genuine interest in gardening, although this rarely extended to physical work on their part. With teams of gardeners employed on most large estates and in grand London homes, they mostly held just a watching brief – albeit an appreciative, if critical, one. The key social events of the summer were all conveniently staged within 70 miles of the capital. Next on the agenda was a visit to the Derby, the world's most prestigious horse race. Whilst this was very much a day out for Londoners, it was the rich and influential who provided the runners. Although Wednesday June 4 was damp and misty, record crowds gathered on Epsom Downs to witness the first running of the Derby since the war. The area was clogged with traffic as open-top buses and charabancs jostled for position. As ever, dress defined social status. Cloth caps and the odd boater or two peered across to the grandstand, where top hats and tailcoats dominated. The event was given additional status, as this was the first race meeting attended by the King since the end of the war. There were 13 runners, and their owners included a lord, a baron, three knights of the realm, an admiral and a Rothschild. The hot favourite was The Panther, although Paper

Money, ridden by Steve Donoghue, was widely tipped to win. During the war the course was used by the military and had been churned up by constant heavy motor traffic. Rain led to further deterioration, with some jockeys declaring the course to be dangerous. Unfortunately for favourite-backers, The Panther became agitated at the start and the race was delayed until he joined the other runners. His chance had gone. As they rounded Tattenham Corner, Donoghue had Paper Money in the lead, with the outsider Grand Parade handy in second place. Halfway down the straight Grand Parade edged ahead but was challenged by Buchan, a 7/1 shot ridden by Jack Brennan. In an exciting finish Fred Templeman, riding Grand Parade, managed to hang on by half a length. The winner, owned by Lord Glanely, was returned at 33/1 making the bookies very happy. The owner's winnings were £6,450 (about £320,000 at today's values).

In contrast to the hustle and bustle of Derby Day, Royal Ascot provided an ideal opportunity for the rich and well connected to mingle with their own kind and be watched enviously by crowds of onlookers. The 'sport of kings' appealed to the working man just as much as to the aristocracy, and an important part of the appeal of racing was the heady mix of spectators, viewing each other at a distance without actually rubbing shoulders. Two strictly defined groups looked at each other with equal interest and amusement. Sandown Park was the first course to introduce enclosures. It was a place where a gentleman could take a lady without fear of them hearing coarse language or witnessing uncouth behaviour, a form of social apartheid. Royal Ascot was possibly the pinnacle of the social scene. Each day the royal procession arrived on the course from Windsor. There were outriders dressed in vivid scarlet and gold uniforms, and postillions sporting grey wigs and jockey caps. The gentlemen raised their top hats whilst the ladies in their expensive finery curtsied. The Royal Enclosure was packed with the great and the good but even here some of the 'new rich' began to appear. Smartly togged up, it was difficult to tell them apart from those whose birth ensured their continued inclusion.

Lawn tennis was a favourite participation sport for the well breech'd. Many of London's finest houses boasted a well-tended court. June 23 witnessed the thirtieth staging of the Wimbledon Championships. It was a very low-key event compared to the modern era. It was the first Grand Slam event of 1919 and the first championship to be held since the outbreak of war. Gerald Patterson, an Australian known as 'the human catapult' due to his athleticism, defeated his fellow countryman, Norman Brookes, in the men's final. Interest centred on the women's singles, where a young Suzanne Lenglen struggled to beat Dorothea Lambert Chambers – an Englishwoman twice her age – in three sets (10/8, 4/6, 9/7). A crowd of 8,000, including the King, watched as the youngster tried to smash her way to victory against a wily opponent, who frequently passed the precocious French star at the net. After the glasses of champagne had been quaffed and plates of strawberries consumed, the blazer and boater came out as the privileged army moved on to Henley for the Royal Regatta. In 1919 the event was named the Royal Henley Peace Regatta. It drew crowds from around the world and spectators lined the towpath on the Thames to witness five days of top-class international competition. As ever with the leading social set, the sport was secondary to the partying and being seen.

With social occasions coming thick and fast, some were already thinking ahead to the Hunting Season – but the show had to go on and there were still a couple of events requiring attendance. 'Glorious Goodwood' was more relaxed than Royal Ascot and more refined than the Derby meeting. The five days of racing were capped by a lavish house party given by the Duke of Richmond at his beautiful Goodwood House. This had become an annual tradition, popularised by the attendance of the late King Edward VII. For many it marked the end of 'The Season', and saw them rushing back to London prior to the trek up to Scotland for the grouse shooting. For those keen on sailing it was down to the Solent for the Cowes Royal Regatta, which immediately followed Goodwood in early August and finished before the 'Glorious Twelfth'.

'Glorious' was a recurring theme in the lives of the fêted aristocracy, returning to their glorious London mansions if only for a brief stay. Yet, problems were mounting. Some were being forced by increased taxation to sell at least one of their homes. Would it be London or the country estate? This problem was solved, in part, by the hunger for land in London. Old residences were being demolished to make room for blocks of flats and more hotels as, seemingly, the world headed for London. Formerly the prime location in the capital had been Park Lane, but greatly increased traffic noise had reduced its desirability. Despite this, and the increased taxation, many leading families hung on grimly to their London homes. Londonderry House on Park Lane was considered to be perhaps the foremost private home in London. Owned by Viscount Castlereagh, it boasted the most spectacular staircase in the country, leading into a grand ballroom and beyond to a fabulous dining room featuring an astonishing collection of priceless silver. The walls were lined with family portraits. Against this ultra traditional setting the society beauty, Lady Diana Manners, turned up to a formal function one evening in February 1919 wearing fancy dress. The age of 'bright young things' was still on hold so soon after the war and the response of onlookers was as cold as the Canova marble statues staring down from their plinths. The charmless Hilton Hotel now occupies the site of this former bastion of the British aristocracy.

Just down the road from Londonderry House was another palatial mansion, Dorchester House, whose days were also numbered. Built in the style of an Italian palazzo in the 1840s, it was probably the showiest house in London. Leased to the American ambassador before the war, he hosted receptions there for thousands to celebrate Independence Day. During the war it became a military hospital and afterwards it was thought to be too large and expensive to run and was sold in 1926. The site is now occupied by the Dorchester Hotel. Grosvenor House was another Park Lane mansion that bowed to change. It had been used as an auxiliary hospital since 1916 and the Duke of Westminster didn't take up residence again after the war. No doubt daunted by the task of restoring the building to a family home, he decided to sell it to a new breed of property developers. The building was demolished and the site occupied by yet another luxury hotel.

Another favoured location for the aristocracy was Piccadilly. Devonshire House, with its fabulous crystal staircase, had been in the same family since 1696. Unfortunately for the 9th Duke, by 1919 the tax man came calling. The grand parties were now just a memory. With death duties of over £500,000 and other inherited family debts, he was forced to sell not only the house but much of his antique collection as well. Enter the wealthy industrialist and property developer, Shurmer Sibthorpe, who paid £750,000 for the house and, importantly, its large garden, for redevelopment. It was a sign of things to come. The blue bloods retreated, for the time being, to leafy squares and the moneymen started a long and ongoing defacement of London. So the aristocratic families pitched their tents in the likes of Belgrave or Eaton Square. Huge in modern terms, these houses were still able to accommodate a sizeable troop of servants but on a significantly smaller scale than previously. The move from palaces to terraced houses (no matter how grand) must have been a bit of a shock. With some having to forsake London altogether, it was good for them to know that properties like Wimpole House at 22 Arlington Street were still spacious enough to hold The Three Arts Ball in February 1919.

'Old money' had generally been adaptable when confronted by social change. Staying in a luxury hotel offered many advantages after 'cashing in their chips' and selling their London home; no huge wage bill and greater flexibility in deciding when to come up from the country. Previously it had been like a military operation to organise, now it was possible to stay in luxury, for the most part in the company of like-minded people. But where was it best to stay? Well into the Victorian era visitors to leading British cities tended to stay in lodgings, ranging from the well-appointed and comfortable to barely disguised brothels. Brown's Hotel claimed to be London's first hotel, although this is disputed. It opened in 1837 but 25 years earlier James Mivart opened the doors to what was to become Claridge's in Brook Street. By 1919 the choice for visitors to London had expanded. The most prestigious of these still operate from their original premises, although under much-changed ownership. With hundreds of hotels available in London the upper crust tended to opt for those that, in addition to offering great comfort and good food, also attracted the 'right kind' of guests. Claridge's certainly earned its reputation for understated luxury and impeccable taste. The Savoy was also much favoured. With its wonderful views over the Thames it attracted the younger set from the grandest families and found particular favour with wealthy Americans. Brown's in Albemarle Street continued to attract royalty, whilst Rudyard Kipling found its quiet atmosphere conducive to writing, completing several books whilst a guest. The Ritz opened in 1906, but by the end of the war it was considered to be stuffy and out-of-date. Coal fires were still lit in the bedrooms during the winter. The rooms with baths were tiled from floor to ceiling but the pedestal washbasins had not been replaced in 13 years, leaving a few cracked and stained. The décor in the bedrooms also looked tired, with brightly coloured rugs the only relief from the white walls that dominated. The hotel boasted a really grand ballroom but lacked a good band, and the young were drawn to the new Embassy Nightclub in Bond Street.

Dowdy or not, all age groups gathered at The Ritz for afternoon tea. The Palm Court was always packed in an era when, as Barbara Cartland confirmed, 'we were allowed to have rounded figures,' although she reckoned the cakes at Günters were better, if the setting not half as grand. Society beauties would station themselves in high chairs by the balustrade, with a good view of the foyer to see who was coming in. It was a chance for once to meet young men without a chaperone. Even the 'also ran' man could afford half a crown for tea and the chance to meet an heiress or two. According to Barbara 'The Ritz stood for stuffiness and standards.' (She didn't say what standards.) The Carlton was a no-no, being a gathering place for businessmen. The Savoy was rather fast, some others frankly scandalous. Summing up Cartland and her girlfriends was a popular song:

Children of the Ritz,
Sleek and civilised,
Frightfully surprised,
We know just how we want our quails done
And then we go and have our nails done...

There was now a huge selection of hotels to choose from across the British Isles, many of them former coaching inns. For those seeking an exclusive place to stay a series of grand hotels had mushroomed in the major cities. The Adelphi Hotel in Liverpool was rebuilt in 1912 and soon acquired a reputation for excellence as a place where even the grandest in the land were happy to stay. In the centre of Cardiff, the Royal Hotel was the first in the city to offer similar standards of comfort. At the beginning of the 20th century a rash of grand hotels opened across the country, in response to the growing demand for five-star accommodation. For some, the pace of change was too rapid. Wary of new-fangled electric lighting, some requested candles for bedside reading and were adamant that washbasins in bedrooms were unhygienic. 'When I need water, I will call for it,' was the cry. These old stick-in-the-muds were fighting a losing battle as hotels strived continuously to modernise their premises in pursuit of this very profitable and growing segment of the market.

The year 1919 represents a cusp in British life; a pause before a slow but irredeemable change in society really took hold. Back in London the 'in crowd' were beginning to acquire the cocktail habit that would sweep the country and come to represent the 'Roaring Twenties'. In fact, the first American bar had opened in The Criterion in 1878. They even imported Leo Engel, their own American bartender. The craze for cocktails had returned by 1919 and soon swanky hotels were opening American bars. Foremost was The Savoy, where Ada Coleman mixed the cocktails, having started there in 1903. It was reckoned she fixed the best dry martini outside New York. As the dapper, immaculately dressed men and their fashionable escorts sipped at their cocktails, they were doubtless unaware that they were now witness to a gradual erosion of their way of life. The age of deference was in decline, particularly in London. Fewer servants were available to attend to their needs and there was confusion caused by the effects of modernisation and technology. No wonder they needed a stiff drink. And yet outside of this gilded magic circle, life for most remained little changed from the turn of the century.

4

WHAT ABOUT THE WORKERS?

*Less than a mile away from swanky Park Lane, a fifteen-year-old
girl would awaken to the sound of metal wheels rattling outside
her window. That young girl was my mother, the year 1919.
The noise she heard was barrow boys, fit and strong young
men employed by older traders. They cursed and shouted as
they careered down Church Street to get the best pitch for the
day. The comforting smell of freshly baked bread would waft
upstairs, her father (my grandfather) having been baking batches
of steam loaves and trays of rye and pumpernickel bread since
5 o'clock. Only those who couldn't afford a white loaf bought
wholemeal bread. She'd serve in the shop until lunchtime and
then, on her afternoon off, set out towards Edgware Road.*

Church Street was one of thousands of markets scattered across
the country. A place for working people to hunt for bargains.
In Belfast, Birmingham or London the patter of the barrow boys
was much the same, only the accent differed. Furtive-looking
traders would assure the punters that everything they were selling
was 'knocked off, that's why it's so cheap, darlin'!' They probably

weren't offering stolen goods but it drew in a crowd. Church Street was lined with stalls selling everything imaginable. Fruit and vegetables were the most popular. Vendors bellowed out the bargains: 'Did I say sixpence a pound? I tell you what, 'ow about fourpence,' but canny housewives demanded the shiny apples and plump tomatoes from the front of the stall, rather than the over-ripe ones at the back. Displays of dress fabrics, knitting wool, lengths of elastic and cotton reels all jostled with caged birds that fluttered and squawked. A dark-skinned gypsy might offer to read your fortune, whilst an exotic Indian claimed to be able to predict the future by assessing the bumps on your head. A wicker chair set on the busy pavement advertised 'Tooth extraction for sixpence, painless for a shilling', the difference paid for an assistant to beat a drum to drown out the screams of the patient. Butchers in bloodstained aprons sharpened knives whilst cats scurried beneath the stall looking for scraps.

Fighting through the familiar rushing crowds, a few pausing to look fleetingly in the shop windows, the baker's girl would turn into Edgware Road and head towards Marble Arch. Here a sea of cloth caps greeted her, only occasionally punctuated by a bowler. Clothes defined a person's social background and the caps, bowlers and homburgs all told a story. Only the trilby, worn at a cheeky angle, nearly defied stereotyping, except that those wearing them often acquired a dubious reputation. Not a top hat to be seen, these being more the preserve of the City and Mayfair. The odd twirled umbrella, but far more pasty-faced men with 'roll your own fags' fixed firmly in their mouths. The sound of Gaelic music emanated from an Irish pub and (mostly) red buses growled and roared as they pushed their way past the clanking trams. (Only mostly red because a few 'pirate', unlicensed buses worked the capital.) Motorcars spluttered and revved their engines as they fought for space with a few horse-drawn cab drivers, who pulled at their reins and cursed, most of them unaware their days were numbered.

At Marble Arch she might pause and glance right to Park Lane, and Mayfair beyond; a different world of unimaginable wealth. Oxford Street was already a retail Mecca and Selfridges rose like a classical temple dedicated to mammon. Shoeshine boys plied their trade and uniformed nannies pushed their prams, heading for Hyde Park. Elegant ladies entered the stores, leaving a lingering waft of expensive perfume hanging in the air. In the space of a few yards two different worlds merged. Oxford Street, offered a nod to that developing commercial world, whilst working class Marylebone looked on enviously, unable to join in the spending spree. People living in Marylebone had to work hard to make ends meet, but they were lucky compared to those confined to Britain's worst slums.

The debate in the House of Commons on the 1919 Housing Bill highlighted many of the acute problems being encountered. In addition to an overall housing shortage it was reported that almost 400,000 houses were classed as being unfit for habitation. It was reckoned that roughly 3 million people were living in overcrowded conditions. Over 750,000 of these were in London. London was constantly changing, and respectable well-to-do areas gradually declined before deteriorating into slums. Essex Street in Shoreditch was highlighted. Formerly home to fairly well-off tradesmen, it had become a street of mean tenements. In one house there were 31 people living under the same roof, sharing one outside toilet and a single water tap. In that street almost 800 people were crammed into 29 houses. This was fairly typical of many of Britain's industrial towns and cities. Families existed in Dickensian conditions, crowded into alleyways and courtyards where the sun never penetrated. People shared beds, sleeping head to toe. It was not unusual to find six people sharing the same cramped bedroom. In Soho, Jewish tailors slept under the counters of their shops. Making his maiden speech the Labour MP John Davison, who had been a sanitary inspector prior to entering parliament, insisted conditions in Smethwick and much of the Midlands were just as dreadful as any in London. Even worse conditions were to be found in Glasgow, Belfast and the major cotton towns.

The wet, unsanitary conditions produced generations of small, skinny, underfed children, many of whom continued to walk barefooted. People with rickets were not unusual and, together with returning injured soldiers, they formed their own disabled army, referred to by that term we can no longer accept, 'cripples'. Life for poor families, even those with jobs, was demanding. Dreadful conditions at home, and often no easier in the workplace. The optimism enjoyed after the armistice soon evaporated. Many assumed the pre-war demand for British goods would revive and the shipyards, mines, mills and factories would soon be working flat out to meet demand. But the industries that had made much of Britain prosperous in the 19th century were now in decline.

Cotton had been the most successful pre-war export, capturing over 60 per cent of the world textile market. The war had restricted the import of raw cotton. Shortage of labour, with men away serving in the trenches, opened up opportunities for competition. Goods produced in India and Japan were now undercutting British manufacturers. They were using modern machinery, developed during the war, leaving British manufacturers to carry on with out-of-date equipment. Mill owners were slow to wake up to the dangers. They relied on the superior quality of British goods, which was fast becoming an illusion. Little attention was paid to the working conditions in the Lancashire cotton mills. The noise of the machinery was deafening and the air had to be kept hot and humid to prevent thread breakage. The thick airborne cotton dust caused many workers to succumb to lung disease.

Before 1914 Britain led the world in shipbuilding, but over the course of the war the US and Japan had built up substantial merchant fleets by creating modern shipyards and increasing their manufacturing capacity. In Europe, Sweden and Holland had also increased their manufacturing output. With the conflict over, all these countries offered formidable competition for British yards. Orders were cancelled, and shipbuilders joined cotton workers on the dole queues.

Coal had underpinned Britain's 19th-century economic superiority. Again, foreign competition made inroads by using modern extraction techniques. Lack of investment in Britain's coal industry made production slow and expensive. Miners had to work in horrific conditions. Men in South Wales and Durham were often working seams only 18 inches thick. This required them to lie on their sides in filthy water, hacking away with picks. They were supported by young school leavers, whose job it was to haul the coal from the face, often working by candlelight and trusting that the wooden pit props were sound. Roof collapses and explosions were a constant worry. Whilst it was dangerous and physically demanding work, a miner still earned about double the wages of a farm labourer.

In the shipyards of the Tyne and the Clyde, riveters were paid by the 100 they knocked down and a skilled man could earn as much as an engine driver. Riveters worked in pairs, one right handed, one left, supported by a 'holder-up' who held the rivet in place after a 'heater-up' had tossed it to a mate from a coke fire. Working sometimes hundreds of feet above ground in all weathers, or tied to scaffolding, these men certainly earned their money. So, too, did the miners and the factory workers. The fully employed could enjoy at least some leisure time. Watching football, ballroom dancing and racing pigeons all featured strongly, but hard work and real austerity dominated most workers' lives.

Some of the worst working conditions were to be found in British docks. The casual nature of the employment caused tension and resentment. Each morning men gathered, hoping to get work either loading or discharging a ship's cargo. Their employment could vary from a few hours to several days, depending on demand. Their earnings were controlled by forces unique to the shipping industry, winds, tides and bad weather affecting the movement of cargoes. Whilst seasonal arrivals, such as bananas, produced an increase in the number of dockers required, at other times there was just not enough work to go around. With no continuity of employment most dockers relied on their women folk to supplement the family income. There were frequent outbreaks of violence as men vied for the opportunity to work. A transport workers' Court of Inquiry in 1920 referred to this system of employment as being 'discreditable to society' and recommended it be 'torn up by its roots'. Despite this condemnation the government just sanctioned a further investigation. Trade union leader Ernest Bevin confirmed that: 'They recognised the demoralising effects of the uncertainty of employment of the casual worker, and expressed the opinion that the time had come – the industry must be radically reformed!' It would be, but not just yet.

Despite a fall in the number of servants working after the war they still numbered more than a million. Rather better off than their urban cousins (they did at least get fed each day) many still endured a life of endless drudgery. It was only the grandest houses that continued to employ a full retinue of staff. Not for them the cosy life depicted in *Downton Abbey*. Junior servants endured hideously long hours and harsh living conditions. Whilst butlers were key figures in the running of a grand house, it was the master's valet who enjoyed the closest relationship with his employer, similar to that of a lady's personal maid. The duties of a valet extended well beyond the laying out of his master's clothes each day. He made all the travel arrangements for his master, accompanying him on trips both at home and abroad. The trust extended to him often resulted in the valet being responsible for the payment of his employer's bills. He became the 'gentleman's gentleman', assuming much of the grandeur of his boss. He was frequently privy to his master's weaknesses and foibles, and as such his discretion was absolute. A unique bond was often formed between them but it rarely extended to true friendship. It was still an era where everyone was expected to know their place.

Butlers always seem to be depicted as discreet and pompous, or bumbling drunks. The butler was the most marketable servant, much prized by rich Americans. He needed a detailed knowledge of wines and spirits, and was a welcome visitor to the local vintner where his orders were much valued. As well as acting as 'front of house' at great banquets he was also the house manager and administrator, taking responsibility for the staff serving under him. Footmen were only retained by the very grandest houses as their role had largely disappeared. Chauffeurs replaced coachmen as motorcars took over from carriages, and it was female staff who now tended to serve at table. On the estates, gamekeepers and gardeners still enjoyed full employment. The cutback in female servants was not as drastic as they were cheaper to employ. Top of the pecking order was the housekeeper. Known as 'Mrs' even if a spinster, her word was law. She needed managerial skills to oversee the work and the emotional upsets of her staff. She would normally meet with the lady of the house each morning to arrange the smooth running of the establishment for the day.

A nanny was usually employed and, at a time when young children tended to see their parents only in the evening before going to bed, nannies frequently became a mother substitute. Often they were retained by the family long after the children had grown up, seeing out their days in genteel poverty in a small room in a huge house. The role of governess has also been stereotyped in fiction, perhaps not as unfairly. By implication the governess was educated and had often come from a good home but fallen on hard times. Her pay was paltry but governesses, particularly those who were bi-lingual, were still in demand. At the menial level were the housemaids whose number was generally dictated by the size and grandeur of the house. Their duties were never-ending and the hours long. This kind of servant was deserting in droves to work in shops and factories, where the pay was better and the work generally less arduous. Kitchen maids also worked long hours but, over time, they acquired skills that made them employable in other houses, sometimes becoming a cook in their own right with the ability to increase their earnings to above £50 per year.

For those living in the countryside but not in service, living conditions were generally extremely basic. Outwardly idyllic villages often had a spartan way of life. Theddingworth, a sleepy village in Leicestershire, had a population of fewer than 200. It was described just after the war as being largely self-contained, with a butcher, tailor and blacksmith. It was seemingly virtually untouched by modern life. The terraced cottages normally had two small bedrooms. The living room had a brick floor, with a few rag rugs scattered around in an attempt to keep out the damp. There was no electricity and water had to be drawn from a well in the garden. The kitchen didn't even have a sink. Washday was a chore, with few even owning a copper to boil the clothes. Instead, in the back yard cold water and soap were applied to the clothes, which were then slapped and beaten against a stone. Creases were flattened out with a smoothing iron, designed with handles that tipped forward to give greater pressure. Meals were taken at a scrubbed pine table, and the only other furniture would be a couple of Windsor chairs. For those living in the cottages, life was extremely precarious, often dependent on the whim of their employer. The rural hierarchy was strict and unchanging. At the bottom of the heap was the labourer. A man who started as a pigman or cowman was likely to spend his whole working life at the same job. Though life for the urban and rural poor was very different, they each suffered deprivation. Poor living and working conditions were further aggravated as livelihoods began to be challenged by advances in technology. Wheelwrighting was just one of the old trades under threat. When times get really tough there is a need for scapegoats, and immigrants came under fire for taking jobs that should have gone to British workers. Sound familiar?

There is a myth perpetuated by modern politicians that Britain has always welcomed immigrants. This is nonsense. For centuries each new wave of foreigners has been abused and often attacked, the newcomers' language, religion or physical differences highlighted and denigrated, before, in time, they were assimilated into society, often through inter-marriage.

Religion was still a major factor in British life. Catholics were generally viewed with great suspicion but rifts went much deeper, particularly in rural England. Church and Chapel folk rarely befriended each other and even shopping was undertaken along denominational lines. Chapel-goers would never allow any religious instruction other than at their own place of worship. It was only at the first Remembrance Day services that religious differences were temporarily set aside. Grief was universal and didn't discriminate between faiths.

Britain 100 years ago was predominantly white and wary of all foreigners. Pockets of exotic incomers tended to live close to the great ports. Soho in London was an exception, being an area that for centuries had attracted people from around the world. There were three immigrant groups who continued to attract hostility and prejudice: the Jews, Italians and Irish (although as Ireland remained part of Britain until 1922, the Irish were not strictly speaking immigrants). It was chiefly religion that set these three groups apart. Each group had arrived in large numbers during the 19th century to avoid pogroms or starvation, and much of the animosity towards them remained.

Jewish immigration into the East End was by now well established. By the 1880s a vast number of the world's Jews came within the empire of Czar Alexander, and it had been made clear that they were no longer welcome. Forced to live in settlements in areas that stretched from the Baltic to the Black Sea, which included much of Poland and eastern Russia, they started to emigrate. Many went to America, but the population of British Jews had risen to about 250,000 by 1919. Most settled in London but there were sizable Jewish populations in Manchester, Leeds and Glasgow. Jewish neighbourhoods had evolved, peopled by distinctive men wearing black hats, long hair and beards. They chatted in Yiddish and opened their own shops and kosher butchers.

By 1919 some of the original immigrants in the East End had become successful and were heading for the leafy suburbs of north London. For many Jewish families, however, life continued to be harsh. Jewish women arriving unaccompanied were at risk of being duped into a life of prostitution. Promises of marriage fell through, and it became impossible to break away if you became victim to one of the organised gangs that controlled these women and girls. Often, at least initially, it was a life of toil in a sweatshop. Many Jews worked in the clothing industry or in cabinet making or shoe production. Few worked for non-Jewish businesses, as this would have required them to work on Saturdays. The fact that Jews worked on Sundays caused massive resentment. They were accused of unfair trading whilst the rest of Britain enjoyed their Sabbath. It didn't seem to register with the non-Jewish population that they benefitted when the Jewish establishments were not working on Saturdays. In the East End over half of the workshops employed only a handful of workers. Houses that had previously been built for middle class artisans were divided and sub-divided to form overcrowded workshops. Newcomers, known as 'greeners', worked for a pittance until they became established in the community. The workshops were not only the backbone of the ready-made clothing trade but also supplied some of the leading haute couture houses situated in the *bon ton* parts of the West End. The invention of the sewing machine in the mid 19th century made mass production easier, meaning unskilled labour could produce clothes quickly and to a high standard. The arrival of the band-saw had a similar effect on the manufacture of domestic furniture. At the same time an aspiring and growing middle class was providing a market for ready-to-wear clothing and reasonably priced furniture.

In a way that resonates today, the Jewish community was willing to work harder and do jobs that were unappealing to most British workers. Despite – or perhaps because of – this work ethic they were accused of being greedy, dishonest and filthy. Certainly, the Jewish community was prepared to endure discomfort and hardship that few Britons would have entertained. Their looks and language, and the fact that they tended to live close to each other, kept them apart – and many felt aloof – from their British neighbours. Stories of some extraordinary successes fuelled jealousy: people like Simon Marks of Marks and Spencer and the Moses Brothers, who developed their Houndsditch rag and bone business into a chain of new clothing stores that became Moss Bros. There were legendary financiers and bankers such as the Rothschilds who, although courted by royalty and politicians, were denied more general approval. A grudging admiration, maybe, and certainly not one afforded to the Irish.

The mid-19th-century potato famine had seen mass emigration from Ireland. Most headed for America but those making the trip to Britain often arrived unwashed, unhealthy and destitute. Irish tinkers and gypsies have been travelling to Britain for centuries. The latter arrivals worked on the dirtiest projects for the lowest pay. They often worked in gangs, digging canals and building roads. They did the work no one else would do. They came by sea, from Ulster to Scotland, from Dublin to Liverpool and from Cork to Bristol and London. A hundred years ago each of these cities had a sizable Irish population. They lived mainly in foul smelling slums, in Glasgow tenements, in Liverpool cellars and in the notorious part of Manchester known as 'Little Ireland'.

In London they were spread widely, with large concentrations along the Edgware Road, from Cricklewood to Kilburn and on to Marylebone. A reputation, often based on caricature, painted them as filthy, lazy and violent. Many were uneducated, unable to read or write. There were constant complaints about noisy, drunken behaviour. The Irish could also be charming and, as the levels of inter-marriage increased, they became more fully integrated. Their entrepreneurial talents were beginning to show and they set up businesses, dealing mainly in dairy and livestock importation. The question of home rule for Ireland continued to create problems. Although Westminster Cathedral (completed in 1903) gave a focal point for Catholics in London, religion continued to be divisive.

If the Jews were viewed with suspicion, and the Irish generally looked down upon, the Italians garnered a very different response, often depending on gender. Many British women found the men exciting and irresistible, whilst their own men folk were wary. Outwardly charming, Italian men could sometimes organise themselves into violent gangs and, from their point of view, they took this action to protect their interests. The largest concentration of Italians centred around Clerkenwell in London. Saffron Hill and Hatton Garden became known as 'Little Italy'. Other sizable communities were to be found in Glasgow, Manchester and Bedford. Their reputation for being involved in organised crime dated back to Fagin-like organisers, who sent youngsters out on the streets to steal. They also controlled buskers by selling them barrel organs that had to be paid for in instalments deducted from their takings. They were sent out to race meetings and holiday resorts so, over time, barrel organs became a familiar sight and sound on our streets in places as far afield as Liverpool, Sheffield and

Newcastle. Organ grinders often had a chained monkey to draw the crowds. The Italians also included skilled tradesmen whose expertise was in short supply. Their tilers were in great demand, completing work in St Paul's, Westminster Abbey and Brompton Oratory. Further contracts were undertaken at the Tate and National Gallery, whilst work carried out at the Bank of England confirmed their status as unquestioned leaders in their field. Small workshops produced figurines and statues for the growing gift market.

The hotel industry was the largest employer of Italians. Italian cafés in Clerkenwell were already popular, the first Italian delicatessen had been trading there since 1878. Now thousands worked as waiters or in the kitchens of Britain's grandest hotels and restaurants. Increasingly Italians turned to the production of food. Initially, barrows loaded with cheese, pasta and wine were wheeled onto the streets, some of it strange food that very few British people had encountered before. Serving abroad in the forces, however, had introduced some of the more adventurous to the delights of foreign food, and soon small Italian restaurants were appearing in Soho. Italians had long been associated with the production of ice cream and the front rooms of homes in Clerkenwell were converted into mini ice cream factories. They were frequently filthy and unhygienic and blamed for causing food poisoning and even cholera. Production had moved on from boiling and mixing milk and eggs. Although often still sold from handcarts, successful producers were now opening scores of specialist ice cream parlours. Ice cream was particularly popular in Scotland, where hundreds of parlours were in operation. Violence erupted as favoured sites were fought over. Rival chains were established and turf wars broke out. As in London, it was a dangerous trade to be engaged in and some Italians turned to fish and chips for an alternative livelihood. Alfredo's, in Essex Road, Islington, served as a perfect example of how Italians tailored their businesses to the local requirements. Moving from pasta and ice cream to become a classic British café serving fry-ups, Alfredo's was a local landmark for over 80 years before closing in 2002. It is ironic that it was a British butcher who first saw the national and global opportunities for ice cream production. In 1919 T. Wall and Sons acquired Friary House and grounds in Acton. Initially a sausage factory, the business was sold in 1922 to Lever Brothers. Later that year the first large factory producing ice cream was opened and, of course, Walls Ice Cream continues to be sold today as part of the Unilever Group.

Life in 1919 continued to be extremely tough, but there was more chance for people to better themselves. Doctors, lawyers and accountants were being joined by a growing band of managers and small businessmen, all seeking more pleasant surroundings. For some, the leafy suburbs beckoned.

5

WHAT WILL THE NEIGHBOURS THINK?

There was a whiff of Puritanism attached to being middle class a hundred years ago. This class appeared convinced that whatever they did, thought or felt was right. They viewed the working class as coarse, violent and ignorant, whilst the aristocracy was lazy, immoral and decadent. It was they alone who upheld the virtues of hard work and decency. It was this group in class-conscious Britain that developed snobbery into an art form.

Large numbers of people were neither rich nor poor. They were part of the growing army of the middle classes. Even within this group there were divisions. Money had its place, but so too did accent and dozens of keenly observed social nuances. The upper middle classes set themselves apart from the rest of the tribe. They were aspirational, both in acquiring wealth but also, importantly, status. This relatively small group lived in large houses with extensive grounds and usually employed several servants. They were often self-made men, successful manufacturers and merchants and were joined by lawyers, surgeons and accountants with thriving practices. Whilst these men frequently retained their regional accents, their wives and children did their best to imitate the drawl of the upper classes. Their attempts lacked the authenticity of the trueborn aristocrat, though it didn't stop them trying. Their sons were packed off to public school and they dreamt of their daughters being presented at court. University for this privileged group of girls was not generally an option. A few were sent off to finishing school in France or Switzerland, and then it was back home to search for a suitable husband. Money certainly gave them access to the fringes of the aristocratic set. Some made good marriages, but other free spirits kicked over the traces by running off with the groom or a worker in their father's factory.

Parisians may have laughed at the accents of other Frenchmen, but in the whole of Europe only in England did accent divide people so clearly. A regional accent jarred and formed a barrier in this most socially sensitive group. If you passed the accent test, there were many other hurdles to clear. On meeting for the first time a gentle but searching social interrogation would begin to assess whether a person was worth knowing. Where you lived was a good starting point. A fashionable town house perhaps, or maybe a larger property in the suburbs. Having established it wasn't a three-bedroom semi-detached, it was time to probe further. School flushed out imposters. Only the poor left school at fourteen, just the age when someone from an acceptable background was finding his feet at public school. These schools were also of course an important indicator. Eton and Harrow were normally the preserve of the grandest families but other notable schools, like Winchester or Marlborough, indicated a person worth knowing. Some of the London public schools achieved fine academic results but, for good, solid background, Shire schools like Oundle and Uppingham were admired. There were also schools catering for particularly stupid sons of the well-to-do middle class. These were often run from magnificent old houses with stunning grounds, offering a beautiful setting for a sub-standard education. If this new acquaintance spoke properly, and had attended a reasonable school, then what about his military background?

The war took a great toll on junior officers. Many who previously wouldn't have been commissioned were elevated to officer status. It was unlikely, however, that anyone from a middle-class background would have been commissioned in any of the Guards regiments. Most outfits were acceptable, other than the Labour Corps. But there was more to explore. Did he know which cutlery to use at a banquet? Was his tie knotted correctly? Surely he didn't wear brown shoes with a lounge suit? Was he amusing without being too clever? Worse still, was his wife? Well-read and clever women were considered a real bore!

So, there is our upper-middle class man. Clubbable, able to hold his drink, and an inveterate snob. He plays golf, where the professional and stewards show him the respect that is his due. His son attends his old school, where he plays cricket and rugger (soccer is for the working class). His wife organises the servants and changes into a suitable dress to welcome him home from a hard day's work. If our imaginary man worked in London he would probably live in one of the suburbs, made possible by the underground spreading outwards from the centre. The Central line finally made it as far as Ealing in 1920, work on the extension having been suspended during the war. Advertisements extolled the virtues of living in the semi-rural retreat of Golders Green, quoting *Sanctuary*, a poem by William Cowper. He might even have ventured further into Metroland, a suburban area made possible by the extension of the Metropolitan railway, roughly defined by land north of Wembley and stretching onto the Chilterns. The concept of 'Metroland' became acknowledged in 1915, with the publication of *The Metro-land Guide*. The directors of the railway understood the potential for colonising existing villages and hamlets by building stations and providing regular services to central London. The magazine pointed out the advantages of being able to travel to and from the City 'without a change of carriage! At Baker Street it is possible to link up with the underground electric system, so there is every facility for expeditiously reaching any part of London. Other cities, like Glasgow, are also spreading outwards with the help of extended railway links.' They weren't just providing transport links: Metropolitan Railway Country Estates Ltd started building houses on its own land in 1919.

The war had applied the brakes to the continued spread of the suburbs, and the ongoing shortage of raw materials and labour ensured that this hiatus continued until the early '20s, when urban development again gobbled up rural land and quickly destroyed the country lifestyle that so many craved. As American journalist, William Vaughan, concluded: 'Suburbia is where the developer bulldozes the trees, then names the streets after them.' Everyone wanted to become middle class; well, not everyone but a sizeable number who had recently escaped from dreary backstreets and slums. These urban dwellers included shopkeepers, office workers, teachers, foremen and skilled tradesmen. Their ambitions for housing were more modest than their richer, better connected, middle class cousins. Modest semi-detached villas were more in keeping with their lifestyle. They probably had a 'daily' to help with the housework. Although the lady of the house rarely went to work, it was her job to make sure the house ran smoothly and that the children were supervised. The couple would make sacrifices for their children to go to a private school. They were drawn into the game of keeping up appearances for neighbours and friends. The housewife's role was frequently organised into a regular routine. With no refrigerator, shopping was time-consuming and had to be done daily. Tradesmen would call, always going to the back door. A weekly order was taken by a salesman from the local grocer. He would carefully write down all 'Madam's' requirements, which would be delivered the following day by a boy riding a tricycle, the order contained within huge wicker panniers. Monday was washday, achieved with the help of a steaming copper. Thursday was normally set aside for baking, to make sure there was a well-stocked larder for the weekend.

Meals tended to follow a set routine. Sunday was the highlight, when a roast and three vegetables were served. Monday was cold meat and salad, by Tuesday the remains of the roast had been reincarnated as a stew or an anglicised curry. British cooking was in the doldrums, both in homes, hotels and restaurants (unless a foreign chef was involved). After a spot of light dusting in the living room, it was time for this wife to change into a frock and look as attractive as possible to welcome 'hubby' home.

Before the advent of the wireless much leisure time was devoted to reading. (The first *Radio Times* was published on 28 September 1923, so there wasn't much to write home about on the airwaves before then.) Newspapers and magazines were enjoying record sales, and books were available from lending libraries. This was a generation with a thirst for knowledge, with many taking an active interest in politics. Other than going to the 'pictures' or attending sporting events, it was a time of home entertainment. Many crowded parlours were not complete without an upright piano. Visiting friends and family would often involve a 'sing-song' around the piano, or listening to a supposedly talented soloist, drawn from their midst, perform. Entertaining was rather formal, and generally revolved around teatime. Tea, sandwiches and cakes, rather than an evening supper, was the norm. Families tended to live in the same neighbourhood and moving many miles away was unusual. The exception was a growing group of young women who headed for India in search of a husband.

With so many young men having been killed and maimed in the war, the chances of marriage for females had become severely restricted. Suddenly, the prospect of the colonial life of the Raj had added appeal. Young women with friends or relatives living in the colonies booked one-way tickets to faraway places in search of romance, or at least marriage, hopefully both. Here, single men from the colonial staff and army personnel who were also denied the company of the opposite sex, warmly welcomed them. Initially overwhelmed by an endless round of parties and glamorous balls, many romances led to nuptials. Afterwards, rather than an ongoing social whirl, the young women found themselves stationed with their husbands in some remote outpost, enduring searing heat, basic living accommodation, and boredom punctuated by tropical illnesses. Gradually, most of them acclimatised and became the backbone of the faltering Raj.

Back home, in 1919 Britain, the war had disturbed but not broken down the immense social divide. Britain was still a deeply conservative country and generally one of conformity. Vast swathes of the public still attended church each Sunday. Although criminals robbed banks and fought each other on racecourses, most people were unaffected. Shame was a potent emotion and controlled behaviour. Society was very judgmental and this acted as a brake. 'What will the neighbours think?' applied across the social chasm. Most remained immensely proud to be British, despite the first signs of a weakening influence. It was as if the country was taking a deep breath before plunging into a new world it didn't fully understand and was ill equipped to take advantage of. Technology and mechanisation were about to transform life, yet deep in rural Britain, old customs still prevailed.

6

OLD HABITS DIE HARD

At the end of the war the population of Great Britain was just in excess of 40 million. Most people congregated around London, the ports, and the major industrial cities and towns. With so many men serving in the forces the countryside was stripped of key agricultural workers, which soon had an impact on food production. There had been panic buying of food at the outbreak of the war, leading to shortages of even basic requirements. Britain relied heavily on imports of food with an estimated 80 per cent of wheat, 40 per cent of meat and virtually all sugar coming from overseas. U-boat activity led to millions of tons of merchant shipping being lost, creating additional shortages. Despite this, the government showed a reticence to introduce rationing. Continual shortages led to an outbreak of scurvy in Scotland and the North of England.

A poor harvest in 1916 led to a further worsening of the situation. Food prices had risen by more than 60 per cent since 1914. Rationing was finally introduced for sugar, and by April 1918 it was extended to such basic items as butter, margarine and jam. Whilst urban dwellers had been encouraged to grow

their own food on any patch of available land, at least
country folk were generally self-sufficient, growing their fruit
and vegetables and picking berries from hedgerows.

The rhythm of life in the countryside still mirrored the gradual changes in the seasonal landscape. Away from the city, the crowds and the constant rush, a sense of calm prevailed. In villages and hamlets, the fields and hedgerows surrounding them remained much as they had done for centuries. A picture-postcard Britain caught in a time warp, a temporary pause before change accelerated to alter both life and the landscape. Cars were already a regular sight, bumping along country lanes, and mechanised tractors were beginning to replace the teams of plough horses. Despite the threat of modernisation, country folk remained faithful to their way of life and many of the old customs were still celebrated.

Most villages continued to be self-contained units with a shop, pub and bakery. As so many young men had been killed in the war those lucky enough to return wasted little time in marrying their sweethearts. Courtship remained rather formal and regulated, as it had done for centuries. There were few secrets in such closed communities. 'Walking out' together was expected to lead to marriage. The pressure from family and friends was considerable. An engagement was followed by a period of planning for the marriage that was expected to be a lifelong commitment. Chastity before the wedding and fidelity thereafter was expected, although rarely openly discussed (probably just as well with visits to French brothels often a recent memory for the returning groom). The outward symbol of the bride's purity was the white dress she wore, together with a head-dress of flowers, her face hidden by a veil. For those widowed during the war and marrying for a second time a white dress was not an option. With money scarce, most village weddings were simple affairs. The reception was usually held at the bride's parents' home, where food was laid out and only beer and soft drinks served. There was no honeymoon and the happy couple usually started their married life in a spare room in one of their parents' cottages. Next day it was back to work as usual.

With no effective birth control it didn't usually take long before there was another mouth to feed. When the young woman 'fell' pregnant she was given advice handed down through the years, much of which was contradictory. 'She's carrying all round so it'll be a boy.' Maybe not! 'The girl is overdue and all in front so it'll be a girl.' Another old wives' tale reckoned that the most virile men tended to have daughters. Childbirth remained a serious health risk for both mother and child. Babies were usually delivered at home by the local midwife. Stillborn babies were buried at dusk amidst great secrecy, in a corner of the churchyard, with only the sextant and midwife (wearing a black shawl) in attendance. When babies survived they were given an egg for luck. The contents of the egg were blown out and the shell painted and tied round with a ribbon, pink for a girl and blue for a boy. Babies born out of wedlock were still referred to as bastards, so for any baby born 'by the light of the moon' the outlook was bleak. In remote parts of the country low belling still took place; in a period of self-righteous condemnation people suspected of adultery were subjected to the constant crashing of metal trays and kettles outside their house, and sometimes forced to flee the area.

Despite the ongoing risks attached to childbirth, families were large by modern standards. Having seven or eight children was not unusual, and the mother was tied to a perpetual round of household duties. The eldest children were expected to help, and often ended up looking after their elderly parents. For village children life revolved around school and helping in the house and fields, particularly at harvest time. Sunday was devoted to attending church and Sunday School. Little time was given over to play, as there were always tasks that needed doing; going to the farm to collect milk, or picking mushrooms or blackberries. No chance to gather food could be ignored. Many households kept chickens and a pig, whilst growing vegetables wasn't just a hobby but a necessity to keep food on the table. In winter those without land of their own to tend often went hungry. A meal of bread with tea and a spoonful of sugar sometimes had to do, whilst hot water spiced with pepper and salt was drunk to ward off the cold. Freezing weather brought misery for the rural poor, so much time was devoted to collecting firewood. Manual work was physically draining, particularly when it was common for a man to exist on just a hunk of bread and an onion or a scrap of cheese. Apples (wrapped in newspaper to preserve them) were a valuable source of winter food. Damsons were layered with sugar and eventually became nourishing syrup. Vinegar was the poor man's sauce for savoury dishes. It was also used for washing meat in summer to mask any unpleasant smell. What was served at mealtimes depended on what job you did:

> Ham and eggs for plasterers,
> brickies, bread and cheese,
> what will the poor old painter do
> when leaves fall from the trees?

All but the very poorest set the table four times a day. If things were good a fried breakfast would be on offer. Lunch (or dinner, as the midday meal was called) was the main meal of the day. Children came home from school and some men were able to take a rest from work. Tea tended to be just bread and jam, whilst supper was more bread but this time with cheese. Life for working country folk was frugal and tough by modern standards. Home-brewed beer and wine produced from the hedgerows offered some cheer, but it was a life of unremitting labour for all the family. H.E. Bates in his autobiography *The Vanishing World* described a rural world that we still like to believe in: 'The scene was utterly idyllic. Time had covered the lacerated cliffs of stone with grass and thyme, and wild rose and elderberry, and odd bushes of hawthorn. Above it rose many fruit trees in their full bearing and prime.' A wonderful vista but few were able to spend much time admiring the view.

Illness was a constant worry as most were unable to afford a visit from the doctor, so old remedies were employed with varying degrees of success. A bad cut was stitched using a needle boiled in water and using any thread to hand. It was a case of 'look away and grit your teeth'. Embedded thorns were drawn out using a hot kaolin poultice. Although eventually effective, the repeated application often left the surrounding skin red and raw. Children suffering with bad chests wore a vest of brown paper, either soaked in linseed oil or goose grease. Keeping a potato in your pocket helped cure rheumatism. Washing your hands in the water used for boiling eggs or potatoes was believed to cause warts, for which the full moon could provide a cure. One method involved rubbing a small piece of meat on the wart and then burying it. As the meat decayed the wart would supposedly slowly disappear. A baby's eyes could be protected by squeezing the juice of germander speedwell into them, presumably whilst ignoring the child's squeals. (The blue flowers had always been a good luck charm for travellers.) Gold and copper were thought to have healing powers. Sore gums or unsightly styes could be cured by rubbing them with a gold wedding ring.

Folklore still exercised its influence on rural life. Witchcraft continued to linger on in the fringes of rural beliefs. With no electricity in most villages, lighting was poor and tales of ghosts and hauntings persisted. Phantom coaches were heard cantering down uneven country roads, and ghostly huntsmen rode across muddy fields as dusk closed in. Children grew up believing in the bogeyman, an undefined horror lurking in the shadows that would come and get them if they misbehaved. Traditional old wives' tales were often acted upon and many survive. People continued to turn their money over when there was a new moon so their wealth would grow as the moon got bigger. It was considered unlucky to look at the moon through glass. It is still supposed to be lucky if a black cat crosses your path, but if you kill one it brings seven years of bad luck. An old rhyme, popular a hundred years ago, related to crows:

One crow sorrow, two crows joy
three crows a letter, four crows a boy.
Five crows silver, six crows gold,
and seven crows a secret, never to be told.

We continue to believe that if a money spider settles on you, it foretells money coming your way. Less well known is that you must never kill a robin, as it was he who tried to pluck a thorn from Christ's crown, which is how he acquired his red breast. Old beliefs also applied to fruit and flowers. Young girls plucked at daisy petals reciting, 'he loves me, he loves me not'. If a child wanted to know what job they would do when they grew up they would eat plums and place the stones on the edge of their plate reciting: 'Tinker, tailor, soldier, sailor/Rich man, poor man, beggar man, thief.'

It was a long-held belief that when entering a house you should always go in and out by the same door, otherwise a friendship would be broken. If you left your own house and forgot something you had to go back inside, sit down and count to ten. Passing on the stairs was considered to be unlucky. It was unlucky to give gloves as a gift so you always had to pay for them, even if only with a copper or two. This applied to knives too, otherwise the present was thought to cut a friendship. Crossed knives even today predict a quarrel. A very costly tradition related to the breaking of a cup or glass as it necessitated the smashing of another two. Spilling salt was thought to bring bad luck but could be avoided by making the sign of the cross in the spilled salt and then throwing it over your left shoulder (where the devil was lurking). Mirrors are an ancient symbol of magic and breaking a mirror was thought to bring seven years bad luck. Mirrors were covered during thunderstorms and doors left open in an attempt to let the thunderbolts out. In times when personal hygiene didn't rank so highly, it was thought to wash on New Year's Day was to wash your luck away. It was also considered really unlucky to wash blankets in May, as it would wash one of the family away. As Friday was believed to be the day of the crucifixion you were not allowed to cut your nails or, bizarrely, to turn a mattress.

In modern society we struggle to cope with death. A hundred years ago people generally died much younger and child mortality remained high. It was normal for friends and family to gather to view a body, still lying on the bed, with freshly picked flowers placed in the hands. The body was prepared for burial by a local woman who attended to all those who died in the neighbourhood. In some regions of the country salt was placed on the chest and feet of the body to mask the smell when it was buried and ensure that animals were not tempted to dig up the grave. Children were actively encouraged to touch the corpse in the hope that it diminished their fear of death. For many the reverse was true. Before the burial, all the mirrors in the house were covered with black material and the body taken out feet first, to stop the death spirit looking back and beckoning another member of the family. Old customs were slow to die and many processions returning from the interment came to the deceased's house by a different route, so preventing a potential ghost returning with them.

There were other deaths to be endured by the rural community. Mechanisation was beginning to kill jobs and sideline ancient and skilful trades. With the introduction of tractors the ploughman's job was at risk. Dating back centuries, the first Monday after the Epiphany (January 6) was designated 'Plough Monday'. The ploughboys would pull a plough around their town or village singing in pubs and on the streets, expecting to be given money. They blacked up their faces and, if they were refused money, they daubed the door of the offender with red sheep dye. Their traditional song varied across the country, often starting 'Pity the poor ploughboy'. The custom probably dated back to mid-winter rites when the darkness was fought off by lighting fires and creating lanterns made from swedes. A ploughman's song, still sung a hundred years ago, went:

Think of the poor ploughboy – only once a year
give him tuppence ha'penny for a pint of beer.
If not that, tuppence will do.
If not, three ha'pence will do.
If not, a penny will do.
If not, then a ha'penny will do.
If not that – well God bless you.

That last line of the song was often far less polite, and frequently 'Plough Monday' ended in unruly behaviour and fights.

In common with the plough many other trades and occupations suffered a gradual decline. Wheelwrights were considered amongst the most skilful tradesmen and their craft, stretching back to ancient times, required them to serve a lengthy apprenticeship. But cars and tractors had no need of wheelwrights. Strangely, some of the trades thought to be in most jeopardy still thrive today. It was thought that the car would replace the horse, leaving farriers and blacksmiths with no work. However, in certain parts of the country hunting kept the farriers busy with fox hunting entering its most popular age. Horses continued to work the fields well into the 1920s and dray horses longer still. Horses had been central to country life for centuries and they were not about to be abandoned, as riding became an increasingly popular leisure activity. (There are still something approaching 950,000 horses in Great Britain today).

Thatchers were also thought to be under threat. The government's housing plans envisaged rows of modern council houses, even in rural communities. Who would choose an old-fashioned thatched cottage by choice? Many did, and continued to enjoy the advantages of a thatched property that was warm and cosy in the winter and blissfully cool in a heatwave. Thus the ancient craft of the thatcher survived and flourished. On the farm the waggoner, cowman and shepherd were safe in their jobs for a time, until the modernisation of farming overtook them as well. The general farm labourer was at the bottom of the pay scale but also had skills, many of which have been lost over time. Today, most hedges are butchered by tractors but a hundred years ago the ancient craft of laying a hedge was commonplace. Of course it requires great skill and time, both of which are now in short supply. Then, the hedge was cut and laid to provide a double brush on both sides. A single stake was driven into the hedge and the top secured with binders, usually of hazel. Once the hedge was laid, each side was trimmed, leaving a neat and pleasing hedge line.

The bringing in of the harvest was central to the wellbeing of a village. A successful harvest was often celebrated with food and drink supplied by the farmer or landowner. A bumper crop was acknowledged with a song as the last load of corn, decorated with ribbons and boughs, was brought home in triumph:

> We've ploughed, we've sowed
> we've reaped, we've mowed
> we've got our harvest home.

Thanksgiving services were celebrated at the local church. Harvest festivals, dating back to pagan days, were held on the Sunday of the Harvest Moon that falls closest to the autumn equinox. Churches were decorated with food and seasonal fruit that was distributed to those most in need at the end of the service.

After the harvest came the ancient right of gleaning. This was a practice dating back to the Old Testament, which allowed for the collection of leftover crops from the farmer's and landowner's fields. This gave the needy the right by law to forage. By 1919 the poor were joined by schoolchildren and their parents in what had become something of a social event. By tradition, no gleaning could take place until three sheaves of corn were left in a stack in the middle of a field. This indicated that the farmer's rights were temporarily waived. No one was allowed into the fields until the church bell was rung at 8 o'clock the next morning. Grain was collected in sheets and then taken to the local miller. The stubble was sharp and scratched the ankles. A version of this tradition continues into modern times, although today the food is collected from supermarkets and distributed to those in need via a food bank.

After a horse, a pig was the most valued possession in the rural community. If you had the space for a sty you could feed a pig on household scraps and vegetable peelings and the animal would provide valuable food for the family. Where possible it paid to keep two pigs: one for sale to the local butcher with the proceeds used to pay for feed for the second. When the pig was killed, the liver and kidneys were the first to be eaten. Then some fresh meat was cooked whilst scraps and trimmings were used to make brawn. Food was shared with friends and neighbours who returned the favour when their own animal was slaughtered:

Health to the man who kills a pig
and sends his neighbours fry,
and after that, a leg of pork,
and then a big pork pie.

Some people salted the carcass to preserve the meat longer. It was not unusual to find hams hanging from beams throughout the house. Chickens were also a source of food and were easy to keep. Eggs could be sold and, if you were lucky enough to own a pig and a few chickens, you were on your way to being self-sufficient. An apple tree was a bonus whilst hedgerows were the source of nourishing berries.

We still obsess about the weather, although a hundred years ago it was even more important. Weather lore has been passed down to us and still contains many truths:

Red sky in the morning,
shepherd's warning.
Red sky at night,
shepherd's delight.

Still pretty reliable. How about:

When the moon is on its back
then the weather will surely crack.

Without formal weather forecasts these old sayings formed a rudimentary kind of knowledge. Throughout the year weather on certain days was believed to indicate the weather to come. 'If Candlemas Day be fair and bright,/ no more winter is in sight. Or 'If at Candlemas it be rain,/ winter is gone and won't come again.' Candlemas is the second day of February, a rainy month, hence: 'February weather, all mire and muck,/ three white frosts and then pack up.' Each month has its own rhymes, many dating back to antiquity: 'A cold May and a wet June/ makes all things come in tune.'

With no television or tablets children had to make their own entertainment, and many of the games they played had been passed down through the generations. Some, like 'Cat's Cradle', still keep children amused today. Many games centred on hunting each other, chasing across fields pretending to be foxes or huntsmen. The game of 'Tiggy Wood' involved being chased, but if you touched wood you were safe from capture. In previous times touching wood was believed to offer protection against witchcraft. This superstition lives on today in the sayings 'touch wood' or 'knock on wood', still thought to bring good luck. The most ancient of the surviving games frequently involved sticks and stones, as they were always available for play. A basic game involved hitting a stone with a long stick (an early forerunner of golf). Hopscotch is still played today, although in slightly different variations depending on the area of the country. A common form saw the traditional pattern chalked onto the pavement and a stone kicked onto each number in turn, which then had to be reached by hopping. The stone had to land in the centre of a square without touching the sides otherwise you lost your turn. The game was very competitive, involved any numbers of children and could keep them occupied for hours. Marbles was a Victorian game that became really popular with adults as well as children after the Great War. It could be played in the schoolyard or even in gutters. Where improvisation was needed, games were cobbled together using old tins or empty milk bottles left lying about. If you couldn't afford a football, a pig's bladder stuffed with straw made a good substitute. Perhaps the oldest game of all was carried out in silence, and known in southern counties as IK AK OK. The two contestants faced each other and produced a hand from behind their back. In the game, a clenched fist represented a stone, an upward palm, paper, and two fingers pointing forwards, scissors. Stone blunts the scissors, whilst scissors cut paper but paper wraps the stone.

Old rhymes survive the passage of time, including well-known ones like 'Sticks and stones will break my bones', but how about this from Dorset:

> Corum, borum, bingle lock,
> three wires in a clock.
> Sit and spin and turn the wheel,
> diffy, daffy man afield.

Children like to be frightened and were influenced by the tale of Little Red Riding Hood. A popular game queried, 'What's the time Mister Wolf?' At first the wolf is friendly, 'One o clock' he replies, then 'two o clock', before suddenly shouting 'Dinner time' and chasing the children who have been creeping up on him. Another chasing game was 'Sheep, sheep, come home'. An adult plays the shepherd and asks the children what they are afraid of? 'The wolf' they reply. He hides behind a bush and calls:

> The wolf's gone to Devonshire
> and won't be back for seven years.
> Sheep, sheep come home.

The children, acting as sheep, advance slowly then suddenly the wolf leaps out and chases the screaming children.

The country year was dominated by the seasons and Christian tradition. Shrove Tuesday is the last day before Lent. The 40 days before Easter had traditionally been a time for fasting, although no longer so strictly observed. Previously it had been a time to use up butter and eggs, which were forbidden during Lent, leading to the tradition of making pancakes. The pancake bell was sounded in village churches, calling people to confession. The pancake tradition continued but by 1919 fasting and going to confession were not observed by the majority of people. Valentine's Day was celebrated but its origins are open to interpretation. Over time it became known as a day of romance and love that is declared secretly. It was also a day of pranks, like knocking on the door of someone you were attracted to and then running away. This was a forerunner of the unsigned Valentine's card. On Good Friday all the shops closed and everyone was expected to go to church, whilst April Fool's Day was thought to be a survival of celebrations marking the spring equinox. May Day was celebrated with dancing, singing and the crowning of the May Queen. Male Morris dancers wore breeches and white shirts decorated with ribbons and they all carried handkerchiefs and bells. The girls were usually dressed in white broderie anglaise dresses. The blonde girls had blue hair ribbons and sashes, whilst those with dark hair wore pink. The dances were very complicated and required hours of practice before they were performed in public. The accompaniment was usually a single accordion or a cobbled-together band. Crowds would be drawn from the surrounding area. The dance, which had local variations, featured the clashing of staves, fluttering of handkerchiefs and the tingling of bells, creating a scene generally associated with English village greens.

Despite the overall resistance to change in the countryside, there was to be no halting the advance of technology and mechanisation. Frank Lay was typical of many returning village soldiers. Having survived four horrific years at the front he attended a final parade where he was presented with the Distinguished Conduct and the Victory Medals. 'All through the bloody war for a couple of bloody medals,' he said, then, cheering up, added, 'Still I came through wonderful well and never a scratch. I was one of the luckiest (that) ever went in.' He had done his bit for King and country and he hoped the King appreciated it. Medals and the King were of little interest to another group of returning servicemen. Violence and discipline were, however, key attributes for success in the criminal world.

7

THE DARK SIDE OF THE STREET

The poor are always with us, but so too are criminals. The fear of thugs, crooks, fraudsters and murderers cast a shadow over post-war Britain. Returning servicemen had been brutalised by constant exposure to the violence of war. Newspaper reports of robbery and murder confirmed the view that Britain appeared to be in the grip of a frightening crime wave. Addressing the problem Sir Nevil Macready, the Commissioner of the Metropolitan Police, conceded 'special measures are under consideration.' He was particularly concerned about the younger men. Often unemployed before joining up, he felt that the war had encouraged them to 'take life lightly'.

They had no sense of responsibility, with many finding it difficult to settle back into civilian life. They had become institutionalised by army discipline and yet were expected to resume their lives as if nothing had happened. Despite this, Sir Nevil advocated 'severe sentences' for any returning troops found guilty of crimes, adding it was no use them pleading they had 'done their bit'. Whilst the young were a worry, of greater concern were the professional criminals. Many of those who had served were returning with stolen or captured guns. Despite the obvious dangers these posed Sir Nevil was against arming the police or even resorting to the use of dogs, believing that old style methods (a quick whack with a trusty truncheon) would be enough to maintain law and order. Some of the gang leaders, however, weren't about to lose any sleep because of anything Sir Nevil could try. They already had a handy number of police and a few judges on their payroll.

Many provincial towns and cities were blighted by organised crime but London and the South East were home to the most notorious and violent gangs. The most feared of these was led by Charles Sabini (known as Darby). He was born in Saffron Hill, Clerkenwell (known as 'Little Italy') the youngest of six brothers, and by his early 30s he had emerged as their leader. Unlike his brother Joseph, Darby avoided serving in the war. He used the time to build his power base and acquired a reputation as one of the most feared men in London. Of only medium stature he still managed to create an air of menace. Neatly turned out, he favoured dark suits, always worn with a waistcoat. His trademark collar-less white shirt rather spoilt the sartorial affect, as did a cloth cap that was rarely taken off. His English mother, a devout Catholic, influenced him in ways not normally associated with a hardened gangster. He detested blasphemy and swearing generally. He also insisted that women were treated politely and with respect. Perhaps it was due to his upbringing that he never became involved with prostitution. He was a complex man and, for someone involved for decades in violent crime, he was surprisingly squeamish. Although razors were the chosen weapon of the gangs Darby avoided using one, preferring a cosh or a knuckleduster. He wasn't averse to whacking someone over the head with a chair leg either.

After the war, horseracing was booming and the Sabini gang moved in to establish a lucrative protection racket. At this stage they concentrated on the southern courses, particularly those close to London. Their business model was simplicity itself. Violence. Outright, blatant violence. Pay up or get beaten up. Darby Sabini recruited a small army of hard men, some bordering on psychotic. The group contained a number of Jews from the East End, a variety of misfits from the Italian community and other criminals who had returned from service abroad. Money was demanded from every bookie on the course. Querying the gang's demands was likely to lead to hospitalisation, the destruction of your pitch and your punters deserting, as they wanted to steer clear of trouble. It was easier and less painful to pay up. Adding insult to injury the bookie also had to pay for everything that allowed him to trade, even down to the chalk he used to write up the odds. In the 1920s there were a series of turf wars as rival gangs tried to muscle in on the act. These included The Elephant Gang from the Elephant and Castle, together with Billy Kimber and his Birmingham gang of *Peaky Blinders* fame. The Sabinis were spreading their influence to nightclubs and other enterprises they felt were worthy of their 'protection'. Other criminals were not spared. If a known robber had made a big haul they could expect a visit from the Sabinis, demanding a cut.

Despite their good contacts within the police, occasionally one of the gang received a prison sentence. Then it was time for the bookies to make a further donation to ensure that the imprisoned man's family didn't suffer whilst he was 'inside'. The Sabinis' influence continued to expand and for years found rich pickings in the West End. The extent of their control of the underworld during the inter-war years is unlikely to be seen again. Graham Greene based his gangster, Colleoni, in *Brighton Rock* on Darby Sabini. Darby was imprisoned during World War II as an enemy alien. This infuriated him as his son was serving in the RAF as a pilot. His son was killed and, devastated, Darby retired to Brighton, living out his life in middle-class respectability.

Gang warfare was certainly not confined to London. In Glasgow its roots lay in religion rather than purely financial gain. Glasgow had always been a predominantly Protestant city until the mid-19th century when there was a huge influx of Irish Catholics escaping famine and lack of employment. The shortage of jobs led to an increase in tension. The Glaswegians resented the new arrivals who were prepared to work for less money. Glasgow already had a reputation for being a tough place to live. Accommodation was in short supply, forcing families to live in crowded, filthy tenements. Many were around an area south of the River Clyde known as the Gorbals. Religious animosity, unemployment and crowded housing all made for a brew that was bound to cause trouble. The gang wars were a constant backdrop to Glasgow life, gaining it a reputation as Britain's most violent city. Segregation was absolute, and territorially based around the Gorbals and other working-class areas. Although there were many street gangs across Glasgow, two of them encapsulated the hatred felt between the Protestants and Catholics. The Bridgeton Gang was better known as the 'Billy Boys'. Their base was less than a mile away from staunchly Catholic territory controlled by the 'Norman Conks' gang (named after the Norman conquerors). For decades these gangs fought each other in an ongoing series of pointless battles.

An inquest into the death of a well-known actress on 8 January 1919 focused the attention of the public on drug abuse. Billie Carleton had been found dead at her Savoy Court apartment after appearing at the victory ball held at the Royal Albert Hall. The circumstances of her death caused a sensation and probably led indirectly to the Dangerous Drug Act of 1920 that implemented controls over the supply of opium, morphine, cocaine and heroin. These drugs had previously been freely available. Conan Doyle's famous detective, Sherlock Holmes, was described as frequently injecting himself with cocaine, which at the time scarcely raised an eyebrow. Now a perception was growing that the smart set in London society was sinking into a moral morass; a feeling that was endorsed as details of Billie Carleton's life emerged. At the age of 22 Billie had appeared to be on her way to stardom, at least until drugs entered her life. Plucked from the chorus by C. B. Cochran in 1914 to star in a review, she was described as being 'a delicate beauty', and having a good stage presence. Unfortunately, she also had a thin, weak voice and was given to rolling her eyes in a melodramatic way to express emotion, which may have worked in silent movies but was rather lost on the stage. It was during the run of the review *Watch Your Step* that Cochran got word of Billie's liking for drugs and promptly fired her. He relented in 1917, giving her a small part in *Fair and Warmer*, starring Fay Compton. This was followed by a leading part in *Freedom of the Seas* at the Haymarket Theatre. Things were looking up, on the surface anyway. The fact that a relatively minor actress could afford to live in a swanky Savoy Court apartment hinted at a life that didn't actually match her outwardly demure image. The gossip suggested she was a 'kept woman' who attended shocking orgies involving sex and religious rites. *The Tatler* caustically summed her up as having 'cleverness, temperament and charm. Not enough of the first and perhaps too much of the latter.'

Poor Billie was found by her maid, and at her bedside was a gold-coloured box containing cocaine. The inquest revealed that the cocktail of drugs that killed her was supplied by a dance instructor and costume designer with the unlikely name of Reggie de Veulle. He was an unsavoury character who, it transpired, had previously been involved in a homosexual blackmail case. It appeared that Reggie had purchased the drugs from a Scottish woman called Ada, an incendiary fact being that she was married to a Chinese man, Lau Ping, who lived in Limehouse. With the ongoing suspicion of foreigners, the British press went into overdrive. A beautiful British flower killed by an inscrutable Chinaman. 'Beware the Yellow Peril', screamed the press. In the event it was Ada who was sentenced to five months hard labour whilst her husband escaped with a £10 fine. Reggie de Veulle was charged with manslaughter. The jury chose to ignore the judge's advice in his summing up and found him not guilty. Pleading guilty to procuring drugs, he was sentenced to eight months in jail without hard labour. The scandal unleashed a huge surge of anti-Chinese sentiment. Although there were only a few hundred Chinese living in Britain they were universally condemned, accused of running opium dens and spiriting English girls abroad to a 'fate worse than death'.

The Chinese tended to congregate around the major British ports but Limehouse in London was singled out as being a dark and squalid den of iniquity. A shadowy figure had arrived in London and became the main supplier of drugs to the upper classes until his deportation in 1925. Brilliant Chang was well named. Suave, good looking and highly educated, he took over the running of his uncle's restaurant at 107 Regent Street in 1918. It provided a perfect base for him to ply his trade of

'Chinese delicacies'. Later he opened a restaurant in Gerard Street that was probably one of the first Chinese restaurants in what is now Chinatown. Chang was the first major drug dealer in 20th-century Britain, a baton that has since been taken up by numerous others who seek to profit from other people's misery.

Late in 1919 a driver was ambushed on a deserted road near Maidwell, Northamptonshire, by two men wielding guns, highlighting the problems caused with so many unlicensed weapons in circulation. A gun featured in the most famous murder case of the year, an unsolved mystery that still rumbles on a hundred years later. There is little doubt that the case would have been solved today with the help of improved technology. In May *The Times* reported a spate of robberies carried out by men 'grown callous after four years' experience of killing'. Within two months of the article there was a report of a death that was to niggle away at public nervousness. On 5 July 1919 an attractive 21-year old factory worker was riding her bicycle on a visit to her uncle's cottage in Gaulby, a village set in the rolling Leicestershire countryside. The rough road caused a wheel of her bike to loosen, making it dangerous to ride. She was joined by a man riding a distinctive green bicycle who offered help. Finding he didn't have a spanner he accompanied her to her uncle's home where the wheel was fixed. They left together at 8.30pm. Half-an-hour later, a farmer discovered the body of Bella Wright lying next to her bicycle. The police called a local doctor who, with the help of a torch in the rapidly fading light, confirmed her to be dead. Astonishingly the police concluded she had died from falling off her bike. Another case solved. Well, not quite. The following morning PC Albert Hall returned to the scene, uncomfortable with the doctor's perfunctory examination and declaration that

Bella had died from a fall. Her uncle had already described the stranger with the green bicycle as 'unnerving'. It didn't take long for the constable to find a number of clues. There were smears of blood on the top bar of a nearby field gate. Unfortunately, despite recent rain, there were no footprints but on ferreting around on the path he discovered a .455 calibre bullet. Surely they couldn't have missed a bullet wound? By 6 o'clock the next morning it appeared that the body had been all night at the police station, seemingly without further examination. It was when the constable was washing the girl's mud-splattered face that he discovered a small entry wound to her head. This was obviously no accident but a cold-blooded murder. Now the police started to piece together the circumstances leading up to the crime and to search for the mysterious stranger who had been riding the green bicycle.

Despite the presumption that the suspect lived locally the police failed to locate him. Wanted posters for a man of medium height in his 30s were widely displayed, producing no leads. It appeared the trail had gone cold. Then seven months after Bella's death a barge carrying coal on the River Soar became obstructed by what was later identified as the handlebars of the missing bike. A witness came forward to say he had seen a man toss the bike into the river a couple of days before. This eventually led to the discovery of the remainder of the green bicycle. An attempt had been made to erase the serial number but enough remained for the police to identify the owner.

Enter Ronald Light, a character who could have been drawn from central casting. He was 34, rather dapper and with a colourful past. Despite the advantage of a prosperous background he had been in trouble as a youth. He was expelled from Oakham School for sexually harassing an eight-year-old girl. This set up a recurring pattern of improper interference with young girls. He was also suspected of arson. This dubious record didn't stop him from obtaining a commission in the Royal Engineers in 1914. Two years later he mysteriously resigned his commission and rejoined the army in the ranks as a gunner, serving on the Western Front. Like many in the artillery, he suffered deafness and from shellshock.

Just before his arrest, a gun holster and bullets were discovered in a local canal. The bullets matched the one that had killed Bella Wright. It appeared all the odds were stacking up to convict Ronald. The trial was held at the imposing setting of Leicester Castle. It featured two legal heavyweights. The prosecution was led by Sir Gordon Hewart, the attorney general. Opposing him was Sir Edward Marshall Hall, known as the 'Great Defender'. On the advice of his learned barrister Light opted for an unusual ploy in that he admitted all the charges made against him except the actual killing. Certainly the revolver was his, as were the holster and bullets. Importantly, he came across positively in the witness box, well spoken and seemingly at ease. Marshall Hall made a convincing case that the death was just as likely to have been caused by a rifle using the same calibre bullet but fired from a distance. It was noted that youngsters had been seen firing at birds in the vicinity and the sad episode could have been caused by persons unknown. Marshall Hall also suggested that a shot at close range would have caused considerably more damage to Bella's face.

None of the defendant's dubious past was revealed in court. Rather, the defence was able to paint a picture of a man who had been a teacher and an engineer prior to the war and had suffered for and served his country well. The newspapers appeared to be generally impressed by Light, an ex-army officer accused of killing a factory girl. It seems astonishing to us now, but class distinction and prejudice was never far below the surface in 1919. Why would a man from such a good background kill for no apparent motive? No one came forward to say they had seen Ronald on that stretch of road that evening. The 'Great Defender' made his case and sowed the seeds of doubt in the jury's mind. Ronald Light was duly acquitted. Unsolved mysteries always intrigue. Subsequently several books have been written about the case. Whilst opinions vary the consensus is that Ronald Light was probably guilty, but doubts continue. Avoiding further publicity, Light changed his name and moved to Kent where he married an older woman and lived to be 89.

Another murder that still resonates today took place in Liverpool in June 1919. Liverpool, like many port cities, had a relatively large ethnic population who generally lived in harmony with each other. As in Glasgow this tolerance broke down with the return of servicemen hoping to get their old jobs back. With unemployment high some turned on the black population of seamen whom they accused of taking their jobs. Rumblings of discontent broke into outright violence when two white men were stabbed in a dockside pub. Although the sailors injured were Scandinavian, it led to a mob attacking hostels and lodging houses traditionally occupied by black seamen. With the threat of escalating violence the police were called and two officers apparently received gunshot wounds. Charles Woods, a young Bermudan sailor who had had nothing to do with the disturbance, was walking home when he was chased by the mob down to Queens Dock where he either jumped or was thrown into the sea. A gathering crowd hurled stones and rocks at him yelling 'Let him drown.' He did. The mob showed him no mercy, shouting and cheering as he floundered. The inquest was a farce. It was stated that the dead man was 'reasonably believed to have fired at the police' and the stone that hit him had been 'thrown from the middle of the crowd' whilst a police officer had tried to rescue him. False statements were recorded and subsequently no one was held accountable or even criticised. Attacks on the black community continued in an atmosphere of hatred, with several hundred black seamen having to be given police protection. Racial and social prejudice were alive and well in Great Britain, adding to the general unease in the country.

The British public loves a good murder, getting a voyeuristic thrill by reading all the gory details in the press. During 1919 the hangman was kept busy, dispatching over a dozen killers. Many of the murders were committed by returning servicemen whose homecoming was ruined by discovering their wives or sweethearts had been unfaithful. Harry Gaskin married his wife, Elizabeth, in 1913. It was never a love match; she gave birth two months later, telling poor Harry that the child wasn't his. Following a spell in jail, he was dispatched to fight for king and country in 1916. After his demob he returned, hoping to mend fences and make a new start. Elizabeth promptly left and went to lodge with her parents in Hednesford. In his absence his wife had given birth to two more children. A man of some persistence, Harry tracked her down and pleaded with her to come home. She insisted she had fallen for another and wanted a divorce. The couple was seen arguing outside the local colliery on 19 February and Elizabeth was never seen again. She was reported missing but when the police interviewed Henry he denied all knowledge of her whereabouts. He eventually broke under questioning and led the police on a grim hunt for the various parts of her dismembered body. He had strangled her in a fit of rage as they walked in the local woods. On 8 August 1919 Henry Gaskin was executed at Winson Green prison in Birmingham. His executioner was John Ellis, who saw over twenty years' service, which included the dispatch of Dr Crippen.

This is one of the sad, forgotten footnotes to a war whose effects were profound and far-reaching. From the most humble to the highest in the land the shadow of war hung over everyone, including members of the royal family.

8

THE KING

It was the worst imaginable start to the New Year for the royal family. On 18 January 1919 Prince John, the youngest child of King George and Queen Mary, died at Wood Farm, an outpost on the Sandringham Estate. He was just 13 years old. For years it had been assumed that the young Prince had been abandoned by his family and erased from history. This was only partially true. Prince John was born at York Cottage on 12 July 1905. He was named John despite it being considered an unlucky name by the royal family, as the youngest son of Edward VII, bearing the same name, died after surviving only one day.

At his birth John was sixth in line to the throne, behind his father and four older brothers. He was christened at St Mary Magdalene church and grew into a big, good-looking child with a shock of blond hair. Although he spent most of his time at Sandringham, all seemed well. He was a boisterous but seemingly perfectly normal child. Although the relationship between the parents and children of the aristocracy one hundred years ago seems strange and aloof to us now, there are signs that 'Johnny', as he was known, was quite a favourite. The Prince of Wales (later King George V) was a strict disciplinarian and boasted that all his children were obedient 'except Johnny'. It was Prince John alone who normally escaped punishment. It appears that the young Prince's unusual behaviour was already being noticed prior to his first epileptic attack, which occurred at the age of four in 1909. It must have been very frightening, not only for the young boy but also for those witnessing it. Although very big for his age it became obvious that the child was slow to learn and something was not quite right. As he grew older the attacks became more frequent and frightening, as he was very strong and difficult to control when he was having convulsions. He began to show signs of what today we might associate with autism and had obsessional repetitive tendencies. An estate worker commented that he would sit for hours surrounded by a pile of farthings that he would painstakingly place into a box, one by one.

Back in 1919 epilepsy was widely thought to be a mental condition rather than a neurological disorder and considered a cause for alarm and embarrassment, even shame. This was particularly true for the royal family, as it was deemed important for the general population to look up to them; 'normality' (or the appearance of normality) was essential. The young Prince was driven to London to see specialists. The blinds were drawn in the car he was travelling in for fear he might have a fit in public. He was rarely seen in public after the age of seven. Queen Mary continued to visit her youngest son and he still attended the traditional Christmas gatherings at Sandringham House, but his behaviour and fits were proving to be not only frightening but an embarrassment for his siblings. To understand the attitude of his family towards young Johnny it is helpful to look at his own parents' background and upbringing. How is it that children born of the same parents develop such different characteristics and personalities? Within the royal family King Edward VII was a larger-than-life character, a lover of good food, wine and glamorous women. By contrast the life of his son (the future George V) was dull. He enjoyed simple pleasures and remained faithful to his wife, yet, in turn, his eldest son Edward (the future Edward VIII) shared a love of a lifestyle similar to that of his grandfather.

The future King George V was the second son of the then Prince of Wales (later Edward VII) and Princess Alexandra of Denmark. He was born amidst the splendour of Marlborough House on 3 June 1865. It coincided with Britain being at the height of its imperial power. Queen Victoria had been on the throne for almost 30 years but was rarely seen in public as she continued to mourn the death of her husband four years previously. Intermarriage within Europe's royal families meant that Prince George was a cousin to both the future Emperor of Russia, Czar Nicholas, and the future German Kaiser, Wilhelm II. As a child he was surrounded by relatives speaking German. His father spoke English with a deep guttural accent. When George was baptised at Windsor Castle there was little expectation that he would become King. This was to affect his upbringing. His parents followed the Danish tradition and believed that their children should be brought up simply. His mother was very popular with the public for her unaffected manner and she did her best to dilute the overbearing Teutonic influence. Luckily for her it appeared that Queen Victoria generally approved of this method of upbringing, although she felt that Princess Alexandra (known as Alix) allowed the children too much freedom. Most aristocratic Victorian children were given only limited access to their parents but Alix veered in the opposite direction. She was a cloying presence who seemingly never wanted her children to grow up.

Both parents were guilty of not providing an adequate education for their children. No doubt influenced by the rigid regime inflicted on him, Edward and Alix never guided their children towards literature and the arts. Lady Cavendish noted that the royal children were '...equally lacking in a love of learning or intellectual curiosity.' Both George and his brother struggled. Albert (known as Eddy), George's older brother, was declared to be vacuous, lazy and unable to concentrate, traits that were to re-occur in George's youngest son many years later.

George was hardly a star pupil either, and it was decided that naval training would teach both the Princes all they needed to know. As young teenagers they were dispatched to serve on the naval training ship HMS *Britannia*. At last Prince George found real meaning to his life. He loved the structure of naval service. But Prince Eddy struggled. Despite his obvious shortcomings, Prince Eddy and his younger brother spent the next three years aboard the corvette HMS *Bacchante*. 'Join the Navy and see the world' certainly applied to the young royals, as they visited much of the vast British Empire including Hong Kong, Singapore, Ceylon, Gibraltar, Egypt and the West Indies. Back home, the dour Queen Victoria bemoaned the fact that her grandsons didn't speak French or German. It was not disclosed if she also disapproved of the tattoo of a dragon on Prince George's arm that he had acquired on a visit to Japan. No matter, the young men were now shunted off to Lausanne in an attempt to make them bi-lingual. The results were predictably bad and besides, George had developed a lifelong suspicion of all things 'foreign'.

He had an unshakeable Christian faith and was a regular reader of the Bible (but of very few other books). Perhaps it was his rigid naval training that led him to be a fanatic about uniforms and decorations, backed up by obsessions with punctuality and formal etiquette. He had become something of a bigot and loathed witty people and intellectual conversation. Even as a young man he was suspicious of anyone with imagination. He distrusted those he deemed 'clever', particularly women, a fault not uncommon amongst the aristocracy of the time.

Prince Eddy was now packed off to Trinity College, Cambridge, in the vain hope that they would be able to engage his brain. His mother's favourite, he was variously described as charming and sweet-natured or, more accurately perhaps, as listless and gormless. His concentration span was minimal, whilst any conversation he undertook tended to lose its thread and the original thought never developed. His tutors despaired and were saved by him being commissioned into the 10th Hussars.

His behaviour began to cause concern. He was not the first (or last) royal to be suspected of indiscreet homosexual affairs. He was also seen in the company of totally unsuitable women. It was deemed time for him to be married off. Europe was scoured for a mate and eventually Princess Victoria Mary of Teck was declared suitable material. The daughter of the Duke and Duchess of Teck, she was known as May and had been brought up in England. She was well educated, spoke French and German fluently and was interested in the arts. But would she be interested in the dim and wayward Eddy? Pressure was put on the couple to make a go of it, if only for the good of the country. So, after a proposal made at a house party held at Luton Hoo, she became engaged to her second cousin, once removed. This was not to be a marriage made in heaven. In fact it was not to be a marriage at all. Just weeks after the engagement, following a day's shooting at Sandringham, Eddy went down with the 'flu. Crowds gathered at the gates as news of his worsening condition and subsequent death from pneumonia spread. Just six days after his 28th birthday Prince Albert, Duke of Clarence and second in line to the British throne, died. It may well have been a blessing in disguise for he was obviously unsuitable to become king. Subsequently letters to his doctor suggested that he might have been suffering from venereal disease. He was also later suspected of being 'Jack the Ripper', in a book written by Patricia Cornwell. Whatever the truth, Prince Eddy was poorly equipped to take on the onerous task of becoming King and Emperor of India. Stand by for the boring but eminently more suitable Prince George.

Having moved up the royal pecking order, George's mood on recovering from a serious bout of typhoid was doubtless improved by being awarded a substantial Civil List grant for his expenditure. He was also allotted his own London accommodation in St. James's Palace, together with York Cottage on the Sandringham Estate, and given the title of Duke of York. Now pressure was transferred to George in an attempt to see him married. Marrying for love was not an option. If nothing else the royal family were distinctly pragmatic. Mary Teck was considered suitable, both for Eddy and as a future Queen, so why look any further? She was not tainted goods so the shy young couple were actively encouraged to get engaged. This they duly did, and just a year after Eddy's death the couple were married at the Chapel Royal in St James's Palace. Perhaps theirs was a good case for an 'arranged' marriage as they grew to love each other deeply, despite their inability to outwardly show emotion.

Whilst York Cottage was a relatively modest house, George was always happy staying there. He preferred the life of a country squire, away from the bustle and political infighting of London. It prompted Harold Nicholson, his official biographer, to write 'He may have been alright as a young midshipman, and a wise old King, but when he was Duke of York he did nothing at all but kill animals and stick in stamps!' He did find time however to father six children. Prince Edward was followed by Albert, Princess Mary, Henry, George and finally, in 1905, Prince John. After the death of Queen Victoria, George and his wife made a number of official visits to far-flung parts of the empire and also to the provinces in Britain. In November 1901 he was created Prince of Wales. His father was anxious to prepare him for his future role as King and he was regularly allowed to view state papers. Extensions were made at York Cottage to accommodate his growing family. He was always happiest when staying at Sandringham. He had become a first-class shot and found blasting pheasants from the sky the perfect way to spend a day. His other passion, stamp collecting, began when his father handed over a collection already made by his uncle, the Duke of Edinburgh. The now Prince of Wales continued to make a huge number of additions throughout his life until it was reckoned to be one of the finest collections in the world.

A small, spruce, bearded figure, the Prince of Wales could be charming but also, on occasions, arrogant and dismissive. Strangely, he was most relaxed and informal with children other than his own. Much has been written about his cold and emotionally cruel treatment of his offspring. It is a common modern trait to criticise behaviour that we find abhorrent today and yet was commonplace a hundred years ago. His own harsh upbringing had done nothing to diminish his love for his father. He had been frightened of him and felt that this was something his own children should feel of their father. It was not unusual for aristocratic children to be presented to their parents by their nanny only fleetingly, in the evening. Children were to be 'seen but not heard', a mantra that was generally upheld. Obedience and discipline were expected of the royal youngsters and they lived a relatively spartan existence. The young Princes Edward and Albert (later George VI) shared a small bedroom, with iron beds lined up close to each other. Though mostly ignoring them as babies, the King was to become a feared martinet to his sons. He showed a much softer, loving side to his daughter Princess Mary, who was undoubtedly his favourite. Lacking in any intellectual interests himself, George imposed a strict regime on his sons. Their education was nonetheless chaotic and latterly left to a tutor, Harry Hansell, who was conscientious but dull and unable to inspire. Later Prince Edward declared himself to be 'completely self-educated'. Like his father, at the age of 13, Prince Edward, (known to his family as David) was packed off to Naval College at Osborne. George believed that nothing could beat a naval education. Soon Albert was sent off to Osborne too, before moving on to Dartmouth Naval College.

On 6 May 1910 King Edward VII died. George was devastated. 'I have lost my best friend and the best of fathers... I am heartbroken and overwhelmed with grief, but God will help me with my responsibilities and darling May will be my comfort, as she has always been.' Later in the year an extraordinary rumour relating to the King began circulating.

A Belgian-born journalist, Edward Mylius, published an article in a Paris newspaper stating that the King had married his Queen bigamously. Mylius claimed that George had already married the daughter of Admiral Sir Michael Culme-Seymour whilst stationed in Malta. Winston Churchill, the then Home Secretary, had been made aware of the allegations by the intelligence service. The paper, edited by American Edward Holden, was little more than a scandal sheet. Published in English the headline screamed 'Sanctified Bigamy'. The article claimed that the unlikely bigamist had abandoned his true wife and entered into a sham marriage with the daughter of the Duke of Teck. It was claimed that the admiral's daughter was the true Queen of England. It was obviously necessary to halt the rumours circulating and Mylius was arrested and charged with criminal libel. At the trial it was stated that the King had not been in Malta at the time the marriage had supposedly taken place and was in no way responsible for any children outside of his marriage to the Queen. Mylius was found guilty and sentenced to 12 months in prison. The King wrote in his diary: 'The whole story is a damnable lie... I trust time will settle it once and for all.' Well, not quite! On release from jail Mylius went off to live in America, beyond the reach of British law. There he published another version of the story with additional claims that the couple had indeed met, and were seen dancing together at the time. Even then there was a thirst for any hint of royal scandal, but George remains an unlikely candidate for a bigamous marriage.

George was 44 when he became King and Queen Mary reflected that the quieter, easier times were over: 'Everything will be more difficult now.' Not only did they have the distasteful libel accusation to deal with but a new Parliamentary Bill that sought to limit the power of the House of Lords. An arch conservative, the King was worried at the prospect of the aristocracy losing their power and influence. The days when the monarch could dictate events had long gone, and the 1911 Act was important in realigning the powers of the Commons and the Lords. The King took some comfort blasting away at the pheasants on his Sandringham estate, but he continued to fear change.

Prior to the coronation a Festival of the Empire was held at Crystal Palace. Timed to take place 60 years after the Great Exhibition of 1851, it provided a focal point for the population to celebrate the power of Britain and its empire. There was a lavish opening concert featuring the London Symphony Orchestra, a military band and a massed imperial choir of over 4,000. Every patriotic musical button was pressed, including Edward Elgar's *Land of Hope and Glory*, together with his version of the National Anthem. The nation's chest swelled with pride. An historical pageant was held over three days, involving 15,000 volunteers. The event was organised by Frank Lascelles, who later in the year was responsible for the breathtaking Coronation Durbar, held in Delhi. The London pageant set out to illustrate the extent and development of the empire. In a sense it was a piece of naked propaganda in an increasingly unstable world.

A little-remembered athletic and swimming event was also held in London, featuring athletes from Australasia, South Africa, Canada and Great Britain. This can be seen as the forerunner to the British Empire Games, which eventually emerged as the Commonwealth Games. Events on the track were confined to sprints and the 120-yard hurdles, together with races over 880 yards and the mile (which was completed in 4 minutes 46 seconds). The Australians dominated the swimming events, whilst a British win was recorded in the Middleweight wrestling.

By June the country had been fully primed to enjoy celebrations surrounding the coronation of King George V and Queen Mary. Huge crowds lined the streets as the royal coach made its way from Buckingham Palace to Westminster Abbey. Over 50,000 troops were on hand to march in procession and to line the route. Camps for the troops had been set up all around London. Colonial and dominion troops were billeted separately from their British colleagues and their turbans and brightly coloured uniforms brought gasps from the crowds. Most would never have seen Indians or black troops before, but how they cheered. Westminster Abbey had been closed for a month to allow pews to be removed and replaced with individual chairs in order to accommodate the 6,000 invited guests. Never missing a trick, the chairs, each with a carved coronet, were available for purchase later.

The King found the service beautiful and impressive, but a terrible ordeal. He recorded in his diary, 'It was grand, yet simple and most dignified and went without a hitch. I nearly broke down when dear David (Prince Edward) came to do homage to me, as it reminded me so much when I did the same thing to beloved papa, he did so well. Darling May looked lovely, and it was indeed a comfort to have her by my side as she has been ever to me for these last 18 years.' He was anxious for his shy wife to become a more dominant figure in the public's perception, as his consort. Later the couple appeared on the balcony of Buckingham Palace. In official photographs they appear wearing full regalia, with Queen Mary sporting a new crown containing the famous (supposedly unlucky) Koh-I-Nor diamond.

Within a month the new King was in Wales to celebrate the investiture of his eldest son as Prince of Wales. Aged only 17, the future King Edward VIII had yet to cause his father the concern that was shortly to develop over his wayward behaviour. The King always had difficult relationships with the leading politicians of the time, as well as his children. Even Henry Asquith, whom he eventually came to admire, he described as 'not quite a gentleman'. His view of David Lloyd George was always damning, and yet it was the MP for Caernarfon Boroughs that came up with the idea of the investiture. It had its origins back in the 14th century, but the re-introduction appealed to the King, who overcame his distaste of Lloyd George by agreeing that the ceremony should take place at Caernarfon Castle. The King was satisfied, and of his son he declared: 'The dear boy did it all remarkably well and looked so nice!' These compliments were about to dry up over the next few years as the 'dear boy' found that amusements other than dressing up in 'a preposterous bib' were far more exciting.

Prior to the Great War the King was frustrated by his inability to influence matters as a constitutional monarch, and worried about the inevitability of war. At a meeting with the foreign secretary, Sir Edward Grey, on August 2 1914, just two days before Britain went to war, he made his views clear. Grey still maintained that he 'could not possibly see what justifiable reason we could find for going to war'. The King was said to have replied, 'You have to find a reason Grey.' He continued, 'If we don't go to war Germany will mop up France and, having dealt with the European situation, would seek to obtain domination of the country.' This conversation was recorded by Sir Edward Grey's nephew, Sir Cecil Graves, following a meeting with the King in 1933. If these were the King's sentiments then he was very much in tune with most of his subjects, as the mood in the country had become increasingly bellicose. On 4 August the King held a Privy Council meeting to declare war on Germany. He recorded, 'A terrible catastrophe ... but not our fault.' The King and Queen appeared on the balcony of Buckingham Palace to wild and enthusiastic cheering from a huge crowd stretching up the Mall. They were not able to predict the disaster that awaited.

It was important for the royal family to be seen to be 'doing their bit'. Prince Albert (the future King George VI) was already serving as a midshipman on board *HMS Collingwood*. Prince Henry was packed off to Sandhurst, whilst the young Prince George followed the well-worn path to Osborne and Dartmouth Naval College. The Prince of Wales was kept out of trouble by serving on the Western Front, understandably as a non-combatant officer. The King made frequent visits to the front, which increased his popularity across the country. With Prince Albert seeing action at the Battle of Jutland in 1916, this feeling was underscored.

A year earlier the King had been injured on a visit to France. His tour was about to finish when he was thrown from his horse whilst inspecting a wing of the Royal Flying Corps. The sudden cheering from the troops caused his horse to spook. It reared, slipped in the mud and fell backwards. The King was trapped beneath his frightened mount. He suffered a double fracture of his pelvis that continued to give him discomfort for the rest of his life. Unsure how serious his injuries were, the medics didn't want to move him any great distance until a full prognosis was made. General Sir John French, concerned that being so close to the front line meant the King was being exposed to unnecessary danger, tried to convince the doctors to move him. The King's reaction was succinct, 'Tell Sir John to go to hell.' The King continued to visit the troops, and by the end of the war it was reckoned that these trips numbered in the hundreds. A seemingly uncharismatic, dull man, he obviously had a sense of duty. A further insight into his complex personality can be found in his decision to give up alcohol in 1915 for the rest of the war. He was a lover of good wine but wanted to be seen sharing the deprivations brought about by war. Meals served at the royal residences were plain and frugal. Balmoral was closed down and shooting much reduced. This was wearing a hair shirt, royal style. Here was a King who, for all his lack of intellectual rigour, was far more complex than generally understood. Despite his seemingly cruel and unemotional attitude to his children when they were young, he was fundamentally a decent man when judged by the accepted standards of the time.

By 1917 the King was aware that his family's Germanic name was forming a barrier between him and his people. The shop windows of businesses bearing German names were being broken and yet the royal family was saddled with Saxe-Coburg Gotha. The King was loath to disown his heritage even when the author H. G. Wells spoke of 'an alien and uninspiring court'. The King replied, 'I may be uninspiring but I'll be damned if I am an alien.' Here was a man who had given up drink and lived a truly spartan life, who had no new clothes made for him throughout the duration of the war and was seldom seen in anything other than khaki. Perhaps it was the air attack on London, undertaken by a Gotha G.IV bomber, which finally swayed him. Although no public criticism of his family name had surfaced, this was not true of his cousin, Prince Louis of Battenberg. His name was duly changed to the more English-sounding Mountbatten. It was the King's private secretary, Lord Stamfordham, who came up with the inspired name of Windsor. On July 17 the proclamation anglicising the royal family name was made, to wide approval.

Earlier in the year the King again showed a degree of independence when he declined the advice of his cabinet to give refuge to the deposed Russian Czar and his family. The royal cousins had always been close and enjoyed holidays together. His refusal to offer asylum was certainly hard-headed, but possibly wise. Amidst the hardship and sacrifice of war would the rescue of a despotic royal dynastic leader really sit well in war-torn Britain? Nicholas and his family were left to their fate with the Bolsheviks. Their brutal deaths no doubt caused the King and his Queen heartache.

By 1919 the King had ruled for nine years. He was uneasy. So much had changed. There was a growing fear that revolution could spread to Britain (that fear perhaps part of the refusal to help the Romanovs) and he found himself the head of a democratic monarchy, something that previous monarchs had despised. He was alarmed that the aristocracy was no longer accepted as the natural ruling class, and that many were forced to sell off their family seats. There were tanks and troops on British streets, Ireland was a mess, and the socialists were gaining political traction. The natural order of things was being turned on its head, overseen by a prime minister he disliked and distrusted. The king was impervious to the Welshman's legendary charm; the man represented everything he loathed, he was immoral and lacked gravitas. The feeling was mutual. Lloyd George thought the King was an old fashioned reactionary. Their relationship continued to be tense and uneasy.

Despite the broader picture and their seemingly distant and uncaring role as parents, it must have been a shock to be confronted with the death of their youngest son so soon after the euphoria experienced with the ending of the war. They would have been aware that Prince John's fits were becoming more frequent and severe. He died either in his sleep or of a particularly violent seizure on 21 January, depending on which report you believe. It appears his parents did motor down to Sandringham once they heard the news. Showing a softer side than is usually attributed to her, Queen Mary recorded in her diary that the news was, '...a great shock, though for the little boy's restless soul, death came as a great relief.' Later, writing to a friend, she appeared genuinely touched, 'It is a great relief as his malady was becoming worse as he grew older, and he has thus been spared much suffering. I cannot say how grateful we feel to God for having taken him in such a peaceful way!' His elder brother (the future Edward VIII) offered these thoughts in a letter: 'He was more of an animal than anything else. That I should be plunged into mourning for this!' He did apologise later to his mother for his callousness, but mourning was not going to affect his social life! Many myths surround young Prince John. One was that there was no mention of his death in the press, as it was suppressed by the royal family. In fact the whole of the front page of the *Daily Mirror* for 20 January 1919 was devoted to the young boy. Under the heading 'Death of youngest son of King and Queen' were photographs showing John riding a pony, on a bicycle, with a toy car, and on a trip to London Zoo. The 'invisible Prince' was laid to rest at Sandringham after a funeral attended by a turnout of estate workers. He occupies a modest grave, largely forgotten but not totally erased from British history.

He was obviously not the first member of the immediate family to exhibit either physical or moral problems. King George's eldest brother, Eddy, would have been a disaster for the monarchy and the country. The King might have mused that even royalty, like the rest of us, can choose their friends but are stuck with their relatives. His eldest son was already showing his true colours and the King was not impressed.

9

THE ERRANT PRINCE

The Prince of Wales was the first shining star of the newly created House of Windsor and a British obsession with the lives of the royal family continues to this day. King George V had done much to nurture the popularity of the royals. Dull he may have been, but he was visible, making regular visits around Great Britain and abroad. After the reclusive Victoria the public generally looked upon Edward VII, her son, with affection, but his lifestyle was so lavish that it set him apart. Viewed fleetingly at a race meeting or some grand state occasion, it was as if this larger-than-life character was being played by an extravagant thespian. By contrast, George had the bearing in public of a benign squire.

Enter Prince Edward, who was thoroughly modern in his outlook, which was a problem for his father. George felt threatened by modern attitudes. An arch traditionalist, he was appalled by much of his eldest son's behaviour, his attitudes and his outlandish dress. It was these very qualities that appealed to the British public. Although small in stature, Edward was good-looking and informal, such a change from the stiffness and formality of the King and his Queen, who never seemed at ease in public. Opinion was more polarised when it came to the young Prince's love life. His ongoing attraction to older married women caused his parents genuine distress, and elicited censure from the more conservative members of society.

The Prince was to experience three great loves in his life. It is quite normal for a young man to think he has fallen hopelessly in love in his early 20s, but not usually with a woman who is 12 years older and married with two children. Lady Marion Coke was the daughter-in-law of Lord Leicester, whose estate at Holkham was close to Sandringham. The two families visited each other regularly. Although the Prince of Wales was serving as a non-combatant officer in France, he enjoyed regular leave and it was in 1915 that he met Lady Marion. A passionate and impressionable man, Edward was not always able to differentiate between his liking for sex and real love. His introduction to sex was in an Amiens brothel with a young prostitute called Paulette. He was to have numerous affairs during his long life but now he was experiencing gut-wrenching, all-consuming love for the first time. Presumably Marion was flattered by his undivided attention when he was home from France. Whilst away he bombarded her with letters. Discretion was the watchword in all adulterous affairs undertaken by the aristocracy. Like most young men this was not a lesson that the young Prince had yet learned and the gossip was becoming an embarrassment and source of anger and disappointment for his parents. Lady Marion was to provide the template for the other great loves of his life. As well as being married, she was small, slender, lively and with a great sense of humour. The affair lasted three years.

What was it in his make-up that continually drew him to older women? Many theories have been advanced but the most likely references his upbringing, and particularly his relationship with his mother. Even before her marriage the future Queen Mary was described as being 'withdrawn, (having a) reserved manner and a cool, even temperament'. She wasn't an emotional person, seemingly quite unable to show outward affection except in the letters she sent to members of the family. The King was often harsh and hectoring in his dealings with his children. The Queen, distant yet controlling, attempted to exercise authority over the Prince well into adulthood. What his parents wanted was to make him an ideal Prince – in their eyes at least. His younger brother Prince Albert (later George VI) was subjected to similar treatment, which in his case might have contributed to his unfortunate nervous stutter. As a young boy Edward was probably the stronger character and gave the impression of not being particularly frightened or intimidated by his parents. Who knows what doubts and frailties we pass on to our children via their upbringing? There is no doubt that the King was utterly devoted to his children, and wrote to Edward of their 'ideal relationship'. Unfortunately, as the boys grew to manhood his wish to control and dominate them intensified. Their mother found it impossible to give her children the love and affection that in most families is taken for granted. She was described as being 'very cold and stiff and very unmaternal!' She had 'nothing of the mother at all!' She didn't reserve this coolness just for her children. Her inability to communicate extended to everyone she met. She was outwardly emotionally barren, as awkward with the highest in the land as with her mystified staff.

The King was given to periodic impulses regarding his son's upbringing. These tended to be connected to physical activity rather than an emphasis on formal education. Edward, like all his class, learned to ride as a child. It was a skill required for

state occasions but it was also important for him to be seen
on the hunting field. The Prince was an enthusiastic and brave
rider without showing any great natural ability. Caddying for
his father encouraged his love of golf, whilst the King personally
taught his sons how to handle a gun. By 1919 tensions were
building, however. The Prince did not always approve of the way
his father treated staff. The King was given to sudden, ill-judged
tirades. Edward as a young man was polite and generally sensitive
towards those he came into contact with. He did show some
dissent at the clothes he was required to wear at his investiture
as Prince of Wales at Caernarvon Castle. There was a family
'blow-up' before he paraded in white satin breeches, a mantle
and a surcoat of purple velvet, edged with ermine.

Following a spell of service in the navy, from which he was
withdrawn before his graduation, it was decided that it was
time for a little formal education and he was packed off to
Magdalen College, Oxford. This was both a surprise and an
annoyance to the prince. His father was well-known for his
suspicion of 'clever' people, a view endorsed by his eldest son.
Edward loved company that was amusing but not intellectual.
No matter, it had been decided that Edward needed to study a
couple of foreign languages and to understand more about the
British constitution. His opposition to the plan was made more
acceptable by the prospect of lengthy vacations, to be spent
in France and Germany. As he would have had little chance
of passing the entrance examination it was tactfully deemed
unnecessary. The poor young man was accompanied to Oxford
by his tutor and an equerry, effectively ruining any chance he
may have had of leading a normal student life.

On arrival at Magdalen in 1912, the Prince was assigned
a selection of eminent lecturers. Their attempts to spark his

interest in constitutional law, politics, history and languages resulted in varying degrees of success. Despite being overseen by the King's 'minders' the Prince was lonely and lacking in true friends. His fellow students had two major advantages; they had (mostly) gained entry on ability and many of them had attended the same public schools, so already had their own circle of companions.

A stubborn streak had developed in the young Prince that was to stay with him all his life. He became increasingly convinced that his judgment on a whole range of subjects was correct, and no amount of persuasion was going to change his mind. This trait would eventually change the face of British history. His intransigence whilst at Oxford centred on his suspicion of people whom he felt were reporting back to his father. Put simply, he wanted the right to pick his own friends. Whilst the Prince was not a prize pupil, he did discover another talent and a life-long absorbing interest. Having been brought up in a world of stiff collars, morning suits and formal dress, he began expressing his personality through his choice of clothes. He started wearing flannels and sports jackets, favouring bright colours and large, bold patterns. His interest was not as casual as the clothes he wore, but an absorption that verged on an obsession. He became a fashion guru and trendsetter. At Oxford he started wearing plus fours and, shockingly, trousers with 'turn ups'. On a trip to France he was reported to have been seen wearing purple trousers and a light blue shirt and on another occasion sporting bright blue trousers, a vivid yellow shirt and blue shoes. This was a young man making a statement in an attempt to break away from – what? His fated responsibilities perhaps.

Despite the King's disapproval of his behaviour, and Edward's initial dislike of Oxford, he returned for a second year. He had now made friends and entered fully into student life, devoting time to wining and dining and even to playing football for the college second eleven. Golf and beagling took up much of his time, and he joined the Officer Training Corps as a private. This was probably a good introduction to service life and in November 1914 the Prince of Wales left Oxford to join the army. Two months before, he had attended his first ball and discovered another of his lifelong interests – dancing. Being small in stature with a good sense of rhythm he was a natural. He loved the nightlife. Gone was the reticent student who had arrived at Oxford. He records in his diary his love of going out and of dancing the night away. How many of those young men attending that ball survived the next four horrendous years?

Initially, on the outbreak of war, Edward had been denied his wish to join up. He wrote to his father expressing his growing distress at not being allowed to serve. For once the King agreed with him and the Prince of Wales joined the 1st Battalion of the Grenadier Guards. After initial training at Brentwood the battalion was to be posted overseas, but Edward was transferred to another unit that was to remain in Brentwood. Infuriated, Edward went straight to the top by approaching Lord Kitchener. There is no doubt about his sincerity in wanting to serve just like any other junior officer. He pleaded with Lord Kitchener saying 'What does it matter if I get killed? I have four brothers.' It was explained that his getting killed was not the issue. The problem was him getting captured and being used as a bargaining tool. A compromise was reached and Edward was sent to France to work in the office of Field Marshal Sir John French. Despite being given a succession of desk jobs the Prince never stopped in his efforts to get to the front line and the trenches. Finally, in September 1915, his persistence was rewarded. He was appointed to the staff of Major General Lord Cavan. This was to be his first real taste of war close-up and it ended in tragedy. Whilst accompanying Lord Cavan to the divisional front line his car was hit and his driver killed.

The Prince soon acquired a reputation for bravery. It was noted that wherever there was heavy shelling the Prince of Wales would suddenly appear. Kitchener's biographer reported, 'It proved impossible to keep him out of the front line.' Yet still Edward complained that his employment was 'just artificial'. It appears that the Prince, although frustrated, was intent on testing himself. Despite sometimes appearing rather diffident in company he was convinced of his own ability and showed no apprehension or fear of any physical challenge. He was not exposed to the daily risks encountered by those in the trenches, but it was not through lack of trying to be treated the same as any other young officer. He was often seen riding his bicycle, inspecting camps and forward positions before returning to make his report. The suffering of those serving made a huge impact on him. Despite enjoying more leave than others the Prince was appreciated by the ordinary tommy for 'mucking in' and seemingly not seeking special treatment. He was also popular for being more approachable than many of his fellow officers.

When the Prince did come home on leave it provided an opportunity to forget the horrors of war, if only temporarily. Pamela Lytton reported, 'No girl is allowed to leave London during the three weeks of his leave and every mother's heartbeat is high!' Unfortunately, their dreams were not about to be fulfilled. The Prince had already fallen in love. Again, this was no youthful infatuation. It was on one of his bike rides early in 1917 that the Prince visited a British Red Cross unit. Fascinated, he watched as a nurse gave her undivided attention to a shell-shocked soldier. He was told that she had spent hours with the young man attempting to get him to speak. Just one word, she was convinced, would help release him from the torment he was enduring. Standing back in the shadows Edward was captivated, not only by the nurse's beauty but also by her compassion. Later, apparently, the soldier pointed at her as she entered the ward and uttered quite clearly 'darling'. He was not the only one to be entranced. This was no ordinary nurse. Rosemary Leveson-Gower was the daughter of the 4th Duke of Sutherland. The Prince of Wales was totally smitten. At the age of 23 he was no longer a callow youth. This was real. He was hopelessly, passionately in love.

The *Illustrated London News* described Rosemary as 'Cheery, kind, ready for any excitement'. That hardly does her justice. Photographs show a dark-haired, rather sultry and soulful young woman, with film star looks. She was unusual in Edward's list of lovers in being of a similar age and unmarried. Their whirlwind romance blossomed and intensified. The King really liked Rosemary, and seemingly approved of her – at least initially. Things changed when society gossip suggested that marriage was a possibility. Alarm bells started sounding at Buckingham Palace. The Prince was furious as he realised that powerful forces with a raft of objections were being activated to curtail the romance. Queen Mary spoke darkly of 'bad blood, a touch of madness in the Leveson-Gower family'.

Look at your potential mother-in-law before 'popping the question' is an old maxim. Unfortunately, Rosemary's mother, Millicent, the Duchess of Sutherland, had left herself open to criticism. In the self-righteous, sanctimonious climate of the day it was deemed that she had remarried in indecent haste after the death of the Duke. Worse was to come. This second marriage was short-lived and ended in divorce. Later, in 1919, she married again, to a known homosexual. Third time unlucky, as this marriage didn't last either. There was more. Millicent's brother, Lord Alastair Sutherland, was considered to be somewhat disreputable, with a gambling habit that led to constant financial problems. It was quickly decided this was not the type of background considered suitable for the future Queen. Within a year the Prince had found a new and even more controversial love in Mrs Freda Dudley Ward.

However fickle Edward may have been, he never forgot Rosemary Leveson-Gower. In a letter later in life he admitted she was the only woman he wanted to marry until he met Wallis Simpson. There is an intriguing and sad footnote to the Leveson-Gower affair. In 1919 Rosemary married Viscount Ednam, heir to the Earl of Dudley and a good friend of the Prince of Wales. They had three sons. In 1929 John, then aged 7, was killed in a motor accident whilst riding his bicycle along Chelsea Embankment. The following year Rosemary was killed in a mysterious plane crash. The aircraft she was travelling in broke up in mid-air whilst flying over Kent. Her remains were discovered in an orchard and could only be identified by the string of pearls she was wearing. The following year the Prince of Wales opened the Rosemary Ednam extension to the Royal Northern Hospital in Stoke-on-Trent.

With the ending of the war the Prince of Wales was stationed in Belgium, attached to the Australian Corps. He visited occupation troops in Germany before finally leaving the army in February 1919. If Rosemary had caused the King to have sleepless nights, they were nothing compared to the angst caused by his son's new lover, Freda Dudley Ward. She was married to William Dudley Ward, a Liberal MP and whip. They had two children and already lived separate lives. Her meeting and introduction to the Prince of Wales came about purely by chance. With her husband closeted at the House of Commons, she was out for a stroll with a man rejoicing in the name of Buster Dominguez (supposedly a South American diplomat). As they entered Belgrave Square in March 1918, an air raid warning sounded. There had been a raid the previous night and pedestrians started to run for cover. The couple noticed an open door and followed the noise of a party in full swing. As they sheepishly entered the hallway partygoers were spilling down the impressive staircase on their way to the cellar. They were quickly invited to join the guests by the hostess, Maud Kerr-Smiley. Not knowing anyone they stood rather awkwardly on their own when out of the blue a dapper young man joined them. Ignoring Buster he started an animated conversation with Freda. He established that she was staying in London with her mother-in-law. He lived in London too, he informed her, although he also spent some time in Windsor. Surely the penny must have dropped? Apparently not. When the all-clear sounded the uninvited guests made to leave. A flustered Mrs Kerr-Smiley insisted they join the party, at the request of his royal highness. Good night Buster! Life is full of unlikely coincidences. It transpired that Maud Kerr-Smiley was the sister of Ernest Simpson – later to be married to Wallis.

Freda danced with the Prince until the early hours. She was not high-born but the daughter of a Nottingham lace and tableware magnate. Her marriage to William Dudley Ward was not untypical of the time. He came from a relatively poor aristocratic family whilst she brought money to the marriage.

He was an Olympic rower and Cambridge Blue. It appears Freda had already taken a number of lovers before the Prince of Wales arrived on the scene. There was never any secret about Freda's relationship with the Prince. They were constantly seen together at parties or dancing at the Embassy Club. Lady Cynthia Asquith described Dudley Ward as 'a pretty little fluff'. She fitted the mould admired by Edward. Dark, petite and with a strange, catchy, high-pitched voice. She was completely natural and not in the least snobbish or stuffy. She treated everyone the same, from royalty to maids or shop assistants, which set her apart from many of her class. Above all these qualities was her sense of discretion. She never made any public comment about the Prince during or after their 16-year friendship.

Edwards's love for Freda at times betrayed his immaturity. Some found it pathetic that he was so abject in his desire to please her (a trait that continued in his relationship with Wallis Simpson). During 1919, if he was in London, he would call on her every day at about 5 o'clock in the afternoon, often returning later in the evening after attending some official event. He found it difficult to let her out of his sight. Wherever she went he followed. Letters sent to her underline his immaturity. They are almost childish. In one he starts 'My vewy, vewy own precious, beloved darling'. He refers to himself as her 'poor little boy' and then to her, rather creepily, as his 'very own, darling, beloved little mummy'. Even assuming it was meant as 'baby talk' banter it does appear that he saw her as a mother figure as well as a lover. Surely a rather uncomfortable combination? In the midst of all this adoration he found time to have other passing affairs, including a fling with Lady Thelma Furness, another brunette beauty. Despite these dalliances it was still Freda Dudley Ward who dominated his life.

With the relationship becoming common knowledge Freda became persona non grata in royal circles. The King was furious but also bewildered by his son's choice of partner. Why, when he could pick virtually any well-connected girl or Princess from across Europe, would he choose a married woman with two children? King George had bullied and intimidated Edward as a child, but he was now trying to impose his will on the Prince as an adult. Edward refused to listen. They were so different in character and outlook and the generation gap was evident to all. Like so many parents the King and Queen were worried for their son's future. It transpired that their worries were well-founded. Although she couldn't have known it at the time, Freda was creating a precedent that would eventually lead to Edward marrying Wallis Simpson. He declared that he would 'never marry except for love'. He also stated, bizarrely but truthfully, that he would 'never again find attractions in anyone who was not already a married woman'. It was these thoughts that were eventually to lead him to commit constitutional suicide.

Freda Dudley Ward must rank as one of the most interesting and influential royal mistresses. Beyond her obvious physical beauty, she was charming, intelligent and, importantly, totally discreet. Although their affair only lasted five years, they remained firm friends until 1934. Enter Wallis Simpson. Edward was beguiled, some even thought bewitched. From that moment on, Freda Dudley Ward was history. She was suddenly and brutally frozen out, her calls were refused and years of shared confidences pushed aside. For the Prince of Wales love was compulsive and all-consuming. Despite living into her late 80s Freda never divulged anything about her affair with the young Prince of Wales. She married Pedro Jose Isidro Manuel Ricardo

Mones. She obviously had a liking for South Americans. Perhaps Buster Dominguez should have hung around a little longer.

Although King George V famously didn't get on well with his prime minister, it was Lloyd George who suggested that the Prince of Wales should undertake a series of visits to the Commonwealth. This was to underline Britain's thanks for the contribution these countries had made to the war effort. It also took Edward away (at least for the time being) from the embraces of Mrs Dudley Ward. Before leaving for Canada in August 1919 Edward acquired (or more accurately was given) his own residence, York House, a wing of St James's Palace. It was an ideal location but it was tired-looking and filled with gloomy Victorian furniture. With the help of Freda Dudley Ward the rooms were re-decorated. For a time a portion of the rambling house was occupied by Edward's cousin, Louis Mountbatten, until his marriage in 1922. Early in 1919 the Prince made a series of tours throughout Britain, including a six-day visit to Wales. He increased his popularity in the principality by attending the fight between the 'Welsh Wizard', Jimmy Wilde, and his American opponent, Joe Lynch. After the fight he entered the ring to congratulate Wilde on his victory. His approachability and his seeming concern for the underprivileged was beginning to further widen his popularity. He was appalled by conditions on the Kennington Estate (which he owned via the Duchy of Cornwall), which led to a substantial amount of money being spent on improvements. The Labour Council reckoned that the Prince was one of the best landlords in the country. There were rumblings from establishment figures that he was becoming too accessible and in danger of removing the necessary gap between the Prince and the public, so essential to maintaining the respect required. There was still trouble with his family. His parents' view of his behaviour and general attitude erupted when the King declared him to be the worst dressed man in London. Queen Mary doubtless agreed, although she was emotionally adrift from her sons whilst finding some comfort in her closer relationship with her only daughter, Princess Mary.

The Prince sailed to Canada aboard *HMS Renown* with mixed feelings: away from the criticism and straitjacket of court life, but also from his obsessive love of Freda. On his arrival in Canada it soon became clear that the tour would owe its success to the Prince of Wales, moving freely through crowds, smiling and shaking hands with those nearest to him. Here was a modern prince, quite unlike anything seen before. Of course there were the formal events to attend but even here he displayed a common touch. His good looks didn't go unnoticed as young women struggled to get close to him. The first royal sex symbol had arrived. The writer, Compton Mackenzie, summed up the gulf between father and son when he wrote, 'King George has all the talents but none of the genius of royalty. If his son may have lacked some of the talents, he had the genius of it beyond any except a dozen Princes in the history of man.'

He toured Halifax and Charlottetown, and went on to Québec, where he boarded a train that carried him over vast swathes of Canada, across a wild, deserted countryside, taking in all the major cities as well as stops at small towns. Everywhere crowds gathered to cheer him and applaud. In all the major cities he made the expected speeches and attended luncheons and dinners. He spoke well, although there was diffidence, a sense of vulnerability that appealed greatly to the ladies attending. More to his liking was the time he spent in the wild in the company of Indian guides, joining them to fish for trout. He won wide appreciation by mounting a bucking bronco and staying on board. He was brave and enjoyed physical challenges. His trip was covered in minute detail by the press from around the world, which had the effect of turning him into a type of global superstar. It was noted that he showed real empathy with every serviceman who had seen action in the war, and paid particular attention to a number of war widows who were introduced to him. His obvious popularity drew a reprimand from his mother, who wrote: 'I see you gave your left hand as the right was swollen (due to constant handshakes), this does not sound dignified though no doubt the people mean well.' It seemed he could seldom win his mother's praise. Luckily his father stepped up to the plate on this occasion, writing to Edward in October, 'I offer you my warmest congratulations on the splendid success of your tour, which is due in great measure to your own personality and the wonderful way you have played up.'

With the Canadian tour successfully completed it was now time to get his first taste of America. After a few days in Washington, where he visited President Wilson, he spent time in Sulphur Springs and enjoyed a few rounds of golf. He impressed the locals with his ability to turn somersaults from a diving board. None of this was to prepare him for the welcome he was to receive in New York, where he was given the freedom of the city. He drove in an open car to a ticker tape welcome, passing along Wall Street, which was decked with flags. *The New York Tribune* reported the raucous response of the crowds. 'They drowned out the sound of brass bands with the din of their voices, shouting their welcome. They observed the decorations, hung along Lower Broadway with blizzards of torn paper, they fought the heavy police guards to get close to his car and in the Aldermanic Chamber at City Hall, they broke through to cheer him frenziedly.' This was perhaps the first inkling that Britain had produced a valuable global asset in the young Prince. The British establishment was still to be convinced. Surely there was (as Queen Mary had already suggested) something rather undignified about this hysteria? The *New York World* understood the reasons when reporting that 'It was not crowd psychology that swept him into instant popularity but the simple something called personality.' Earlier one of the paper's reporters had wired 'New York will fall in love with this lad,' and it did! He was variously described as 'a good sport' and 'a prince with no pretensions'. This was so different from the formal, buttoned-up attitude of his parents. The Prince of Wales was pointing the way towards a new post-war Britain that was slowly emerging. A time of gradual transition.

10

BEFORE GETTING BACK TO NORMAL

The celebrations marking the end of the war had been raucous but somehow hollow in London and the other major cities, and muted elsewhere. People deal with grief in different ways but this was a totally new experience, a whole nation bound by a shared dark thread. This was exposed each Sunday as millions attended church services. Black dominated. Dresses, coats, ties, armbands. A pale face glimpsed beneath a veil. The empty sleeve of a jacket tucked neatly into a side pocket. The vacant seat in the front pew where before the war the local landowner's son had knelt in prayer. The congregation wanted to return to normal life, but the tentacles of war proved slow to release their grip.

Although many churches were still full on Sundays, overall attendances were falling. The faith of Britain had been tested and, for many, churches of all denominations had been found wanting: too many jingoistic sermons, and sometimes not enough pastoral care. The clergy had to tread carefully as so many of their parishioners had been killed or wounded. By 1919 there was a groundswell of opinion asking 'what was it all for?' Was the world a better place? It certainly didn't seem so. Bereaved families wanted answers but there were none, other than faith and it was faith that for many was being questioned. Just as in the commercial markets, there was a gap to be filled. There was no lack of contenders as a small army, mostly women, sought to bring peace of mind to the grieving. Were they genuine comforting angels or money-grabbing charlatans, happy to fill a void for cash?

Prior to the war spiritualism had fallen from the height of its Victorian popularity, but the bereaved grasped at any opportunity that encouraged their hope of making contact with deceased loved ones. Gladys Osborne Leonard claimed she had developed psychic powers as a child, but kept quiet about it for fear of ridicule. She subsequently became a singer and actress (skills which may or may not be significant depending on your point of view). It was whilst touring with a theatrical company that she took part in a series of séances. Initially, there was no contact with the spirit world, but eventually she was supposedly introduced to her guide, through whom she would be able to contact the dead. For the sceptical it is difficult enough to believe this stuff but her guide stretches this doubt to breaking point. Bizarrely, the name spelt out at the séance was Feda, a young Hindu girl. She had been married to Gladys Leonard's great grandfather and had died bearing him a son in 1800. Feda claimed she had looked after Gladys since she was a child. So it was goodbye to the theatre and hello to the mystical – perhaps shady is a better term – world of spiritualism. Her calling to help and comfort the bereaved happily coincided with the outbreak of war. We are asked to believe that it took some persuasion for her to take money for her sittings though, reluctantly, she accepted. Her consultations, she claimed, were just as beneficial as any visit to a doctor. By the end of 1914 she had already built a formidable reputation and a healthy bank balance. Her sittings were reported to produce comforting and positive results. She was kind, approachable and convincing. A potential superstar, waiting for a break.

On 14 September 1915 Second Lieutenant Raymond Lodge was killed on the battlefield just outside Ypres. He was the son of Sir Oliver Lodge, the well-known physicist who was a key mover in the development of radio. Ten days after his son's death Sir Oliver's wife attended a sitting with Gladys Leonard. On cue Raymond sent a message, 'Tell father I have met some friends of his.' Sir Oliver was an expert on electromagnetism, airwaves and 'syntonic tuning', which he patented. It's perhaps surprising that a man of his background and an eminent scientist was a believer in the supernatural and convinced by Gladys Leonard, an ex-theatrical trouper. His book *Raymond, or Life and Death* was published in 1916 and created a sensation. Reviews were mixed, with some critics resorting to ridicule. In the book Lodge claimed that the spirit world was much like our own. There were people existing in a comforting British countryside, with trees and flowers. Additionally, in this heaven-like existence there was no disease and the soldiers who had been killed met up for a smoke and a nip or two of whisky. The book spawned a glut of new mediums offering their brand of comfort to the bereaved.

Mrs Leonard organised public meetings that helped thrust her further into the limelight. She attracted the attention of Sir Arthur Conan Doyle, creator of Sherlock Holmes. Celebrity endorsement was as important 100 years ago as it is today. Surely the backing of so many eminent men (including those with a scientific background) proved that she really was able to contact the dead? Conan Doyle had been interested in the afterlife for years and described himself as a Christian spiritualist. It is often thought that Conan Doyle was influenced by the death of his son, Kingsley, who died of pneumonia in October 1918 after being seriously injured two years previously. Perhaps it was the general carnage in 1916 that led Conan Doyle to believe that spiritualism was a 'new revelation', sent by God to bring solace to the bereaved. His children's nanny appeared to have psychic powers and she prompted him to meet Gladys Leonard, a tall, elegant woman with a fair complexion and brown hair tied back in a bun. He was obviously impressed:

> The greatest trance medium with whom the author is acquainted is Mrs Osbourne Leonard. The outstanding merit of her gift is that it is, as a rule, continuous. It is not broken up by irrelevant pauses but it flows on as if the person alleged to be speaking were actually present. The usual procedure is that Mrs Leonard, a pleasant, gentle, middle-aged, ladylike woman sinks into a slumber, upon which her voice changes entirely and what comes through purports to be from her guide Feda.

There is a hint of doubt here, but Conan Doyle went on to write *The New Revelation*, published in 1918, and followed in 1919 by *The Vital Message*, in which he outlines his belief in Christian spiritualism. The views of the public were deeply divided. A core of people wanted to believe the mediums that promised contact with their dead relatives; others were convinced that vulnerable people were being duped by trickery and autosuggestion. Despite the need to honour the dead, there was a fear that the effects of the war threatened to overwhelm optimism for the future. So was Leonard an out-and-out fraud, or was her spirit guide Feda a 'typical hysterical' secondary personality, as historian Ruth Brandon concludes in her book *The Spiritualists* (1983)? No one can be sure.

There was a desire for life to return to normal, but what was normal? Life in Britain had changed and it was time to establish new norms. As families were reunited or came to terms with their loss, the first steps were faltering. Nature, in the form of a calming walk in the country observing the slow changes in the seasons, or pottering in the garden, helped some to gradually lighten their mood, as did the escapism of a visit to the local picture house or watching a football match. There was a new world to look forward to, spearheaded by ground-breaking technology and evidenced by more cars on the roads and the occasional sight of an aeroplane high in the sky. Many felt that change should be welcomed and embraced.

Part 2

BRITAIN AT PEACE

11

THE SILVER SCREEN

The British have always been good at queuing, standing patiently in line for buses and trams, at the butchers or bakers, in the queues caused by rationing. Now people of all ages waited in line with a sense of anticipation and excitement. In the rain or hot summer sunshine they queued for a chance to watch their favourite film stars. A trip to 'the pictures' became a central part of the nation's enjoyment. Throughout the year millions would join in this ritual. Turnaround was swift, with those queuing outside quickly filling vacant seats as the audience of the previous screening departed. The silent screen continued to astonish and enthral a public hoping to be transported to a different world. Comedy, romance and melodrama were all on offer at a price everyone could afford. There were more than 500 picture houses in London alone, with a proportionate spread throughout the rest of the country.

The first public film show in Britain took place in London in 1896. Two rival systems launched on the same day and by the end of the year the two competitors were presenting moving picture shows at the Alhambra and the Empire Theatre, situated close to each other on either side of Leicester Square. Not to be outdone, the Biograph, an American development, was on offer at the giant Palace Theatre on Cambridge Circus. The search was on to find permanent sites for the shows and cinemas, or 'electric theatres', started to appear. As with the nickelodeons in the States, going to the pictures in Britain initially only cost coppers. However, it was not long before the full commercial possibilities for films became obvious. Most of the early cinemas were converted from existing buildings. Shops and offices were transformed into gleaming picture palaces. Many cinemas employed commissionaires to greet the customers, dressed in uniforms more suited to a Ruritanian prince, to underline the sense of glamour. Cinema was an industry beginning to find its feet. It offered the public a rare chance to escape from everyday life and be transported to a world that few even knew existed. Some cinemas had auditoriums as lavish as the grandest theatres, with snacks and cigarettes on sale in the foyer. Others were situated in mean backstreets and became known as 'flea pits'. Initially, cinemas only seated around a hundred people but by the outbreak of war Britain boasted some of the largest and most lavish cinemas in Europe.

With the increased availability and popularity of film shows, concerns were raised by the government and by local authorities about fire risk. The first fatalities in British cinemas occurred when four children were killed in a stampede at the Electric Theatre Picture Palace in Dartford. Of even greater concern to the authorities was the behaviour of audiences under the cover of darkness. Whilst young couples got to know each other better in the back row, more outrageous behaviour was often underway elsewhere in the building. Enterprising prostitutes moved from the stalls to the balcony, dispensing their services to a willing clientele. These ladies could earn far more during a performance than hanging around on cold street corners. A percentage of their take was normally passed on to all but the most moral cinema managers. For young men home on leave or waiting to be sent to the front, the film being shown was only of secondary interest. There was public outrage. Daughters were banned from going to the cinema. Gradually the police restored decorum, with only a few picture houses still retaining a reputation for lewd behaviour. The usherette's torch shone more often and brightly, and the sex workers reverted to their street corners.

Before the introduction of the cinema organ many of the larger cinemas employed a full orchestra. Sitting in the pit, they would try and interpret the actions on screen with a suitable accompaniment. Smaller cinemas had to make do with a pianist. Most film showings were interrupted by the need to change reels. Frequent delays were caused by a film splitting or unravelling from its reel, which ruined the continuity and was generally greeted with a mixture of booing and cheering. Boisterous behaviour would sometimes boil over into outright aggression and violence. The Teddy Boys of the 1950s were not the first to fight pitched battles in the aisles. This was usually prompted by rivalry between different regiments or units. Violence has always lurked just below the surface in Britain, particularly where tribal interests are threatened. The cinema would screen newsreels from the front or war propaganda films to try and halt bad behaviour. One of the most popular films in 1916 was the *Battle of the Somme*. The audience reacted to it as one, with aggression and abuse directed towards the sight of the retreating Hun. Although troops might occasionally fight amongst themselves they were united in their hatred of the enemy. There was a thin line between the young men's natural propensity to aggression and their patriotic pride in their country, witnessed daily as the audience stood for the playing of the national anthem at the end of the last performance. Anyone attempting to leave was quite likely to be dragged back or restrained. This attitude extended until well after the end of the Second World War.

Building restrictions ensured that almost no cinemas were built during the war. The 1920s were to witness massive new picture houses with the advent of the 'talkies'. Entrepreneurs and businessmen were moving in. The demand for films appeared insatiable and there was huge money to be made. Studio bosses, producers, directors, actors and their agents all vied for public attention. Many films were short in length and relatively easy to produce, though the emphasis was beginning to shift towards longer blockbusters. British films were being made in 1919 but most of the films being shown in Britain were from Hollywood. Whilst crowds continued to flock to the cinemas, the industry was in chaos. There was no formal structure. Filmmakers were selling off distribution rights on a localised basis in return for a percentage of the take at the box office. There was little financial control or accountability. Agreements were open to abuse and there were plenty of ambitious men willing to take advantage. Hollywood produced a string of ruthless moguls quite capable of widening any loophole in a contract to their advantage.

The most powerful man in Hollywood at the time was Adolph Zukor. He was determined to bring some discipline to the industry. Zukor was a Hungarian immigrant who arrived in America in 1899. Living the American dream, he arose from New York's deprived Lower East Side, first opening a penny bazaar before taking over a small theatre. Within ten years he was working as a film producer, which was when he first encountered Mary Pickford and Charlie Chaplin. He quickly realised that there was an opportunity for him to channel his productions through a single powerful distributor. He obtained the backing of the newspaper magnate, William Randolph Hearst, as he moved towards his goal of controlling every aspect of filmmaking, from inception to distribution. A small, dynamic and ruthless man he was to be known as 'The Godfather of Hollywood'. He set out to get control of producers, directors and the stars appearing in his films. He acquired a number of companies, including Realart Picture Corporation and the Famous Players Film Company. The Paramount Film Company was formed to distribute his films. In 1919 Zukor, through his Paramount Film Company, purchased over 100 cinemas. He was now in position to set up a nationwide system of distribution for all his productions. He had formed the basis for what was to be known as the studio system, a far cry from the mess many of his competitors were in.

It was partly this desire for total control that led to the creation of United Artists at the beginning of 1919. The producer, D. W. Griffith, and famous stars Mary Pickford, Douglas Fairbanks and Charlie Chaplin, started to forge their own separate identity with the formation of a new company. Griffith had become particularly aggrieved following the astonishing success of his film *The Birth of a Nation*. Its success was mired in controversy, but he was denied the financial reward he was due. Griffith was a brilliant filmmaker, introducing many new techniques including close-ups and fade-outs. The film was a story about two American families, one that supported the Union and the other on the Confederate side in the Civil War.

The film ran for over three hours and was a brilliant technical achievement but centred on the explosive theme of race. It's often dubbed the most racist movie ever made for glorifying the Ku Klux Clan and depicting African-Americans as sullen, stupid and sexually aggressive towards white women. Millions went to see Hollywood's first blockbuster, but it was so divisive that riots broke out in protest. The subplot to the film was that, despite huge box office takings, the lack of financial control meant Griffith was seriously short-changed. One of the biggest culprits was Louis B. Mayer who owned the lucrative distribution rights for New England. On the proceeds Mayer was able to form his own film company that eventually became Metro-Goldwyn-Mayer. Griffith was swimming with sharks. Something had to change. It did, with the formation of United Artists.

Like many projects started with missionary zeal, United Artists never fully realised its initial concept. Perhaps there were too many inflated egos involved. Mary Pickford and Charlie Chaplin never really trusted each other and their relationship was further complicated by Pickford being engaged to Douglas Fairbanks. They married in 1920 to become Hollywood's first golden couple. Their romantic fire finally burnt out and they were divorced in 1936. United Artists released three films in 1919, the first of which was *Broken Blossoms*. Set in London's Chinatown, it starred Lillian Gish and was considered a box office success, as was *His Majesty the American* starring Douglas Fairbanks. Although the intention had been for each of the stars to make five films a year, financial restraints and lucrative offers from elsewhere restricted their output, but they had made their stand against the overall concept of the studio system. Pickford became increasingly interested in the activity behind the scenes and she proved herself to be an astute businesswoman. Known as 'America's sweetheart' she was actually Canadian, having been born in Toronto. In common with other former silent movie stars her popularity declined with the arrival of the 'talkies'. She finally retired from acting in 1933.

Although Fairbanks was the leading heart throb of the day, Charlie Chaplin was already the most recognisable star of those involved in the formation of United Artists. Aged just 30 in 1919, he had already become a world superstar with films such as *Sunnyside* and earnings reckoned to be in excess of $80,000 a year. Chaplin was born in Walworth, a deprived working-class district of London. His abusive, drunken father deserted the family, leaving his mother to bring up the young chilrden. Lily Chaplin was a music hall performer who developed mental health problems, creating an unhappy and difficult childhood environment for the young Charlie. Despite this he inherited his mother's love of the stage and was performing in public by the age of five. On leaving school he took any job available whilst keeping in touch with variety agents. Eventually he made his acting debut as a pageboy in a production of *Sherlock Holmes*. Moving on, he joined the famous Fred Karno Troupe. The young Chaplin was a keen observer of human behaviour and perfected an art of playing a drunk (there were plenty for him to see staggering around the streets of London), before being spotted by Mack Sennett, the leading film producer.

By 1914 Chaplin was living in the States. It was the year that he established the unforgettable figure of the little man with the bowler hat, moustache and cane, a character he might well have remembered from his childhood. The character was seen to full effect in 1915 in *The Tramp*. The pathos of this downtrodden figure was embraced across the world and cemented in the sad ending of *The Bank*, which followed in 1916. By now there was nothing sad or downtrodden about Chaplin in real life. He was pocketing eye-watering sums making a stream of films to satisfy the seemingly endless demand. Despite the number of short films he made he was a perfectionist, often insisting on countless retakes. The films kept on coming during the war and Chaplin was criticised in Britain for not volunteering for military service. He half-heartedly said he would sign up if called to, and he did register for the American draft. He probably did more for morale by continuing to make films, as he was very popular with the troops when they did have a chance to see him at camps away from the front. There were by now many impersonators of Chaplin, complete with pinstriped trousers and cane, earning money on the back of his fame. It is hard today to understand the impact of Chaplin. As Ignatiy Vishnevetsky writes:

Charlie Chaplin was famous in a way that no one had been before; arguably, no one has been *as* famous since. At the peak of his popularity, his mustachioed screen persona, the Tramp, was said to be the most recognized image in the world. His name came first in discussions of the new medium as popular entertainment, and in defenses of it as a distinct art form – a cultural position occupied afterward only by the Beatles...

That's not just the most recognised person – a US president, a George Clooney – it's the most recognised *image* – Ferrari's prancing horse, the Golden Arches, the Facebook logo.

Hollywood producers didn't take long to realise the massive appeal of comedy and Chaplin, although undoubtedly the most successful, was not without competition for public acclaim. Silent movies lent themselves to a universal type of comedy that many felt would never transfer to talking films. In many ways they were right. Just look at young children today watching films produced a hundred years ago, still squealing in delight at the antics on screen. Harold Lloyd was a contemporary of Chaplin and, along with Buster Keaton, was considered to be the finest exponent of silent comedy. Whilst Chaplin's appeal was based on sympathy for the perpetual underdog, Lloyd relied on action and hair-raising stunts. To set himself apart from Chaplin's down-at-heel tramp, Lloyd started to wear large round glasses and a straw hat to establish his own identity in the eyes of the public. Success brought financial rewards that included owning his own studio. In 1914 he employed Bebe Daniels as his co-star. Many years later she became famous when featuring with her husband, Ben Lyon, in the radio series *Life with the Lyons*. Lloyd and Bebe Daniels, known as the 'The Boy and The Girl', were lovers, before splitting up in 1919. This was a year that Lloyd would remember for the rest of his life. He was still only 26 and in constant demand, but like other stars, he had to go along with the publicity machine that fuelled Hollywood's success. He was holding a fake bomb on the set of his latest film *Haunted Spooks*. Unconcerned by clouds of smoke he smiled gamely for the photographers when suddenly there was an explosion. This was no joke or stunt. A photographer was thrown across the room and part of the roof collapsed. Lloyd was temporarily blinded and his hand was seriously damaged, causing him to lose his thumb and forefinger. For a time it appeared that his whole career was in danger but he recovered and continued to make some of the most memorable silent films. The highlight was probably the sight of him hanging from the side of a skyscraper, clinging to the hands of a giant clock, the people in the street below looking no bigger than ants. Lloyd, together with Chaplin and

Buster Keaton, was about to spearhead a vintage decade for film comedy in the 1920s.

The viewing public tends to be rather fickle in their attitude to famous film stars. Despite the wide acclaim Lillian Gish received for her performances in *The Birth of a Nation* and *Broken Blossoms* her popularity dipped with the arrival of the 'talkies'. Her innocent vulnerability, so admired in her silent films, was suddenly considered old-fashioned and out of touch by an audience that wanted a more 'vampish' approach. She adapted by returning to the theatre and then, much later, appearing in television. Thus she successfully maintained a career that spanned some 70 years.

It was film mogul Cecil B. DeMille who recognised the star potential of the beautiful Gloria Swanson. In 1919 he cast her in the popular films *Don't Change Your Husband* and *Male and Female*, which included the sensational 'lion bride' scene. A rather ludicrous plot sees a group shipwrecked on a deserted tropical island. Swanson was never one to avoid doing her own stunts, but appearing with a live male lion was surely beyond the call of duty, even for her? However, she did so in a fantasy scene that replicated the painting by Gabriel Von Max. Swanson lies prostrate, all flowing gown and feather boa headdress. The lion has his huge paws on her back (he was apparently eating a hidden biscuit). It certainly took a deal of courage as it was reported that the lion killed someone a couple of weeks later (though this is probably just a story dreamt up by Paramount). No matter, the pose shocked and thrilled. Swanson was confirmed as Paramount's leading star and rewarded with a reputed salary of $20,000 a week. Following a long and severe dip in her popularity Swanson found fame again in the 1950 film *Sunset Boulevard*. In it she plays Norma Desmond, an ageing and forgotten silent movie star. It was a brave move as the part had already been turned down by a number of former silent movie stars, including Mary Pickford. For Swanson the gamble paid off and it is probably the role for which she is best remembered, despite her cuddle with the lion.

The year also saw the emerging talent of perhaps the silent screen's greatest director. Eric von Stroheim was in his early 30s when he directed *Blind Husbands*. It was his first independent production, for which he wrote the script and also played a leading role. He had served his apprenticeship observing the work of D. W. Griffith, who continued to be an influence on his output. Born in Austria, the war must have been a difficult time for Von Stroheim, but with peace came the chance for him to develop his unusual and innovative method of making films. He was a difficult and intimidating man to work for. He was not afraid to be hectoring and antagonistic towards his actors and his attention to detail in seeking perfection was obsessive. Gone were the sugary heroines and upstanding heroes, Stroheim presented realistically flawed characters whilst challenging perceived moral taboos. His masterpiece came in 1924 when he directed *Greed*, a tale about the power of money to corrupt. It is ironic that before filming was completed Goldwyn Pictures was merged to form Metro-Goldwyn-Mayer. The new studio bosses took a very hard line with Von Stroheim, insisting on huge cuts to the length of the film. The project was taken over by the studio and cut to two-and-a-half hours. The butchered version was not a success. Von Stroheim's choice of controversial subjects and lack of commercial understanding sidelined him as a director in Hollywood. Greed and the making of money were central to the Hollywood philosophy and there was little room for true artistic expression.

Before the war about 25 per cent of films shown in Britain were made domestically. Four years later Hollywood dominated, with only 5 per cent of films being produced in Britain. As many British films were sentimental romances or slapstick, director Alexander Butler was brave in taking on the controversial subject of venereal disease with his film *Damaged Goods*. There was a genuine fear of a VD epidemic, with servicemen returning home after visiting French and Belgian brothels during the war. The film was dynamite, and illustrated the changes taking place in society. Subjects that previously would have been banned were now being addressed. Whilst censorship in all forms of the arts had many years to run, the movement towards a more open and liberal society was inching forward.

Cinema offered an opportunity for even the poorest in society to enjoy a good night out. Subtitles allowed the audience to fully enjoy the experience. It was estimated that millions were attending each week, with many making two or three visits. Most sat through the entire programme, which included a newsreel and a couple of short supporting films, as well as the main feature. Cinema opened up an entirely new world of romance, comedy and adventure. A chance to see strange far-flung places, but most of all a chance to dream.

12

READ ALL ABOUT IT

The raising of the school leaving age from 12 to 14 in 1918 led to an increase in literacy. Publishing was entering a golden age. With radio still not generally available as a distraction, books, magazines or newspapers captured people's imaginations. Reading offered not only the chance to educate yourself but also to relax and escape into another world. There was no excuse for being left behind. Most towns of any size had a public library, and Boots and other retailers had lending libraries, normally located in the stationery department. Demand stretched from non-fiction to serious novels and cheap thrillers. If that didn't suit there was an incredible selection of magazines and newspapers on offer. On buses and trains, in cafés and at home, people had their noses stuck in a book or some other publication.

There was fierce competition for leadership amongst the popular press, with each publication trying to differentiate itself from its competitors. *The Times* sat aloof above the rest, secure in the knowledge that it remained the choice of those with influence in society and business. The content of their pages reflected this, with court circulars and the births, marriages and deaths of the elite of British society. World news was covered by leading journalists, and their financial reporting and information was only rivalled by the *Financial Times*. *The Times* also carried extensive classified advertisements that, at the beginning of 1919, included requests for information about men missing, presumed dead, in battle.

Elsewhere in the newspaper market another form of battle raged. The *Daily Mail* was locked in a bitter fight with its rival, the *Daily Express*, which had been purchased by Max Aitken (later Lord Beaverbrook) in 1916. Two years later he opened the popular *Sunday Express*. This left those with left-wing tendencies to choose between the *Daily Herald* and the *Daily Mirror*, both serious, well-written publications that usually ignored the more sensational stories favoured by the *Mail* and *Express*, whose targets were the expanding middle-classes and more conservative working-class. *The Express* was unashamedly patriotic and nationalistic in its coverage, a sentiment that reflected much of public opinion so soon after the war. *The Mail* continued to attract new readers with its emphasis on competitions and stunts. Both papers also had regular contributions from well-known public figures and experts on subjects currently in the news. With sports fixtures slowly getting back to their pre-war levels, it was important to have a top-class racing correspondent and tipster. The *Sunday Express* followed a similar format to its sister paper, but more space was dedicated to feminine interests. Beauty tips and articles on film stars found a ready and enthusiastic market. Much of the advertising in these papers was also aimed at women, with a strong emphasis on fashion.

The Sunday papers already played an important role in British life. For once there was time for most to trawl through them at their leisure. The competition for readers was hard-fought. *The People* declared itself, 'a weekly newspaper for all classes'. Photographs were becoming increasingly important for papers, replacing etchings and hand-drawn illustrations. *The People* was strong on stories with human interest, which extended to reports from the divorce courts. News of adultery and scandal pointed a tentative way forward for the publishers. Sex certainly sells but outwardly, for the moment, decorum was being upheld. It was still the age of subtle suggestion rather than revelation. Most of the papers were now devoting space to gardens and home improvement. There was also a page in *The People* devoted to answering readers' queries, a forerunner to an agony aunt column.

The British public has always loved scandal. The *News of the World* claimed a certified circulation of more than 2.5 million and was already reporting scurrilous stories of infidelities. The paper was also running regular features on the music halls, despite a fall in audiences caused by the popularity of silent films.

It was the *Daily Mirror* that boasted the largest daily circulation. Its close relationship with the Labour party and the trades union movement guaranteed it a loyal core readership. The *Mirror* set itself apart by being a tabloid paper rather than a broadsheet and featured more photographs than most of its rivals, thus achieving its own unique identity in a crowded market. It didn't lower its socialist principles to report on high society. Others were not so reticent. The aspiring politician, Duff Cooper, noted in his diary, 'The *Daily Express* and the *Daily Sketch* came out with the announcement of our engagement (to the actress and socialite Lady Diana Manners). The whole front page of the latter was taken up with pictures of Diana...

The evening papers were full of our engagement, especially the *Evening Standard*.' A golden couple, they came to represent the louche lifestyle of the roaring '20s. They married in June 1919 and, although no doubt deeply in love, within months Duff Cooper was having affairs whilst Diana was beginning to show her increasing dependency on drugs.

A book that was started in 1919 but published later proved a sensation, and skewered the lifestyle of the privileged young elite in London. *The Green Hat* was written by an Armenian, then living in London. He had changed his name to Michael Arlen and, despite being educated at public school and mixing in high society, he remained an outsider. He dressed immaculately and had impeccable manners. No matter, he was spoken of behind his back as 'a bloody foreigner' and, as such, untrustworthy. He was about to get his own back. Like Scott Fitzgerald in America he set out to satirise a glamorous set with too much money and time on their hands. Stung by snide remarks by fellow author Sydney Horler, who declared that Arlen was 'the only Armenian who never tried to sell me a carpet', he set out to expose the snobbery and decadence of high society. It was portrayed as sleazy, immoral and ultimately sad. Iris, his heroine, has to endure the suicide of her husband on their wedding night after confessing that he has syphilis. She has a succession of lovers but it brings her no joy. She speaks of her 'soiled loneliness of desire'. Ultimately she kills herself, driving her yellow Hispano Suiza (presumably the H6, inline six-cylinder OHC, introduced in 1919) into a tree. Strong stuff and, although poorly written, it made Arlen a fortune.

The superficial lives of this pampered set were put on hold for a while as a group of poets exposed the grief and suffering created by war. Rudyard Kipling, whose 18-year-old son had been killed in 1915, mourned publicly in his moving poem *My Boy Jack*, published the following year.

"Have you news of my boy Jack?"
Not this tide.
"When d'you think that he'll come back?"
Not with this wind blowing, and this tide...

"Oh, dear, what comfort can I find?"
None this tide,
Nor any tide,
Except he did not shame his kind –
Not even with that wind blowing, and that tide.

Whilst artists and composers had added to the public's understanding of the futility of war, it is the poets whose words still have the same power to affect us today. Novels like Remarque's *All Quiet on the Western Front* and *Death of a Hero* by Richard Aldington add to our understanding, but it is the immediacy of the poems to events that so moves and shocks us.

Siegfried Sassoon was already a household name even before the publication of *Memoirs of an Infantry Officer*. Harold Nicholson described the work as: 'A book of deep beauty and abiding significance'. Famously, in 1917 Sassoon decided not to return to the trenches. He sent a letter to his commanding officer giving his reasons. His *Soldiers Declaration* began 'I am making this statement as an act of willful defiance of military authority because I believe that the war is being prolonged by those who have the power to end it.' This was despite him having been awarded the Military Cross for conspicuous bravery and being recommended for the Victoria Cross. He was known to his men as 'Mad Jack' owing to his lack of concern for his own safety. The government decided it would be problematic to charge a war hero with treason and he was shipped off to Craiglockhart Hospital to be treated for shell shock. Meantime he published *The Hero, Henry Holt* in 1918 and his other influential war poems in 1919. Whilst he was in hospital he met and influenced Wilfred Owen, perhaps the finest of the war poets. Was it the early deaths of Owen and Rupert Brooke that propelled them to posthumous fame? Surely not, for there is no doubting the potency of their work. Owen, like Siegfried Sassoon, had been awarded the Military Cross for bravery. Having been discharged from hospital he was killed by a sniper's bullet just one week before the end of the war. Sassoon continued to champion Owen's work long after his death. A shocking passage from Owens *Dulce Et Decorum Est* illustrates the power of his work:

Gas! Gas! Quick, boys! – An ecstasy of fumbling,
Fitting the clumsy helmets just in time;
But someone still was yelling out and stumbling
And flound'ring like a man in fire or lime...
Dim, through the misty panes and thick green light,
As under a green sea, I saw him drowning.

Sassoon turned his fire on the complacency at home. A verse from his poem *Suicide in the Trenches* reads:

You smug faced crowds with kindling eye
Who cheer when soldier lads march by,
Sneak home and pray you'll never know
The hell where youth and laughter go.

By contrast the poetry of Rupert Brooke is gentle, deeply patriotic and less realistic, yet it continues to be popular well after his death in 1915. He saw little active service but an infected insect bite developed into blood poisoning that resulted in his death. His charm and good looks had already drawn the public's attention to his work. His early death helped to ensure his place in English literature together with lines: 'If I should die, then think only this of me: that there's a corner of a foreign field that is forever England.'

For those seeking an escape from the memory of war there was much to entertain rather than inspire. Whilst the jingoistic adventures of *Bulldog Drummond* were archly described as 'snobbery with violence', it was left to P. G. Wodehouse to caricature the aristocracy. His brilliant characterisation of Bertie Wooster and his butler, Jeeves, proved irresistible to the British public. His two new books, published in 1919, were both best-sellers. Certainly *A Damsel in Distress*, about a golf-loving American composer was popular, but *My Man Jeeves*, a collection of short stories, flew off the shelves. Wodehouse went on to represent a segment of British life with his stories of snobbery, his manner of speech and catchphrases. A comic master, he was particularly good at conveying the elongated drawl and phraseology of clubroom slang. Yet there was more to Wodehouse than parody and it is his gentle debunking of the social scene, with his hapless, chinless wonders and ferocious harridans, which make him one of the great comedy writers of the twentieth century.

Ulysses by James Joyce is considered by many to be one of the finest novels of the twentieth century. For others it is impossible to read. Another avant-garde writer, Virginia Woolf, was not alone in concluding 'I have been amused, stimulated, charmed, interested by the first two or three chapters... and then puzzled, bored, irritated and disillusioned, as by a queasy undergraduate scratching at his pimples.' The book was serialised in America from March 1918 until December 1920. It was finally published in 1922. Any novel based on Homer's *Odyssey* is never going to be an easy read, particularly when the author boasts: 'I've put in so many enigmas and puzzles that it will keep the professors busy for centuries, achieving what I meant, and that's the only way of ensuring one's immortality.' Considered obscene at the time, hundreds of copies of *Ulysses* were confiscated by H.M. Customs. It was considered by T. S. Eliot to demonstrate that 'Joyce was the greatest master of the English language since Milton.'

Less lofty but more readable were the novels and short stories written by Somerset Maugham. He was a prolific writer, known for his gift of storytelling in an uncomplicated and straightforward style. His novel *Of Human Bondage*, published in 1915, had already established him as one of Britain's foremost writers. Whilst successful and rich due to his eventual output of almost 200 published works, Maugham's private life was complicated. Once describing himself as two-thirds normal, one-third queer, it appears that he got his percentages wrong. Despite marrying in 1917 he spent most of his life with his partner, Gerald Haxton, until Haxton died in 1944. Before marrying Syrie Wellcome, Maugham had been cited in a divorce by her former husband, the industrialist Henry Wellcome. The marriage was very unhappy despite them having a daughter together.

Maugham volunteered to serve as an ambulance driver during the war. Instead he was co-opted into British intelligence and worked as a spy in Geneva and Petrograd. Maugham obviously found time to write during the war as his novel, *The Moon and Sixpence* was published in 1919. Based loosely on the life of Paul Gauguin, its central character was an English stockbroker who leaves his wife and children to become an artist. As in other Maugham stories there is an element of autobiographical content.

Agatha Christie was a volunteer nurse in Torquay during the war. It was on observing a Belgian refugee that she created Hercule Poirot. The unlikely Belgian ex-police officer with his outrageous moustache featured in her first novel *The Mysterious Affair at Styles*. She completed the book in 1916 but it was rejected by a number of leading publishers. Eventually, in 1919, The Bodley Head accepted it provided she changed the ending. It was a busy year for Christie as she gave birth to her only child, Rosalind, in August 1919. The book was serialised in *The Times* before its eventual publication in 1920. This first novel marked the beginning of the career of the most successful crime writer of all time.

Whilst sales of books after the war were increasing, the appetite for magazines seemed insatiable. In a crowded market there were dozens of titles available, covering a huge range of interests. There was particular emphasis on titles appealing to women. The cosy, comfortable content provided by *Woman and Home* would shortly be challenged by the British version of *Good Housekeeping*. For the moment the choice was mostly a panoply of knitting patterns and craft projects. Ever conservative in its approach, *The Lady* was considered essential for those wishing to appoint a maid or a housekeeper.

Vogue was almost identical to its American counterpart except for its use of anglicised spelling. *Vogue* had established itself as the fashion magazine by which all others were judged.

It was bought mainly by women who couldn't afford the sleek gowns and dresses illustrated. For most it offered the equivalent of window-shopping. Each edition featured a stunning front cover, many of which have since achieved iconic status. Those wishing to keep up with the social scene made a beeline for *The Tatler*, which covered all the great social and sporting events. There were pages of photographs featuring ladies sitting side-saddle on their favourite hunter or with their husbands at a point-to-point in deepest Leicestershire. If you had a title, a military rank above captain, or at least a double-barrelled name, you had a pretty good chance of being included. There was a striking contrast in how dull and dowdy the ladies appeared in photographs compared to the line drawings of the elegant gowns and dresses regularly advertised. A rival to *The Tatler* was *The Bystander*, which, like many other magazines, sold for a cover price of one shilling. It also combined reports on social gatherings and gossip with coverage of theatre and sport, and often featured short stories written by well-known authors. By 1940, against a background of war, the demand for domestic tittle-tattle declined and the title merged with *The Tatler*.

The Sphere, The Graphic and *The London Illustrated News* were all indirectly in competition with each other and strived to find a speciality that set them apart. Photography had improved dramatically and was important in their coverage of world news. Each title continued to give prominence to leading artists and illustrators, using colour to brighten their pages. *The Graphic* featured artists like watercolourist Helen Allingham and Frank Hall. *The Illustrated News* reported widely on scientific discoveries, and was also one of the first magazines to understand the huge potential of prominently featuring the royal family. *The Sphere*, whilst similar in content, was widely read in the colonies where its detailed news coverage, photographs and illustrations were enjoyed across the empire whilst sipping 'Sundowners'.

As the lady of the house flicked through the society and fashion magazines, the maids were devouring the *Red Star Weekly* or *Red Magazine*, which concentrated on romantic yarns, often recycled from earlier editions. These offered a temporary escape from the harshness and drudgery of their lives and handsome heroes and tender kisses proved irresistible to this army of young women.

Punch was already something of a British institution, having been published for over 70 years and with a circulation of around 100,000. Known mainly for its cartoons, it featured wide-ranging articles on art, science, history and news from around the world. The cartoons were created by the great illustrators of the day, including Heath Robinson and H. M. Bateman, who became the highest paid cartoonist during the 1920s. He was in high demand, also producing work for *Illustrated Sporting News*, *The Tatler* and *Pearson's Weekly*. E. H. Shepard was for a time a staff member of *Punch*. Already a well-known illustrator, he continued to contribute to the magazine throughout the war, during which he was awarded the Military Cross, having achieved the rank of major. It was in 1923 that he joined forces with A. A. Milne (who also worked on the staff at *Punch*) to create *Winnie the Pooh*.

Magazines and cartoons consciously set out to lighten the public mood after the war. There was even a *Happy Magazine* that, as its title implied, only featured stories with a happy ending. This 'feel-good' factor was extended to the important sector of children's books and comics. The publishers obviously recognised the potential for the children's market as a number of new titles were launched at the beginning of 1919. *Tiger Tim* was a cartoon character who particularly appealed to young children. Previously he had appeared in *The Rainbow* but *Tiger Tim's Tales* (later to be called *Tiger Tim's Weekly*) was launched in June 1919. The format was a cartoon strip, with the storyline printed under each individual illustration. *The Popular*, a comic appealing to older boys, was launched six months earlier and contained the usual mixture of adventure stories, including those of the detective, Sexton Blake. Launched at the same time was *The School Friend*, which was best known for the stories of Bessie Bunter, the sister of the famous Billy Bunter, who was the main attraction in *The Magnet*. (Billy and Bessie were a fraction of the literary output of the extraordinary Charles Hamilton. If we assume Hamilton, 43 in 1919, was at the height of his powers, then he probably wrote between 1.5 and 2 million words that year.) *Boys Own* was the most jingoistic of the comics, featuring many tales of the British Empire. *The Captain* also underlined British values and was presumably meant to encourage the next generation of leaders to take their country forward. *Chums*, and its annual produced each Christmas, underlined good triumphing over evil. All the heroes were of course British through and through.

This attempt to mould the young extended beyond the family home and school. Through reading books, comics and magazines children were signposted towards a life of bravery, fair play and service. Girls and young women were subjected to moral guidance from editors and publishers. *Secrets and Fame* was targeted at young working-class women, feeding them a diet of dramatic tales with a strong love interest. Most of the girls' comics revolved around stories of school. Typical was *The School Friend*, first published in 1919. It featured stories like *Bessie Bunter's Busy Day*. Other tales in the first weeks of publication included *The Rivals of the Fourth* and *Out of Bounds*. It was to be a few more years before publishers realised the potential strength of the schoolgirl market, with a raft of new titles being launched in the 1920s. The reading boom continued as a generation that had received a basic education became enthralled by the power of the printed word. For those seeking more strenuous diversion, the world of sport beckoned.

13

THE SPORTING DIVIDE

The leisure industry as we understand it today did not exist in 1919, though many people, even those involved in the most arduous occupations, were beginning to enjoy some spare time to indulge their interests. A perception had become entrenched during the 19th century that the British were somehow superior to all foreigners, particularly at sport, perhaps because the British invented many of the games that later developed into organised sports. There was almost a sense of entitlement, which was being eroded each year as reality began to sink in. It wasn't just in industry and commerce that Britain was being overtaken. In British eyes it was important for the amateur to triumph without appearing to try too hard. This was undermined by the development of professional sport. It induced a sense of queasiness in many, as being paid somehow tarnished the glorious amateur ethos so loved by the British.

A scandal in the US in the autumn of 1919 confirmed these worries. The World Series baseball final is probably the biggest sporting event of the year in America. Unusual betting patterns were noticed on the morning of the game as a raft of money was staked on the Cincinnati Reds (the outsiders) to beat the favourites, the Chicago White Sox. The Reds duly won. Subsequently, eight members of the White Sox team were charged with fixing the game, although after lengthy court proceedings they were acquitted in 1921. Despite the finding, the players were banned for life from playing again. 'The mob', represented by Arnold Rothstein, had organised the scam. It had been made possible by the notoriously mean owner of the White Sox, Charles Comiskey, who had a reputation for underpaying his players and tying them to unfavourable contracts. Although baseball was a mystery to most people living in Britain, the publicity generated by the scandal underlined the doubts generally felt about professional sport. Surely the Athenian spirit went out of the window when money was introduced?

The other great divide affecting sport was one that was impossible to avoid in Britain. Class. Those from different social backgrounds rarely competed against each other. Polo was obviously the preserve of the 'toffs', whilst rugby (rugger) was mostly played by young men who had been to public school. Professional sport did unite the public, but only as spectators, one group enjoying the comfort of the grandstand or paddock whilst the others viewed from packed terraces or enclosures. It was cricket that provided the closest social interaction, but even here it was important for you to know your place.

Cricket was more than just a game for the average Englishman. It was played at almost all schools and was thought to impress on the young the spirit of fair play. The quintessential English scene is of white-clad players caught in sunlight on a village green, with an ancient church in the background. But cut to any backstreet in Sunderland or Birmingham and skinny, scruffy kids could be found playing with an old bat, a tennis ball and using a lamppost as an improvised wicket. The game was a national obsession, much as it is in India today. Cricket was introduced throughout the empire as a means of spreading British values.

Some contend that the reason the game crossed social barriers dates back to the 18th century. Bowling on a hot summer day was considered too arduous for the toffs and landowners, so estate workers were encouraged to bowl the ball for the master to whack around the field. As the game developed, rival teams were formed. Conveniently, over the years, the early influence of gambling on cricket matches was forgotten and by 1919 the game was fully established but segregation continued. Professional players were required to use a separate entrance to the pavilion and they did not share a changing room with the Gentleman players. The term 'Gentleman' implied that the player was a man of means and had no need to work. Every County team was captained by an amateur, even though many were not talented enough to warrant a place in the side. Astonishingly, the annual fixture at Lords between the Gentleman and Players survived until 1962. The game was a draw, with fiery Fred Trueman pitched against the imperious Ted Dexter for the Gentlemen. After this game the distinction was dropped and they are all just players now.

First-class cricket had been largely suspended during the war, although a few representative matches were arranged between various forces teams, held at the Oval and Lords. There was a real desire to get the first-class games reinstated during 1919. County matches were reduced to two days as the authorities were worried that the four-year gap would badly affect attendances. The experiment was not popular and three-day fixtures were quickly reintroduced. It was a strange year for the County Championship, with each County arranging their own matches. Results were measured by the percentage of possible points earned. This weird arrangement led to Yorkshire being named champions although they won less than half of their fixtures, with Kent taking the runners-up spot. Although there were no test matches, a strong Australian forces team played a number of representative games, winning most and reigniting their reputation for being the toughest of opponents in god time for the forthcoming Ashes series of 1921.

The 'them and us' division found in cricket was reflected in the first match report of 1919 in *The Tatler*. The match took place at Leyton, between the Essex County side and a public school eleven. On July 11 the annual match between Eton and Harrow was held at Lords. This, together with the Varsity match, highlighted the social divide, as thousands of top-hatted gentlemen and their elegant ladies paraded in front of the pavilion during the lunch break. Their young sons were also decked out in top hats, morning suits and stiff white collars. They tried to look unconcerned, despite having been heckled earlier by a scruffy band of youngsters as they made their way to the main entrance.

Although Yorkshire won the County Championships, with leading players Herbert Sutcliffe and Wilfred Rhodes, it was Jack Hobbs who became the first major cricketing star after the war. He was awarded a five-year contract by Surrey in 1919, at £400 a year. Hobbs repaid them by scoring in excess of 2,500 runs, at an average of more than 80. He went on to be the first professional sportsman to be knighted, in 1953. He fitted perfectly into the establishment's view of an ideal professional cricketer. His father had been a Cambridge University servant and he knew his place.

He was understated, unfailingly polite and immaculately dressed. Others would challenge the straitjacket of conformity placed on them by society – but not yet.

By late August, from Roker Park to Stamford Bridge, huge crowds of cloth-capped supporters flocked to support their local football team each Saturday. In Scotland, Rangers and Celtic revived their fanatical rivalry. Professional football had been suspended throughout the duration of the war and there was a massive pent-up demand to be satisfied. Even amateur clubs drew crowds that would be the envy of some lesser professional clubs today. Football had become the working man's sport as much as beer was his drink. Armies of supporters with rattles and scarves cheered from the terraces. It was a family game and youngsters were lifted and passed overhead all the way to pitch-side so they could enjoy a better view. There was no obscene chanting and little swearing. Although the atmosphere was tribal and highly charged, it was mostly good-humoured. On the pitch the players wore baggy shorts and heavy leather boots that came up over their ankles for extra protection. Bulky shin guards were essential. The goalkeeper wore a thick woollen polo neck jersey. This was not a game for today's prima donnas. There was no diving and feigning injury. This was a man's game, a tough, no-nonsense, contact sport. It was a game of crunching tackles and hefty shoulder charges, of goalmouth scrambles and hectic action. It was not unusual for a goalkeeper to be barged into his own net as he attempted to collect a high cross. Any ball passed backwards was greeted with howls of derision. Possession of the ball was important but often sacrificed for a long ball, booted down the middle to the muscular centre forward. Technique was secondary to physical toughness and honest endeavour. Often the leather ball became so heavy in wet conditions that it took strength as well as skill to move it any distance. Even the top-class pitches were turned into quagmires or were rutted with frost. Snow did cause matches to be postponed, but as often as not it was cleared and piled up at the side of the pitch. Spectators had to make do on the icy terraces, exposed to all weathers. It could be frightening as the crowd surged forward whenever a goal was scored, testing the strength of the crush barriers. Injuries and deaths continued to haunt football right up to the Hillsborough disaster in 1989 and beyond, though the '20s and '30s were relatively free of outright disaster. The 1923 FA Cup final at the Empire Stadium (Wembley) could well have become one, when an estimated 300,000 turned up to the 125,000-capacity venue. There were many injuries but no deaths.

For those willing to pay a little extra to sit in the stands it meant enduring hard wooden benches, with the view often obscured by steel pillars. Stadiums were spartan by today's standards, epitomised by the smelly, unhygienic toilets. These were often just lean-to shacks constructed of corrugated cladding and set on bare earth. None of these hardships eroded the passion the fans felt for their team. The mill owners and other employers clearly wanted the local team to do well, as production rose or fell depending on the results.

Professional football resumed on 30 August 1919 but it was mired in a scandal that had taken place four years previously. America was not alone in witnessing a betting scam that undermined the integrity of professional sport. The football authorities decided that the 1919/20 season would see the First Division expanded from 20 to 22 clubs. It was expected that the bottom two clubs from the 1915 season would be re-elected whilst the top two clubs from Division Two would join them.

Derby and Preston North End were therefore promoted as planned. Assuming the expected format was adhered to, Chelsea and Tottenham Hotspur (who had finished 19th and 20th respectively) would be reinstated. The decision was complicated by a match that had taken place on Good Friday in 1915 between Manchester United and Liverpool. Missing players already serving in the forces weakened both teams and only 13,000 turned up to watch the match. The game was still important as the result was to affect who would be relegated. Although Liverpool were safe in mid-table it was still possible for United to be relegated. As with the baseball game, unusual betting patterns were detected on the morning of the match. Large sums had been waged on Manchester winning 2-0 at odds of 7 to 1. After the game the referee reported that he had been unhappy at 'the level of commitment from some of the Liverpool players'. They seemed unconcerned at abjectly missing a penalty and then reprimanded one of their own players when his shot hit the bar. It appeared that three United and four Liverpool players had tried to fix the result, saving Manchester from being relegated. As the result of an enquiry, seven players were banned for life. One was killed during the war but the others, with one exception, were quietly reinstated from the start of the 1919 season. Enoch West continued to plead his innocence; his ban was to last another 30 years.

The scandal deepened when neither Liverpool nor Manchester United were fined or reprimanded for any wrongdoing. Things were about to get a whole lot worse. The Football League governing committee had come under the baleful influence of Sir Henry Norris. He was a self-made property developer who transformed Fulham from a country village into a suburban sprawl. A football fan, he became a director of Fulham Football

Club before turning his attention to Woolwich Arsenal. On obtaining chairmanship of the club in 1913 he moved Arsenal to Highbury, on the other side of London, where he had acquired valuable land. By 1919 the ultimate 'Mr Fixit' had been knighted for his military recruitment work and was MP for Fulham. With this level of respectability his influence within the football league was considerable. He managed to persuade the committee chairman, John McKenna (chairman of Liverpool FC who had also been implicated in the fixed match with Manchester United), to propose that Arsenal should be promoted at the expense of Tottenham Hotspur. Yet Arsenal had only finished in mid-table in 1915 and surely had no right to jump the queue? It was argued that Arsenal had been members of the league longer than Tottenham. True, but so had Wolverhampton Wanderers, who finished above Arsenal in 1915. It was suggested that Highbury's proximity to the West End would bring a whole new audience to the game. Surely the committee wouldn't give in to such flimsy recommendations? But they did, by 18 votes to 8. The Tottenham club was incensed to be consigned to the second division and the enmity between the fans continues to this day. This confirmed to many that football and the whole of professional sport was corrupt. In spite of his own ongoing success in making Arsenal a major force in the game, Norris eventually did one deal too many in 1927 and was banned from any further involvement with football.

1919 marked the 30th season of the Scottish Football League. They had also decided to increase the number of clubs playing in their top division. Back in 1916 three clubs had been removed because of the distance other clubs had to travel to play them. With better transport links Aberdeen, Raith Rovers and Dundee were reinstated, with Albion Rovers also being introduced into the top tier. Unfortunately, this revival was short-lived, with Albion Rovers finishing at the foot of the table. Their season was obviously one of wild contrasts as they reached the final of the Scottish Cup, losing narrowly to Kilmarnock. Sensationally, they had beaten Rangers in the semi-final. Of the other newcomers, Aberdeen must have been disappointed to finish only 17th, but Dundee managed to complete the season in 4th place. Rangers dominated the league season, leaving them clear of their arch rivals, Celtic. On October 18 Rangers beat Celtic 3–0 in front of a massive crowd of 78,000. A week later England travelled to Windsor Park in Belfast where the National team drew 1–1 with Northern Ireland. The proceeds of that match were just over £2,000, a record for the venue. Few then would have guessed that football would become the global financial juggernaut it is today.

Boxing has always been associated with gambling. Dark tales abound of fixed fights: eyes nicked with a razor by the boxer's own seconds, fake knockouts and corrupt referees. On one level boxing was a cesspit, and yet it offered an opportunity for young men from deprived backgrounds to seek fame and fortune. At the National Sporting Club the huge social divide was again emphasised, as dinner-jacketed patrons sat puffing at their cigars whilst young men tried to knock each other senseless. If the bout pleased the crowd, they would toss a few coins into the ring. These 'nobbins' had been added to a fighter's earnings since the bare-knuckle days of the Victorians. Away from the plush surroundings of the National Sporting Club, boxing was a popular spectator sport. Most provincial cities had regular bouts. St James' Hall in Newcastle was popular, often attracting Irish boxers who took on the local talent.

Belfast was a hotbed of boxing, with regular bouts held at Celtic Park, Ulster Hall and Grosvenor Park. In London, whilst championship bouts were staged at large venues like Olympia and Haringey, there were a host of other places to watch the latest emerging talent. The Star of David was a common sight on boxers' shorts as young Jewish men tried to fight their way out of the East End slums. They fought in rowdy, often hostile, venues such as the famous Ring on Blackfriars Road or Manor Hall in Hackney. These venues, and many others like them, were bear pits. Fighters were allowed to take fearful punishment that would not be tolerated today. Often a badly beaten fighter would be back in the ring in a matter of days. They needed the money to survive.

Where there was boxing, the gangsters were never far away. Fixed fights sometimes led to crowd disturbances. There was often more money for a boxer if he threw a fight rather than winning it for a modest purse. Whilst fans still flocked to the small venues it was the champions who fuelled the most interest. The heavyweight division has always held a particular fascination for the public. In July British newspapers carried extensive coverage of the World Heavyweight Championship in America, between reigning champion Jess Willard and the relatively unknown Jack Dempsey. Willard had won the title in the 20th round of a gruelling fight in 1915, beating the feared Jack Johnson. A huge man, known as the 'gentle giant', Willard didn't take up boxing until he was 27. Despite a reputation for being a rather negative fighter, relying on counter punching, he had colossal power. Tragically William 'The Bull' Young died the following year after suffering a 9th round defeat to Willard. Jack Dempsey was a hard man who had honed his savage skills by winning bare-knuckle fights in bars where he took on all comers for money. In 1917 he was signed up by 'Doc' Kearns, who became his manager. Although coming from Irish stock Dempsey was marketed as part American Indian because of his 'savage' aggression. It appears that Willard did not take Dempsey's challenge seriously, as he had done hardly any training. A crowd of 45,000 turned up in Toledo, Ohio on a searing hot day. Willard towered above Dempsey as the boxers touched gloves, and the crowd was expecting to witness a long and bloody fight. Despite having a four stones weight advantage it was all over within 10 minutes, producing a result as controversial as when the then Cassius Clay knocked out the intimidating Sonny Liston 45 years later. Willard was overcome by Dempsey's naked aggression. He smashed the champ as if he was in one of his backroom bar brawls. It was reckoned he caused more damage during that first round than had ever been inflicted on a fighter before. Willard was later reported to have suffered a broken jaw and several cracked ribs as he was flattened to the canvas in the opening round. Dempsey left the ring thinking he had won, but the noise of the crowd had masked the fact that Willard had been saved by the bell. This was to prove very costly for 'Doc' Kearns, Dempsey's manager. The fight continued for two more murderous rounds before Willard's corner threw in the towel.

Later it was rumoured that Kearns had bet a massive $10,000 at 10 to 1 for his man to win in the first round. Previously Willard had never been knocked down, let alone knocked out. So why would Kearns risk so much? Stories circulated that Dempsey's hands had been lined with metal tape under the normal bandaging. Nothing has ever been confirmed, but Willard's injuries were certainly unusually severe. Whatever the truth, the 'Manassa Mauler' retained his title until 1926, when he lost on points to Gene Tunney in a close decision in front of a crowd of 120,000. Boxing in the States was a big business but a dubious one, overseen in part by crooks and mobsters.

British boxing was dull by comparison. 'Bombardier' Billy Wells was a popular heavyweight champion, often cruelly known as the 'Horizontal Champ'. During the war he served in France, overseeing physical training. In February 1919 he was scheduled to defend his title against Joe Beckett, whom he had previously beaten. The bout took place at the Holborn Stadium. Beckett was shorter and much lighter than Wells, who was a firm favourite with the bookies. Once again, the unfancied fighter triumphed, with a conclusive 5th round knockout. Although Beckett was really only a light heavyweight, this time there was no hint of a fix. Later in the year, Georges Carpentier, a French boxer with film-star looks, knocked out Beckett. It appeared our heavyweights could only knock each other out and didn't have the ammunition to take on world-class fighters. In the lower weights the 'Welsh Wizard', Jimmy Wilde, and the Jewish Ted 'Kid' Lewis competed and won at the highest level but there was to be a very long wait before Britain could boast of a world heavyweight champion.

Whilst football and boxing were sometimes under a black cloud of suspicion, a breakaway sport had achieved great popularity in the north of England. Its very existence owed much to the recurring theme of social division. Rugby is a unique game in being suitable for players of all shapes and sizes. The tall, squat, powerful and speedy, all have a role to fulfil. As such the game appealed to all classes but it was also very physical and frequently led to injuries. In part this led to the breakaway game. For young, relatively wealthy players injury didn't present a major problem but for working class lads time off work cost money they could ill afford. This led to a semi-professional game developing in the latter part of the 19th century with amended rules. With two fewer players per side, the game required extra fitness and a professional approach to training. From its inception in Huddersfield the game flourished, known until 1922 as the Northern Rugby Football Union. Championship competition was suspended during the war as so many players were serving abroad. On resumption Huddersfield ended the first full season as league leaders but they were defeated in a low-scoring play off by Hull. Huddersfield did enjoy success when they beat Wigan 21-10 in the Challenge Cup final in front of 14,000 fans at Headingley. It was a tough game, played by hard men and set against a bleak background of smoking chimneys and red brick mills. The gulf between the enthusiastic amateurs and the hard-nosed professionals was vast, but at least rugby league was untainted by scandal.

Whatever the sport, refreshment was as essential to its enjoyment as the sporting banter. Sadly, in 1919 food in Britain was far from championship standard, and often frankly scandalous.

14

FOOD FOR THOUGHT

Britain had acquired a reputation for serving some of the worst food in Europe. Wartime shortages increased the need for cooking to be plain and the conflict had increased suspicion of foreigners that extended to their food. British diners preferred a meal of roast beef and Yorkshire pudding rather than fancy food ruined by strange sauces. What was wrong with the meat and two veg enjoyed by all the social classes? If a household could afford it, a roast with all the trimmings would be served on a Sunday, with perhaps cold meat and salad on Monday. Tuesday would see the remains of the joint minced and served with mountains of potatoes. By Friday it was time for a trip to the fishmongers.

The odd cup of tea and a bun in a local café was as near as most got to eating outside their home. Visiting a restaurant or smart hotel was confined to the wealthy or those away from home on business. Anyone seeking foreign cuisine would search around the major ports of Britain where there were a few cafés catering for visiting sailors. There were many Chinese restaurants around Limehouse in London but few Britons ventured in as they had a reputation for being 'fronts' for drug dens. Soho had the widest choice of foreign restaurants, although other, more exotic, attractions led the prudish to steer well clear.

Just as retailers had seen opportunities in an expanding middle-class, the need for mass catering soon became apparent. Tearooms, rather than coffee shops, were what the British public required. A nice cup of tea was essential to life. Mugs of steaming tea accompanied many a meal. Tea was served in the parlour or lounge, along with a slice of cake or a round of cucumber sandwiches in more socially aware homes. Tea was refreshing and comforting, often poured at times of stress or crisis. Tea, it seemed, was a drink for all occasions, and the creation of tearooms would fill a national need. The Express Dairy and ABC Cafés already had hundreds of outlets, but they were about to be outgunned by an organisation that declared its intentions by opening its first branch on a prime site in Piccadilly. Once more, it was Jewish immigrants who were able to exploit and expand a massive potential market.

Isadore Gluckstein and Barnett Salmon had arrived in Britain in the mid 19th century. They established themselves as leading tobacconists, with almost 150 retail outlets. It was Montague Gluckstein, a partner in the business, who identified the potential for a tearoom and restaurant empire. This led to the sale of their tobacconist company, for a mighty £400,000, to Imperial Tobacco. They formed a new public company and the directors included the Gluckstein brothers, Barnett Salmon and a distant relative, Joe Lyons. Joe Lyons created a reassuringly British feel to their cafés and soon became a household name. Their dominance of the tearoom sector was based on a few basic principles. Importantly, prices were always the same in each branch, wherever the location. The waitresses, who became known as 'nippies', all wore a distinctive black and white uniform. The shops, although relatively basic, were more attractive than their opposition. The bentwood chairs and serviceable tables didn't encourage too long a stay as there were normally other customers waiting to be seated. Still, it was a unique experience for many to be served at table. Lyons was targeting a new lower middle-class market that worked in shops and offices. By 1919 Lyons had 184 tearooms. Their ability to bulk buy guaranteed keen prices and excellent quality. The British knew what a good cuppa should taste like. Lunchtime trade boomed as office workers flocked to the shops, and opening hours were extended to meet the demand created by cinemagoers. As J. Lyons & Co extended their selection to include a wide range of catering activities (enough to employ 20,000 staff) they achieved the status of the world's largest catering organisation. Worries about their relative weakness in the north of England were solved with the purchase of two tea suppliers in 1918, including Black and Green, based in Manchester. The inroads into the north saw branches open in Sheffield, Leeds, Liverpool and Manchester, with potential for further expansion. By 1919 Joe Lyons was selling five million packets of tea each week. One in four cups of tea sold in London was supplied by the company.

J. Lyons & Co was also the largest supplier to sporting events like Wimbledon, and responsible for catering arrangements at Buckingham Palace garden parties. It was a major logistical problem controlling the many divisions of the giant company, but they were still eager to explore new areas and identified a gap in the hotel market, particularly in London. There were hundreds of hotels in London, ranging from those with worldwide reputations down to shabby boarding houses in the less fashionable parts of town. What wasn't on offer until Lyons built the Regent Palace in 1915 was modern accommodation in central London, available at a realistic price. The Regent Palace hotel had over 1,000 rooms and offered more than a hint of grandeur. Situated just off Piccadilly and Regent Street it had famous neighbours, with the Ritz just down the road and the Café Royale a couple of minutes away by foot. The hotel cost more than £600,000 and attracted a new clientele. Provincial and foreign tourists were no longer forced to seek accommodation on the outskirts. It was time to rub shoulders with the rich and privileged and enjoy a little cosseting.

Whilst staying in the new hotel, many would have taken a trip to the Corner House on Coventry Street. This was the most audacious example of the introduction to the new mass market of a sprinkling of glitz. The black and white fronted tearooms were a familiar sight to Londoners but the Corner House transported customers into a different world. Rising like a palace this was a place of wonder, somewhere to linger and to be tempted. There were massive pillars and painted murals, creating a feeling of flamboyance and theatre. The initial Corner House was the blueprint for others that were to follow. The ground floor was devoted to a delicatessen. With supplies restored again after the war, open-top counters offered ranges of food previously only available at Fortnum & Mason or in Harrods Food Hall. There were displays of cooked meats, roll mops and Russian salad; there were gateaux and ice cream. There was a huge selection of chocolates (some handmade) and smartly dressed assistants sliced ham and cheese to the customer's requirements. The air of theatre was an important part of the experience.

Every Corner House was built with four or five floors, each with its own restaurant, ranging from a self-service café on the first floor to a conventional silver service restaurant at the top. The intervening floors had various themed restaurants, each featuring a pianist or a small band. The top floor boasted a full-blown orchestra. This was an attempt to transport the customer to a different world in the hope of loosening purse strings, providing an escape from everyday concerns and offering a glimpse of what might be to come in the future. Despite the Corner House not surviving the onslaught of the modern world, the concept was brilliant. Arguably, if updated, it might even find a place in today's highly competitive marketplace. As the newly aspiring consumers left the Corner House back in 1919 they would have been dragged back into the real world on seeing ex-servicemen begging, or selling matches in the gutter, or a couple of skinny, barefoot children, dodging in and out of the clogged traffic. Neither was an uncommon sight across the country.

Second only to the Corner Houses in the public's affection in the Joe Lyons empire was the Trocadero, built on the site of an ancient tennis court in Shaftesbury Avenue that subsequently became a music hall. The building was acquired by J. Lyons & Co and extended in 1902 to include an adjoining building. The Trocadero featured restaurants on each of its floors and was much loved for its afternoon tea dances. This innovation of staging entertainments during the serving of meals was introduced after the war. Later the company employed the impresario C. B. Cochran, who extended the entertainment to include well-known cabaret acts. It must have seemed inconceivable at the time that an organisation as powerful as J. Lyons & Co would falter and ultimately fail, but tastes change and they were not the only household name from that era to disappear.

Another tearoom dynasty, albeit a much smaller one, was being created in Harrogate. It was in 1919 that Frederick Belmont introduced Yorkshire to Continental patisserie. The locals decided they liked it very much and that shop in Harrogate remains open still, with another famous branch in York. Frederick Belmont was born Fritz Bützer in Switzerland. He arrived in England in 1907 and worked for a Swiss confectioner in London, learning his trade. Looking for new opportunities he mistakenly boarded the wrong train, arriving in Yorkshire instead of his intended destination. He found work with F. Belmont, a chocolatier, and saw potential for his skills in the fashionable spa town of Harrogate. He changed his name and became Frederick Belmont. He opened his shop, Betty's, at 9 Cambridge Crescent and was encouraged by his first day's takings of £30. He produced cakes, gateaux and chocolate unlike any seen before in the area and in no time at all Betty's became a favourite destination for anyone visiting the town. Within a year Belmont had opened a bakery and the company, which is still family-owned, runs Betty's outlets across Yorkshire. Here is an example of a small but highly successful enterprise that survived and thrived over the years, whilst a massive corporate giant was buried by its own organisational complexity and changing public tastes.

Finding exceptional food outside London was difficult. Most cities and towns with good railway links sported at least one major hotel. Many of these had been built in the Victorian era and not updated since before the war. They usually had a large formal restaurant, with smartly dressed waiters to serve at table. The food was generally plain and of hugely varying standards. Dover sole could usually be relied on, and there was normally a choice of roast meats nestling under the domed silver servers.

Although many of these old hotels survive today, almost no restaurants outside London are still around from 100 years ago. Even the swankiest London hotels didn't always serve good food. The politician, Duff Cooper, referred to 'a dreadful meal' he'd had at the Berkeley Hotel in February 1919. The Ritz and the Savoy were sometimes more to his liking. The following month he was reporting on a stag night at the Ritz. Each of the 32 guests in the private dining room had a bottle of champagne set before them, just to get the party started. After a meal that Duff declared to be 'excellent', they had what he described as 'a fine old-fashioned evening'. This entailed playing roulette and chemin de fer, during which he won a fine old-fashioned £55. Of course, Duff Cooper and his friends would not have been seen dead in a Corner House, let alone a Lyons teashop. They occupied completely different territory.

Despite Duff Cooper's endorsement of the Ritz there were many who thought the food poor and their wines expensive. Even the shareholders complained of declining standards of service. The Ritz needed a facelift. It had a rather shabby grandeur that continued to attract the highest in the land, who tended to treat it like their club. The Brigade of Guards, who met there regularly, set the tone by insisting that everyone wore a white tie and tails. It was the Prince of Wales who broke ranks by preferring to sport a black tie and dinner jacket. Despite the poor food and expensive wine it was still a good place to take a girl for an intimate late night supper. Sub Lieutenant (later Lord) Louis Mountbatten recalled being, 'very, very star-struck. I was much taken with the lovely Marjorie Gordon, who was in a show called *Going Up* at the Gaiety Theatre. I used to take Marjorie out for supper at the Ritz and afterwards there would often be a note in the social columns.' Restrained publicity such as this, that both the couple and the hotel welcomed, ensured that the Ritz still had the power to attract not just the old brigade but also the young, glamorous set.

Marjorie Gordon was beautiful and impeccably behaved but the same could not be said for all those in the theatrical world. Despite being described as the greatest living American actor, John Barrymore was a rabble-rouser. By 1919 he was banned from the Ritz due to his unacceptable behaviour. It was only when the impresario Sir Gerald du Maurier agreed to stand surety for the star's future good conduct that he was allowed to stay at the Savoy. Generally, the Savoy hosted a rather more colourful clientele than the staid old Ritz. In 1921 huge crowds blocked Piccadilly outside the Ritz in the hope of catching a glimpse of Charlie Chaplin, who was staying at the hotel. The star, encouraged by the crowd, appeared on the balcony. This was considered to be rather unseemly by the management and, for a time, film stars were not welcomed at the Ritz. The Savoy took a very different approach, welcoming the publicity that famous guests brought the hotel. The golfer Walter Hagen stayed at the Savoy after winning the US open in 1919. Whilst there he created something of a tradition that was followed by other champions, including Bobby Jones and Gene Sarazen. Hagen went up to the roof of the Savoy and celebrated his arrival in London by driving a ball across the Thames and into a moored coal barge. Satisfied that he was still striking the ball well he went for a drink in the American Bar before lunching in the Savoy Grill. Cocktails were all the rage and, although other American bars had opened across London, none had the cachet of the Savoy. A great bar requires a great barman, or in this case bar lady. Ada Coleman had been mixing her concoctions since 1903. She had the skill of never forgetting the name or particular tipple of a guest. She continued stirring and shaking until her retirement in 1924. Her most famous cocktail was the 'Hanky Panky', a mixture of gin, Italian vermouth and a couple of dashes of Fernet Branca. It isn't recorded if consuming a couple of the cocktails guaranteed a little hanky-panky or not.

For those brave enough to venture out of their hotel to eat, a visit to the Connaught Rooms in Great Queen Street was a safe bet. For those seeking rather more excitement, a trip to Frascati in Oxford Street would do the trick. The impression on entering was of being overwhelmed by a sea of gold and silver. Here there was more than a touch of Edwardian opulence, with a nod to the future. Rising columns and a grand staircase led to a balcony where diners looked down on new arrivals. To the right of the grand entrance was a discreet grillroom, whilst an orchestra played to diners in the main restaurant, seated amongst palms and dramatic floral displays. Frascati was unique in its theatrical setting, which was unrivalled across the country. It was a place where the food was almost incidental to the glitz and glamour of the décor, a 'must visit' destination, particularly for provincial visitors and foreign tourists.

The food in Soho restaurants was often better, but the setting normally less impressive. Soho was an unfamiliar world, a village within a city. It was almost like travelling abroad whilst staying in London. The sleazy atmosphere was very different from the main shopping streets only a few hundred yards away. Dimly lit streets were filled with shabby looking men wearing trilbies huddling together in small groups smoking. There was an edge and a tension for any visitor new to this exotic area. The smells of coffee, cheeses, spices and cigarette smoke all intertwined. In the shadows, women of all shapes and sizes murmured invitations to passers-by. Suburban matrons and ladies from the provinces were shocked and yet fascinated as they were chaperoned by their husbands from the taxi to the restaurant, while respectable-looking men followed 'ladies of the night' down dark alleys or into scruffy looking tenements. Surely their own husbands had never been tempted? Glancing up from their menus they would have noticed a constant stream of men being led down the same path in bustling Greek Street. And opposite was a French patisserie and a squalid looking Italian café, where men talked as they puffed away on their cigarettes, watchful, as if expecting something out of the ordinary to happen. Restaurant doors would be left open if the night was humid and vague snippets of conversation would filter in from a street full of foreign accents and different languages. If it was a warm night visitors could well imagine that this was not London. With eyes closed it could be Rome or Paris.

South of Shaftesbury Avenue the first Chinese restaurants appeared in Gerard Street, a district later to become known as Chinatown. Elsewhere in Soho there were Spanish, French, Greek, Turkish and kosher restaurants to choose from. Those still seeking entertainment after the meal could go off in search of a nightclub. The choice ranged from lush and expensive to sordid spielers. Here, dead-eyed gangsters and their brassy molls watched mugs being conned out of their money. A marked deck guaranteed 'the house' always won, and it was not a place to argue. Take your punishment and leave. The excitement of visiting a nightclub was heightened by a slight sense of danger. Even the smartest offered only a veneer of respectability, attracting a somewhat raffish set. Some were establishment figures, but imposters playing a part outnumbered them. A strange mixture, not yet quite comfortable in each other's company.

The dawn of the Jazz Age witnessed the arrival of an unlikely figure. Kate Meyrick was the daughter of an Irish doctor. She was abandoned by her husband and left to bring up their six children on her own. What to do? In April 1919 she answered an advertisement placed by George Dalton; '£50 wanted for partnership to run tea dances.' The following month Dalton's club opened in Leicester Square. Dalton quickly disappeared from the scene but Kate identified a potentially lucrative market that we today would describe as 'shabby chic'. Early teething problems led to her arrest for non-payment of fines and she was jailed for ignoring strict licensing laws. This was not to be her last brush with the law, but the future queen of London's clubs was learning her trade. She was gregarious, charming, and prepared to work into the early hours in an attempt to provide a good life for her children. She was at home during the day to welcome them back from school, before going out later to oversee her club.

Moving on from Dalton's she opened a series of similar clubs. She had hit on a formula that worked. Word spread of this eccentric Irish lady, who sat at reception draped in a shawl and who often had holes in her stockings. Inside the club the decor was more suited to a transport café: chipped tables, rickety chairs but excellent champagne at 30/- a bottle and a clientele that included knights of the realm, film stars, politicians and hookers. Her clubs were described as 'absolute sinks of iniquity' but still the customers rolled in. Kate had a guileless charm, but not far below the surface was an astute business brain. From her perch at the entrance to the club nothing escaped her notice. The 43 Club in Gerard Street became known all over the world. Hollywood stars couldn't wait to be seen there. By the time she retired she had made a fortune, although most was

Above left: *The mysterious Gus;*
lover, friend or fiancé?

Above right: *Percy (Persimmon)*
Walker sketched at the front in 1916.

Right: *Prime Minister David*
Lloyd George.

Nurses' contingents in the great Victory March of Allied forces through London.

British infantry of the Southern Command in the London march of 19 July 1919.

Bearers of British infantry colours in the London march of 19 July 1919.

British Standards and colours borne in London's great Victory March of Allied troops.

Left: *The society wedding of Duff Cooper to Lady Diana Manners.*

Below: *Working at the pit face was cramped and dangerous.*

Above right: Young women opted to work in factories, rather than going in to service.

Right: Many farm workers lived in tied cottages.

Below right: School was harsh and discipline strict.

Below: A middle-class family, part of a growing tribe.

Opposite top left: *King George V and Queen Mary talk to wounded soldiers on a visit to Bourneville in May 1919.*

Opposite middle left: *King George and Queen Mary, photographed in 1919 with their remaining offspring.*

Opposite bottom left: *1919 saw the sad early death of young Prince John.*

Opposite top right: *The Prince of Wales, pictured on a trip to Canada.*

Opposite bottom right: *The dashing young Prince of Wales had a preference for married women, a source of angst to his parents.*

Above left: *Brilliant Chang, the society drug dealer.*

Above right: *Glamorous Gloria Swanson was amongst the highest-paid female stars of the cinema.*

Right: Sunnyside *was a blockbuster success for Charlie Chaplin in 1919.*

Rupert Brooke, one of a group of influential war poets still remembered today.

All types of magazines found a ready market in post-war Britain.

Above left: *Jack Dempsey inflicted terrible punishment on Jess Willard during their world heavyweight bout.*

Above right: *Walter Hagen celebrated winning the 1919 US Open Championship by driving balls into the Thames from the roof of the Savoy Hotel.*

The 1919 Tottenham Hotspur team were deprived of promotion to the First Division of English football.

A Sainsbury's advertisement, celebrating 50 years of trading.

The American Bar at the Savoy Hotel, home of the cocktail craze.

The national press celebrated the triumph of British pilots Alcock and Brown.

The iconic painting Gassed, *by John Singer Sargent.*

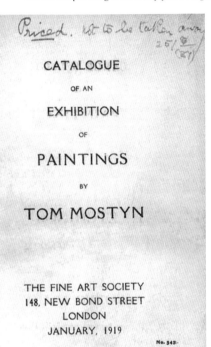

Above left: *The Fine Art Society staged a number of exhibitions by leading British artists.*

Above right: *Margaret Tarrant was one of a number of very talented female book illustrators.*

Right: *The young Ivor Novello was already a household name by 1919.*

Above left: *A Marks & Spencer store, photographed in 1919.*

Above right: *Spedan Lewis, the creator of the John Lewis Partnership ethos.*

Left: *A Moss Bros advertisement, underlining the return to civilian life.*

CHARIVARI.—September 17, 1919.

1914—1919
Khaki to Mufti

Obtain your MUFTI from MOSS BROS., who have the largest, most varied and unequalled stock in London.

LOUNGE SUITS, MORNING COATS, EVENING DRESS, OVERCOATS, TWEEDS for GOLF and Country Wear, FUR-LINED MOTOR COATS, Etc.

Solid leather KIT BAGS, Suit Cases and Cabin Trunks.

Unique Selection of SADDLERY. Also Hunting and Racing Kit.

Prismatic Binoculars by best makers.

MOSS BROS & Co LTD

Naval, Military and Civil Outfitters,

20 & 21, KING STREET | COVENT GARDEN,
25, 31 & 52, Bedford St., | W.C.2.

Phone: 5750-1 Gerrard. Tel. Add.: "Parvet Eano, London."

MOSS BROS.
famous
TRENCH COAT
and Service Kit

Also an immense Stock of
KHAKI DRILL UNIFORMS
are always ready for Officers
serving or proceeding abroad.

Above: *The arrival of motor transport revolutionised society.*

Below left: *A new car required a new outfit.*

Below right: *A chap needed to look the part for his round of golf.*

Left: *Nancy Astor. She was the first woman to take a seat in Parliament.*

Below: *Marie Stopes, whose books on birth control caused a sensation.*

1919 saw the arrival of the 'tubular look'.

Fashion magazines featured ever more extravagant creations. Almost everyone smoked cigarettes.

Above: *Dancing around the Maypole: Britain as we like to imagine it 100 years ago.*

Below: *Blind veterans play leapfrog in the garden of a hostel in Regent's Park run by St Dunstan's in 1919. Set up by Arthur Pearson for blind veterans in 1915, St Dunstan's would come to be known as Blind Veterans UK, under which name it continues today.*

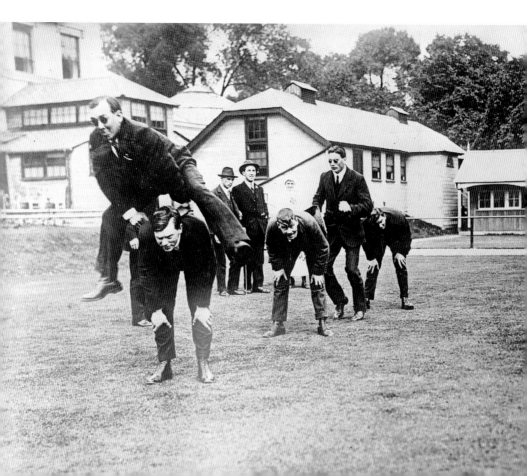

subsequently lost with a series of poor investments. When she died in 1933, all the dance bands in the West End observed a two-minute silence.

A far cry from Kate Meyrick and her louche dives were the traditional gentlemen's clubs, many of which were situated around St James. A depiction much loved by British filmmakers is of an old man asleep in a leather armchair, with an unread copy of *The Times* on his lap and a half-empty glass of brandy handily placed on the side table. Some clubs offered accommodation for country members visiting London, protecting them from the noise, hubbub and distractions of the outside world. Guests were frequently served supper by a waiter older than themselves. Joining one of the most famous London clubs involved a mysterious process never fully explained. Generally it was thought to require a proposer and two seconders. The applicant's name was circulated to existing members and required between 30 and 40 nominees in order to be placed before the committee. The applicant needed to be known by a member in some way – probably by having attended the same school, been in the same regiment, or through a family connection. The process, whilst extremely elitist, allowed for the convivial meeting and socialising of like-minded people. Financial circumstances were far less important than the character and background of the person applying for membership.

Gentlemen's clubs were not confined to London. Each major city or town had their own version, based on their dominant industries or trades. Wool merchants gathered in Huddersfield, whilst the hosiery manufacturers met in Leicester. The principles for membership were the same as for their London cousins. Clubs provided a chance to chat and enjoy a game of billiards or liar dice. It was considered extremely bad form to discuss business and a strict dress code had to be observed. It was rare for a member to be blacklisted. Expulsion tended to be reserved for someone involved in a financial scandal. Financial dishonesty was treated as a mortal sin, whilst a blind eye could be turned where infidelity was concerned.

Billiards, a game dating back to 17th-century France, became popular in gentlemen's clubs, and was adopted and updated in the 19th century with the introduction of pockets rather than hoops. A slate-based table covered with green baize replaced the rough wooden surface. Another important addition was the introduction of the rounded cue tip and the use of chalk to prevent the cue sliding off the ball.

Snooker was invented and developed in India during the days of the Raj. It became popular in the messes and clubs as a diversion from the boredom and searing heat. It was whilst Colonel Sir Neville Chamberlain was serving in Jubbulpore that he came up with the idea. In 1882 he drew up formal rules and in no time the game migrated back to England. It moved quickly from the mess at Woolwich to the clubs of St James's. The game was formalised in 1900 by the Billiards Association and definitive rules were laid down. Soon tables and equipment, manufactured by Burroughs, appeared in the backrooms of pubs. A game that had been invented by the aristocracy was now embraced by the working man. The Temperance Society even created their own snooker halls in an attempt to constrain the drinking and gambling associated with the game. Both billiards and snooker became part of British culture, enjoyed across all levels of society, from the Carlton Club to the Dog and Duck. The lure of a cognac or a pint of stout, and the opportunity to have a wager, proved irresistible. The English

Snooker Championship was started in 1916. It was held at the Orme's rooms in Soho Square and won by Sidney Fry.

Food and drink has always been associated with entertainment. From a stirrup cup at the local hunt meeting to champagne at the theatre or opera, the emphasis was on socialising, encouraged by a drink or two. Whilst Britain was generally slow in its appreciation of good food, those who could afford it enjoyed a diet not contaminated by pesticides and chemicals. What people lacked in 'fine dining' they gained by sitting down together at meal times. For even the poorest this provided a focus for the day, without any of the intrusions that have now relegated the importance of eating together as a family unit.

Whilst the British were slow to appreciate really good food, they did love their homegrown heroes.

15

THOSE MAGNIFICENT MEN IN
THEIR FLYING MACHINES

*Bulldog Drummond was created in a book written in 1919
by H. C. McNeile under his pen name, 'Sapper'. Drummond
represented an essentially British hero, spawned by his
experiences in the war. He was rather posh, gung ho, patriotic
and loyal. Described as 'physically and morally intrepid', he was
manly and invincible. Two men about to make aviation history
were cast in a similar mould. Both had seen active service as
military pilots, involved in what was perhaps the last conflict
where a degree of chivalry was regularly observed by opposing
airmen. This also fitted into the 'Arthurian' values so admired by
McNeile and promoted in British schools.*

Captain John Alcock was a 27-year-old naval pilot who,
according to the *Daily Mirror* 'had a busy and romantic career.
From his earliest days when he started life as a shop boy in a
Manchester works he had taken the keenest interest in motoring
and aeronautical matters.' At the outbreak of war Alcock joined
the RNAS where he helped in the defence of London during
Zeppelin raids. Some time later he was sent to serve on the

Turkish front, where his bravery was rewarded with the DFC. Whilst flying over Constantinople he had been forced to crash-land by the Turks and was captured. He spent the rest of the conflict as a prisoner of war.

Lieutenant Arthur Whitten Brown was a 33-year-old navigator. Born in Glasgow of American parents, like Alcock he started his engineering training early in life. With the outbreak of war he joined the Manchester Regiment, serving in France before transferring to the Royal Flying Corps, where he gained a formidable reputation as an observer. *The Mirror* reported, 'Just as Captain Alcock was eventually captured by the Turks, Lieutenant Brown fell into the hands of the Germans. His foot was injured in the crash and, owing to indifferent medical attention, he now walks with a limp.'

You might think that after their wartime escapades these two young men would opt for a quieter life. No chance, the 'Bulldog' spirit was alive and well and they craved a new challenge. The challenge they were to face was laid down in 1913 by the *Daily Mail* who offered a prize of £10,000 to 'the aviator who shall first cross the Atlantic in an aeroplane in flight, from any point in the United States of America, Canada, or Newfoundland and any point in Great Britain or Ireland, in 72 continuous hours.' The competition was suspended for the duration.

Alcock had spent time whilst he was held captive thinking about the possibility of taking part. On his release he approached Vickers Engineering at their HQ in Weybridge. They had already planned to enter their Vickers Vimy Rolls-Royce Eagle twin-engine plane, which had been built at Brooklands (famous for its motor racing track as well as aircraft). Vickers had been actively looking for a suitable pilot and was impressed by Alcock's enthusiasm and piloting skills. They continued converting the plane, replacing the bomb carriers with extra petrol tanks. Like so many, Brown had been unemployed after being demobbed but he managed to impress the Vickers team with his long distance navigation skills. So it was that the two men were introduced and formed their historic partnership.

The prestige and prize money led to several competitive teams being formed. By the time Alcock and Brown arrived in St John's, Newfoundland, work on the rival Handley Page aircraft was well advanced. Their leader, Admiral Mark Kerr, was a perfectionist and a stickler for detail. Maybe it was this, or possibly indecision, that led to a delay. He was determined that the aircraft would not take off until it was in perfect condition. The Vickers team appears to have had no such reservations. Quickly assembled, the Vimy was declared ready for take-off on 14 June 1919. The plane bumped forward over Lester's Field. It was to be a flight fraught with danger and one that required steely nerves. Weighed down by the extra fuel it was carrying, the plane seemed reluctant to leave the ground. Then, to cheers, it gradually rose, only narrowly missing a row of trees. Of course, he who pays the piper calls the tune. So it was that the *Daily Mail* ran an exclusive account of the flight, told by John Alcock:

We had a terrible journey. The wonder is that we are here at all. We scarcely saw the sun or the moon or the stars. For hours we saw none of them. The fog was very dense and at times we had to descend to 300 feet above the sea. For hours the machine was covered in a sheet of ice carried by frozen sleet. At another time the fog was so dense that my speed indicator didn't work and for a few seconds it was very alarming.

There were lighter moments:

> We looped the loop, I do believe, and did a very steep spiral.
> We did some very comic stunts, as I had no sense of horizons.
> The winds were very favourable north-west and at times
> south-west. We said in Newfoundland we would do the trip in
> 16 hours, but we never thought we would. An hour and a half
> before we saw land we had no certain idea of where we were.
> We believed we were at Galway or thereabouts.

With typical British understatement Alcock continued: 'We encountered no unforeseen conditions. We did not suffer cold or exhaustion, except when looking over the side when sleet chewed bits out of our faces. We drank coffee and ale and ate sandwiches and chocolate.'

It's what Alcock didn't report that makes the flight all the more remarkable. Within an hour of take-off the wind-driven generator packed up, leaving them with no radio contact. It also affected their intercom and heating. A burst exhaust pipe created such a din that they couldn't hear each other, no matter how loudly they shouted. Later in the flight navigation became seriously compromised when they encountered thick fog and Brown was unable to use his sextant. Flying blind must have been terrifying and with the plane tending to be nose heavy they had several narrow escapes. They lost control and headed towards the sea, often flying upside down. Eventually the fog cleared and Brown, now using his sextant, was astonished to find they were still roughly on course. Then came the snowstorm. It blew into their open cockpit, freezing their goggles and stinging their faces. Time for a coffee, which Alcock forgot to mention was laced with whisky. Already drenched and frozen, all their instruments became iced up. They kept going, ignoring all the odds stacked against them. It was 8:40 a.m. on 15 June when eventually they made landfall in Galway. Alcock spotted what he thought was an ideal landing site. They had been riding their luck all through the flight. Now, at the very last moment, it deserted them. As they touched down the seemingly flat field became a deep bog. Both propellers were buried in the mud as they came to an abrupt and undignified halt. They had completed their journey in a little over 16 hours, at an average speed of 115 mph. Rescuers waded through the mud to assist the airmen as they struggled to get out of the cockpit. Both were disorientated and unsteady on their feet. Brown suffered cuts to his nose and mouth but both were in good spirits as they were accompanied to nearby buildings, handing out small mascots to the crowds of onlookers.

Alcock took a flight home to Hendon Aerodrome whilst Brown travelled to England by train and boat. The men, despite their shared triumph, were obviously not close personal friends. However both men were honoured with a reception at Windsor Castle and there was widespread celebration across the country. The worldwide kudos achieved underlined Britain's position in the world. Alcock and Brown were both knighted and invested with the insignia of Knight Commander of the Order of the British Empire. The flight provided a welcome boost for British technology. On arrival in Ireland they had sent a telegram to Rolls-Royce in Derby: 'Congratulations on the performance of the 'Eagle' Rolls-Royce engines, which propelled the Vickers Vimy safely across the Atlantic.' Soon advertisements were appearing in the press 'The first direct Atlantic flight. A triumph for British engineering.'

What a whirlwind few days for the airmen. Back in Ealing, Brown's fiancée declared herself to be 'the happiest girl in London'. Kathleen Kennedy is a 'pretty girl', the *Daily Mirror* reported, who hopes to marry the returning hero 'very soon'. Things were certainly looking good. In addition to the *Daily Mail* award of £10,000, an additional £5,000 was added by a series of sponsors attempting to gain publicity from the epic flight. Everything in the lives of these two young men appeared to be almost too good to be true.

Life, however, can be terribly cruel and fate has an uncanny knack of making a mockery of triumph. In December John Alcock travelled to Paris to take part in the first post-war air show. He was there to demonstrate the new Vickers Viking amphibious aircraft. On 18 December he took off in foggy conditions, which would have held little fear for him after what he had endured on his Atlantic flight. Three days previously he had attended a ceremony at the Science Museum in London at which the recovered Vimy aircraft was presented to the nation. His star was still in the ascendancy. A national and international hero, his glowing future was cruelly cut short when his plane smashed into the ground fracturing his skull. He was rushed to hospital in Rouen where he died. A true British hero in the Bulldog Drummond mould, he was described by a friend as 'the most modest man I have ever met, but he had great confidence in himself.' Arthur Brown lived to be 62. He married Kathleen, his fiancée, in 1919. In the Second World War he served as an RAF training officer. He was also touched by tragedy when his 22-year-old son was killed in 1944, piloting a Mosquito over Holland.

On a lighter note, the day after the Atlantic crossing in June 1919 Thomas Patter, an 88-year-old naval veteran, claimed to be the oldest person to have flown. He was a passenger on a plane that landed on Southsea Common. Previously the record had been held by an 85-year-old woman. Patter stated emphatically that 'he wasn't having that.'

Just as the railways had decimated the stagecoach operators, there was now a fear that the advance of air travel might herald the demise of the passenger liner. British cargo ships still travelled the world but most passenger liners had been requisitioned for military service and were still being re-fitted for civilian use. For the time being those travelling to far-off lands had to slum it aboard cargo carriers. The P&O Line was offering to take passengers on their mail boat sailings to New Zealand via the Panama Canal. The White Star Royal Mail steamers ran a regular service between Liverpool and New York, whilst Cunard had regular sailings from Bristol to Boston via Philadelphia. The Atlantic Transport Line had created a niche market, shipping horses across the Atlantic. By the end of the year advertisements were appearing in *The Sphere*, offering cruises to Lisbon and the Canary Islands. For those opting for northern cruises, Sweden and Norway were also available. For 16 guineas there were organised tours to the French and Belgian battlefields described as 'these hallowed spots'.

The cruise operators could relax and plan for the future, as it was obvious that flights would be confined to short haul. Flights were already available from Hounslow to Paris, with a regular schedule operating every Monday, Wednesday and Friday. Flights to Brussels left on Tuesdays and Thursdays. The price for each destination was 15 guineas, with baggage being charged at 2/6d per pound weight. The flight duration was roughly 3 hours. This was an early indication of the potential for air travel but few would have been able to predict the enormous impact it was going to have on the 20th Century.

Competition between Australia and Britain has always been fierce. Not to be outdone by Alcock and Brown's Atlantic triumph, the Australian government offered a prize of AU$10,000 for the first Aussies to fly from Britain to Australia. It was in May 1919 that rules, in conjunction with the Royal Acro Club, were laid down. All entrants had to be Australian nationals and their aircraft had to be manufactured and constructed within the British Empire. The mammoth journey had to be completed within 30 days (720 consecutive hours). It was also stipulated that the race had to be completed by midnight on 31 December 1920. Hounslow Aerodrome was the designated departure point for land planes, whilst any flying boats had to take off from RNAS Calshot. There were stop-offs and reporting points at Alexandria and Singapore. The final destination was scheduled for somewhere in the region of Darwin.

Six teams took up this incredibly dangerous challenge. The first team to depart experienced a flavour of the problems that would be encountered by most. On 21 October 1919 Captain George Campbell-Matthews and his co-pilot, Thomas Kay, hit trouble almost from the off. They were delayed by poor weather in Cologne and Vienna but much worse was to come. They were captured and imprisoned in Yugoslavia. After their release they hit a snowstorm in Belgrade. Engine trouble and continuing bad weather caused further disruption before they crash-landed in Bali. Time to retire gracefully! Thankfully neither man was injured, but the real dangers of the escapade were further highlighted in a flight that left Hounslow on 13 November 1919. Truly, 13 was an unlucky date, because the Alliance aircraft, flown by Lieutenants Douglas and Ross, crashed into an orchard in Surbiton and both men were killed. The aircraft had flown 6 miles. Roger Douglas had won the Military Cross during the war and, like John Alcock, having survived wartime action met his death in a peacetime accident. Two more teams taking off in 1919 were thwarted in their efforts to secure the prize. Disaster struck when a Martinsyde aircraft containing Captain Cedric Howell and Lieutenant George Fraser disappeared near Corfu. Only one body was ever discovered and poor George Fraser was never found. The competition was inflicting a heavy toll rather than producing the intended glory.

Happily, there was a winner. It again featured a Vickers Vimy bomber, piloted by Ross MacPherson-Smith and his brother Keith. Also on board were mechanics Jim Bennett and Wally Shiers. Their flight took off on 12 November 1919. Flying first across France and Italy, they travelled via Cairo, Damascus and Basra to the Persian Gulf, and then continued across India to Rangoon and eventually Singapore. They arrived triumphant in Darwin on 10 December 1919. They had completed their epic journey in just under 136 hours, at an average speed of 82 miles per hour.

In 1920 a single-engine Acro aircraft astonishingly completed the course in 206 days. The two pilots, with their mechanics, were awarded a second prize of AU$1000. All these insanely brave men were the pioneers in what was to become the hugely successful aviation industry. The early companies trying to run scheduled flights gradually folded due to the high prices they had to charge. It took subsidies, introduced by Winston Churchill as Minister for War and Air, to give the fillip the industry needed. With over £1 million in subsidies made available, the leading aviation companies merged and went on to form Imperial Airways in 1924. This was the forerunner to what was to become British Airways. None of this would have been possible without those 'magnificent men in their flying machines.'

Whilst engineers and scientists were all keen to embrace change, artists were less united in their view of this new world.

16

PUTTING YOU IN THE PICTURE

Long forgotten ancestors peered down from the lofty walls of country mansions and spacious townhouses, their expressions suitably haughty or heroic. Chinless wonders and dumpy dowagers were transformed by the skills of artists hoping for future commissions. In crowded tenements and bleak cottages cheap prints and samplers helped hide the damp patches on the walls. For the most part the British were pretty conservative in their tastes, no matter what social background they came from. They didn't like foreign food that had been 'mucked about' with and they certainly didn't take to pictures or paintings that they didn't understand. Post Impressionism and Vorticism might well be all the rage for the elitist few, but the majority wanted something easier on the eye. The grand, languid style of the Edwardian age lingered on, particularly in society portraiture.

Photography hadn't stemmed the desire of the great and the good to have their image recorded for posterity. Realistic representations of lowlife and aggressive abstracts were now appearing in some of the influential galleries of Bond Street and

Mayfair, but the summer exhibition at the Royal Academy for the most part didn't show much to alarm.

Artists, rather like those connected with the stage, were viewed with some suspicion, fascination and not a little envy. The men tended to wear their hair long and dress outlandishly. Their morals were extremely suspect and their casual lifestyle something of a mystery. True, portrait artists had to tone down their behaviour somewhat in order to be thought safe enough to gain entry to some of Britain's grandest houses, or to be left alone for hours with the lady of the house or their daughters. For the commercially aware artist, portraiture offered the quickest escape from the freezing garret. The ability to create a good likeness usually ensured a regular income. For the best in the genre, fame, fortune and social lionising awaited. There was a constant demand from the aristocracy, from politicians and, increasingly, from the captains of industry. Then, of course, there were their wives, daughters and mistresses.

The arch exponent of society portraiture was John Singer Sargent. He was an American who had studied in Paris before settling in London. His works were generally sympathetic to the sitter. He was able to convey character and mannerisms seemingly with a single flick of a brush. His sitters were flatteringly recorded at ease. It was important for any portrait artist to be able to get their subject to relax and Sargent had a reputation for being charming. Walter Sickert, who sought out the poverty of working-class London, described Sargent as representing 'the wiggle and chiffon school of portraiture'. With this background it is therefore all the more astonishing that Sargent produced one of the greatest works to encapsulate the horrors of the Great War.

Many artists were commissioned by the government to record aspects of the conflict. It had been thought that photography would, in part, drain the other arts of significance. This proved to be a false alarm as artists continued to delve below the surface and present an image of nuance and subtlety rarely conveyed in photographs. It must still have been a shock to this 62-year old establishment figure to be asked to travel to France to observe the fighting first hand. The work was commissioned by the War Memorials Committee of the Ministry of Information, a massive piece to be hung in a hall of remembrance that was never built. Initially, the request from the committee was to produce something underlining Anglo-American co-operation. Sargent set off in July 1918 in the company of the British artist, Henry Tonks.

The two men made their way between Arras and Ypres. There they witnessed much of the second Battle of the Somme. Late one afternoon they saw a line of men returning who had been affected by mustard gas. The dressing station was chaotic, with gassed and bleeding men scattered over a wide area. Strangely, it was Tonks who faithfully recorded this scene in a painting entitled *An Advanced Dressing Station in France*, completed on his return home. Whilst it was undoubtedly accurate, the painting itself appeared muddled and chaotic, and perhaps too factual to capture the imagination of the public. What was needed was a single image conveying the brutality and, at the same time, the nobility and empathy of men in extreme circumstances. This group of blinded men, each reaching out for the shoulder of his comrade in front of him, was both powerful and memorable.

Back at his Tite Street studio in Chelsea, Sargent was not convinced he could produce a painting linking Anglo-American involvement. He already had an idea of the work he wanted to paint, but this required the approval of the War Memorials

Committee. When this was agreed he set to work on a painting of truly massive scale in the autumn of 1918. After making a series of studies the painting was completed in time for it to be exhibited at the 1919 summer Royal Academy exhibition where it was voted 'Picture of the Year'. Although the painting was generally praised, and hit a nerve with the public, as always there were detractors.

Virginia Woolf broke with general public opinion by declaring the work to be 'too patriotic', a sentiment shared with E. M. Forster, who considered it to be 'too heroic'. Winston Churchill praised Sargent's achievement as a work of 'brilliant genius and painful significance'. Although Sargent exhibited other works at the Academy that year, including a painting of the cathedral at Arras, it didn't take him long to link up again with the great and the good. A brief interlude away from the salons of fashionable London and Britain's stately homes had inspired Sargent to create arguably the most iconic vision of the Great War. The picture can now be seen at the Imperial War Museum in London.

Whilst society artists like Sir John Lavery and John St Helier Lander continued to thrive, British art, like the rest of society, was in a period of radical change. This was bought about in part by the direct influence of war. French artist Henri Gaudier-Brzeska was killed in battle aged just 23. He had worked mainly in Britain and, together with Jacob Epstein, had been a member of a radical modernist movement that was shaking up the traditional British art scene. Other artists who survived serving on the front were also deeply affected by their experiences, and this was often reflected in their subsequent work. Whilst some went to France as official war artists, Stanley Spencer served through the conflict as a humble private, witnessing the death and carnage. Much of his subsequent work, created at his home in Cookham, was devoted to the redemption of the dead, albeit expressed in domestic settings.

Christopher Nevison was invalided out of the Medical Corps in 1916, but returned as an official war artist, taking huge risks to record the mayhem. Charles Jagger had a really difficult war, being wounded in Gallipoli in 1915 and then again on the Western Front three years later. The stain of war seeped its way into the art world and was remembered, directly or indirectly, in a huge body of work. It was also responsible for the disbanding of one group of influential British painters and the gentle decline of another.

The Camden Town group was founded in 1911 and included artists who recorded life in an unfashionable and rather rundown part of London. They sought to bring a touch of realism, picturing the mean streets of Camden Town and Mornington Crescent. They only ever held three exhibitions, all in the basement of the Carfax Gallery. Their membership was restricted to sixteen, and each artist was restricted to showing just four of their works. Although forward-looking in their general approach, the group remained true to their British roots. They occupied the middle ground between the traditional and avant-garde. The group included Walter Sickert, Malcolm Drummond and the influential Lucien Pissarro, to add a little French flair. Their demise was hastened by the death of one of their founder members. Late in 1918 Charles Ginner contracted Spanish 'flu. Hearing of his friend's illness, Harold Gilman called round to help nurse him. Ginner eventually pulled through and lived for another 33 years but the unfortunate Gilman fell ill after attending to Ginner and died on 12 February 1919. Some felt the group was cursed, particularly as another founder member, Spencer Gore, had died of pneumonia back in 1914. Gilman's work covered the streets of north London, then expanded into an interest in recording the theatre and the circus, to great effect.

The group had always been rather dismissive about exhibiting at the Royal Academy. Walter Bayes, who was living in Haverstock Hill, broke ranks with a work entitled *Pulvis et Umbra*. The previous year he had completed a painting more associated with the Second World War. Entitled *The Underworld*, it depicted a group of people asleep in the underground at the Elephant and Castle, taking cover during a Zeppelin raid. The work was commissioned by the War Artists Advisory Committee and was purchased by the Imperial War Museum. The group was starting to enjoy commercial success, and with it their objection to showing at the Royal Academy evaporated. Several members were moving away from dingy bedsits to live in up-market Hampstead or Chelsea. The work they produced, however, was far-reaching and important. Robert Bevan memorably recorded the death throes of horse-drawn cabs in the streets and yards close to his home in Swiss Cottage, bringing an English tinge to the influence of French impressionism. His 1919 painting of *Showing at Tattersalls* is now in the Ashmolean Museum.

By 1924 Walter Sickert had moved to the swanky surroundings of Fitzroy Square but it is his lowlife portrayals that define him. His dark, rather creepy pictures of nudes (many of them prostitutes) made uncomfortable viewing. Some were captured earlier, in Sickert's gloomy looking rooms in Mornington Crescent. These oppressive, sexually charged works drew widespread condemnation from the critics, which in no way impaired Sickert's commercial success. He continued showing at the Royal Academy until 1935. He resigned that year as a Royal

Academician in protest at the president refusing to support his friend Jacob Epstein's sculptural reliefs on the British Medical Association building in the Strand.

Youthful idealism often gives way to a more pragmatic view of life, but the members of the Camden Town Group continued to be major influences in British art, from their figurative work to the abstract paintings of Wyndham Lewis. He developed an avant-garde style based on angular, machine-like formations and his work began to be acknowledged by many leading museums and the Tate. This small group of 16 artists widened the understanding of art and influenced future generations. An impressive epitaph.

Another school of British art was also winding down. Its influence had been less dramatic (rather like most of its paintings) but had survived much longer than the Camden Town Group. Newlyn in Cornwall had attracted artists to its shores since the 1880s. It had a special appeal for young, struggling artists. Apart from its natural beauty, living costs were low and it had the added appeal of models that were willing to pose for a few shillings. Over the years many leading artists were drawn to the area, influenced by a thriving artistic community that included a number of talented young women. The sea, artistic freedom and the possibility of romance proved to be a heady mix. High Victorian art was being dismissed by young artists and the idealistic pre-Raphaelites only had a few remaining devotees. The Newlyn School, led by Stanhope Forbes and Walter Langley, created work similar to that undertaken by the earlier Barbizon School in France. On either side of the channel artists became devoted to a simple lifestyle, away from the influence of big cities. Generally they painted outside, in all weathers, catching the natural light.

The outbreak of war saw the end of this idyllic form of life. As Munnings wrote in his autobiography, 'It broke up the easy-going pattern of life.' Since the beginning of the century, when Stanhope Forbes had opened his school of painting, young talented artists had flocked to Newlyn to learn from the master and enjoy an untroubled lifestyle. Laura Knight confessed she had 'never known the joys of youth before'. The body of work completed prior to the war by the artists underlines these feelings. Looked at now, many of the paintings seem to depict a life that was almost too perfect, awakening a feeling of nostalgia for a carefree age that was never to return. The works of Harold and Laura Knight, Alfred Munnings, and Forbes himself hark back to a time of rural tranquility and children playing on beaches, but the war closed that chapter in Newlyn's history. Most of the artists set off to enlist. Ernest Procter left to serve in an ambulance unit in France. This left his wife, Dod Procter, marooned in an almost deserted Newlyn. Harold Knight was a conscientious objector and, as such, he suffered much abuse.

The effects of war led to the Newlyn School's decline. The artist Arthur Newton lost two sons in the conflict whilst Alec, Stanhope Forbes's only son, was killed in August 1916. Many of the artists failed to return after the war and Forbes, to the surprise of many, left the area for good. For a time Harold Harvey and the Procters tried to recreate the past, but it was a forlorn hope. They were joined by Charles Napier and Frank Heath, who continued to paint and exhibit. Over the years Stanhope Forbes brought together an incredible variety of British artists. Few of them set out to shock or fundamentally change the artistic world. They represented an uncomplicated world. It was perhaps apt that the Newlyn School of Art gently vacated the stage, leaving future generations to envy their quiet and seemingly blissful lifestyle.

What does it take to constitute an art movement, group or school? Who knows, but whatever it is John Ferguson, Samuel Peploe, George Hunter and Francis Cadell had it, and thus became known as 'The Scottish Colourists'. True, they were all born in Scotland in the 1870s and were influenced by the French Impressionists, but they were not particularly close friends and only ever had three joint exhibitions during their lifetime. Ferguson and Hunter did make the occasional trip to France together and Hunter also travelled to New York to exhibit his work, on Ferguson's advice. Otherwise the link between them was mostly the French and Continental influence. They brought the vibrancy and colour of Montmartre to an otherwise drab and conservative Morningside. Despite this tenuous relationship many of their still lifes and floral works sit comfortably together. Maybe it is the influence of the commercial modern art market that has linked them more closely than the artists themselves would have. This is certainly reflected in the prices being achieved at auction.

Book illustration could be extremely lucrative and one of the most successful exponents of this art form was Arthur Rackham. His distinctive illustrations hark back to the Victorian tradition. He lived a life of relative simplicity, despite the commercial success that enabled him to buy a substantial house in Hampstead. His extravagances were confined to an evening glass of Marsala wine and a taste for expensive clothes. He wore a polka dot tie, part of his dapper appearance. His amazingly detailed drawings and watercolours created a fantasy world of fairies, goblins, gnomes and elves, against a background of root tendrils and weird trees. It was this unique style that set him apart, and although his work often caused controversy, he stated:

An illustration may legitimately give the artist's view of the author's ideas or it may give the view of his independent view of the author's subject, but it must be the artist's view. Any attempt to coerce him into a mere tool in the author's hands can only result in the most shameful failure. Illustration is as capable of varied appeal as is literature itself.

His illustrations were so powerful that the text of the story, no matter how famous, became secondary. By 1919 he was at the height of his powers and popularity with his illustrations of *Cinderella*. His wife, Edith, was his guiding force, for it was she who initially encouraged him into his fantasy world, starting with his work on the Brothers Grimm. By 1919 he was making regular visits to the States. His work was given greater scope by the improvements in printing and the huge popularity of children's books.

The other giant of children's book illustration was a few years younger than Rackham. Edward Dulac was French by birth, but arrived in Britain in his early 20s. Following a similar career path to Rackham, he produced sketches for the *Pall Mall Magazine* and was commissioned to illustrate *Jane Eyre* by the publisher J. M. Dent. He joined the London Sketch Club where Rackham was a prominent member. He was able to maximise the advances in colour printing, which particularly suited his style and his use of vibrant tones as opposed to Rackham's gloomy, foreboding subject matter. Soon rival publishers were competing for his work. Whilst Rackham was fascinated by Nordic mythology, Dulac was intrigued by the allure of the East, with its mesmerising patterns and dazzling colours. By the end of the Great War Dulac was the most sought-after and successful illustrator in the world. His work leapt from the pages of *Arabian Nights*, perfectly capturing the exotic mystery of the subject matter. Like many before him, Dulac became completely seduced by the allure of all things Eastern, becoming increasingly critical of Western art. He followed the work of archaeologists and became fascinated by first-century Syrian wall decorations. Liberty in Regent Street was similarly influenced and began introducing the British public to the wonders of the Orient. People were fascinated but essentially ignorant of the beauty of art, fabrics and architecture from other continents. It came as something of a shock to many that such genius existed outside Britain.

A small army of British illustrators began to come to the fore, many of them women. Although few are remembered today, they were very talented and provided a cosier form of art that was easy for children and their parents to enjoy. They were generally modest, always seeking to decorate rather than dominate the stories being told. They followed in the footsteps of popular Victorian book illustrator Kate Greenaway. Though they never became part of a school or group their work had a special appeal for children, presenting a comfortable image rather than the challenges of Rackham and Dulac. Many had been formally trained and their work was beautifully executed, although sometimes dismissed as being too twee. Margaret Tempest, who subsequently went on to illustrate *Little Grey Rabbit,* was something of a trendsetter in an age when women artists tended to be patronised. She formed the Chelsea Illustrators Club in 1912 and it remained open until 1939, operating from a wooden Scout hut in the middle of the fashionable West End.

In 1919 Honor Appleton published *Where the Dolls Live*, the latest in a series of *Josephine* books, which were popular at the time. At 40, she was the same age as Mabel Lucie Attwell and it was these two who were to influence younger artists waiting in the wings. Attwell was soon getting commissions from *The Bystander* magazine and it was obvious her work had real commercial appeal. She built up a lucrative outlet by designing greetings cards for Valentine. She painted chubby, happy children – depicted in endless, whimsical situations – that are still popular today. Her work also appeared in advertisements such as one for the Erasmic Shaving Stick, where a cute little girl is pictured standing on a bathroom stool in front of a mirror, pretending to shave, with the tag line 'Daddy knows what's good.' Her work set a high bar for commercial success that few in her field were able to emulate. In 1919 Hodder published *Mary Queen of Roumania* and *Peeping Pansy*, both of which were an instant success with readers.

Honor Appleton, who attended Frank Calderon's School of Animal Painting and the Royal Academy School, never achieved Attwell's level of success but she was a very skilled illustrator. Her *Josephine* books are particularly interesting in that the illustrator viewed the children at ground level, whilst the adults featured appeared only from the knees down. Her work is charming but rather set in a time warp and was criticised for being 'vague' and having 'a pretty romanticism'.

Cicely Barker is still remembered today for her flower fairies that first appeared in 1922. She was largely self-taught and was still completing a correspondence course in 1919. It was obviously a good one as her work was detailed and sensitive, with much of her output remaining in print today. She was very friendly with another of this crop of talented artists, Margaret Tarrant. Tarrant was recognised as an illustrator of real skill from a very early age. Despite winning prizes for her drawing, she frequently doubted her own talent as an artist. However, success wasn't long in coming and her illustrations of Charles Kingsley's *Water Babies* were widely acclaimed. Her delicately executed watercolours and pen and ink drawings defy her lack of confidence in her own abilities. In addition to books, she worked extensively with the Medici Society, who produced greetings cards and gift items. Her work is still available today, charming a new generation with its timeless appeal.

Britain has a fine tradition of equine painting, dating back to Stubbs and Henry Alken. The foremost exponent in the 20th century was Alfred Munnings, a divisive figure to many in the art world for his contempt of modern art. His paintings of racing, of gypsies and of fashionable ladies captured in the hunting field, certainly evoke the atmosphere of their time. Despite volunteering he was excused military service due to the loss of an eye in an accident. Wanting to contribute to the war effort, Munnings was offered the choice of serving in the Labour Corps in Britain or joining a remount unit that recruited and trained horses to be sent to the front. He chose a remount unit that was run by a friend and fellow artist, Cecil Aldin, one of Britain's best illustrators of animals. Aldin's comical studies appeared regularly in books and magazines. Like Munnings he was a great supporter of hunting and was master of the South Berkshire hunt. Aldin was responsible for purchasing thousands of horses to be sent to the front. Hundreds were stabled at any one time at Purley. Few people wanted to give up their prize horses but Aldin's contacts enabled a constant flow to be retrained which, sadly, in many cases led to their deaths. Despite his prominence as a famous artist Munnings mucked in and worked as hard as anyone. He was more often than not taken as a humble groom, rather than a man with connections to the rich and famous who would eventually be knighted and become president of the Royal Academy. Towards the end of the war Munnings was chosen by the Canadian government to go to France as their official war artist. In 1918 he painted the last great mounted cavalry charge by the Canadian army, *Charge of Flowerdew's Squadron*, which is now in the Canadian War Museum.

For every genre, and particularly in portraiture, there were always dozens of competent artists who worked with varying degrees of success. They survived by recording local dignitaries rather than the rich and famous. There was also a group of journeyman equine painters. They often attached themselves to hunts at the beginning of a season, hoping to gain a commission to paint the favourite hunters of the members, or made visits to racing stables. When this source of income dried up they took to the road, calling on farms where, for a few pounds, they would paint the farmer's hack or cob in its stable. They would charge more if the animal was recorded against a background of the countryside. As an additional bonus they often received free board and lodging whilst the painting was being completed.

The series of exhibitions mounted by the Fine Arts Society in 1919 underlined the overall conservatism of the British art market. Early in the year the emphasis was on the war effort. Leading artists featured works created at the front, with studies of Ypres, St Quentin and the Lens-Arras Road. The proceeds from portraits painted by The Duchess of Rutland were given to the Rutland Hospital in Oakham. An attempt to move on was represented by the startling colours of the work of the popular artist, Tom Mostyn. There was also a retrospective of work by Edward Stott, who had died in 1918. The paintings depicted a rather idyllic Britain, caught in a time warp. This cosy view was endorsed by paintings by Ronald Wheelwright and Lucy Kemp-Welch, and with the quaint, sugary watercolours of William Russell Flint.

Artists often, of course, define the era they live in. The 'comfort art' provided by the Fine Art Society 100 years ago was shortly to be engulfed by new, more challenging, work. It is impossible to stop change and artists embraced it, seeking new challenges for the Jazz Age.

17

MUSIC AND ALL THAT JAZZ

*What, back in 1965, linked a pop star with a classical concert
cellist? True, they were both young, attractive, English blondes
who were born within a year of each other, and both had made
recent recordings: one that soared into the Top 10 of the pop
charts and the other still regarded as the sublime performance of
a work that had been sadly neglected since its creation in 1919.
In the 1960s a whole nation of young men fell in love with
the deceptively angelic looking Marianne Faithfull. Her wistful
ditty* As Time Goes By *underlined her faux innocence. By
contrast, Jacqueline du Pré offered the raw emotions of passion,
longing and sadness in her recording of Elgar's Cello Concerto.
Subsequently their lives took them on very different journeys,
both of which were ultimately very sad.*

In 1962 17-year-old du Pré gave her initial performance of
Elgar's Cello Concerto under the conductor Rudolph Schwarz.
The respected critic Neville Cardus wrote in *The Guardian*,
'Those actually present were witness, on the first day of spring,
to an early blossoming and, as such, a beautiful blossoming, in

Miss du Pré's playing, as this year, or any other year is likely to know for a long time to come.' 1962 also saw the screening of Ken Russell's film on the life of Edward Elgar. Suddenly Elgar was revealed as a man of passion whose look of a country squire, teacher or bank manager belied the emotions burning within him. Despite Elgar being best known for his rousing patriotic works like *Land of Hope and Glory*, du Pré was able to explore the complexity of his character in her performance. Her public profile was further highlighted later in 1963 when she appeared at the Proms with the BBC Symphony Orchestra under Sir Malcolm Sargent. By the time of the recording in 1965 she was the acknowledged exponent of the concerto. Unfortunately for Elgar the premiere in 1919 had been a disaster, leaving the work unloved and largely ignored for many years.

Edward Elgar was born near Worcester in 1857. He came from a respectable but rather poor family. Whilst working in a solicitor's office he supplemented his earnings by giving piano and violin lessons. As a young man Elgar was rather introverted, feeling himself to be something of an outsider. Being a devout Roman Catholic set him apart at a time when perceptions were dominated by background, accent and religion. This became painfully obvious when he proposed marriage to one of his pupils. Alice Roberts was the daughter of Major General Sir Henry Roberts. Her family was appalled. The fellow was totally unsuitable on every conceivable level. To start with Alice was eight years older than this upstart. As if that wasn't bad enough he was a struggling music teacher with few prospects to keep their daughter in the manner she should expect, the son of a humble tradesmen and, to cap it all, a Catholic. It just wouldn't do. Alice had different ideas. Despite the threat of being cut off and disowned by the family, she remained defiant.

Alice had huge faith in Edward's emerging genius. She became his sounding board, advisor and mentor. Her organisational skills provided him with much-needed stability, allowing him the time and space to express himself through his music. He was never distracted by having to undertake mundane household tasks. As well as being a devoted wife, Alice acted almost like a business and social organiser, even scheduling in their regular long country walks together. Success was slow to come but in 1899 he enjoyed public and critical acclaim with his moving and evocative *Enigma Variations*. He was developing an individual and recognisable style. The following year he completed his great religious choral work *The Dream of Gerontius*. The premiere in Birmingham was a farce and considered a catastrophe. The amateur choir was under-rehearsed and unable to interpret the complexity of the composition. The conductor was Walter Stockley, and Elgar noted, 'As the music became more chaotic (the choir) slipped hideously out of tune.' Although some critics were able to appreciate the quality of the work despite the awful performance, Elgar became seriously depressed, as the Catholic emphasis of the work drew further criticism from the Anglican establishment.

It is unclear if it was Edward VII or the celebrated contralto, Clara Butt, who approached Elgar to create a rousing patriotic song for the King's coronation. Formerly an instrumental theme from the composer's *Pomp and Circumstance March No 1*, it was to be included in the Coronation Ode as a rousing finale. The poet and librettist, Arthur Benson, was commissioned to write the words, and so the familiar *Land of Hope and Glory* was born. The coronation was delayed due to the King's illness, so the London premiere took place on July 2 1902 at a coronation concert held at the Albert Hall. The soloist was the formidable Clara Butt. Elgar promised it would 'knock 'em – knock 'em flat', and it did. The jingoistic words reflected the times and cemented Britain's belief in its standing in the world. It has since become an alternative national anthem and remains as popular today as it was over a century ago.

Elgar's success continued with his moving *Violin Concerto in B minor, Op.61,* a work that posed its own enigmatic puzzle. During some of the prime periods of his creative powers, associations with a variety of attractive young women inspired Elgar. These infatuations or 'crushes' were often actually encouraged by his wife, who understood that they had the effect of inspiring some of his best work. He wrote a tantalising inscription in Spanish at the head of the Violin Concerto, 'Herein is enshrined the soul of...' There have been many suggestions as to who he was referring to, with the most likely candidate appearing to be an Alice – but not his wife. Alice Stuart-Wortley was the attractive daughter of the painter John Everett Millais and was his focus of infatuation at the time.

By the outbreak of war, Elgar's standing was in decline. Much of his work was considered old-fashioned and rooted in Edwardian nostalgia. Deeply affected by the war, Elgar and his wife retreated to a cottage near Frimworth, in Sussex. Having just recovered from an operation and worried about his wife's declining health, Elgar didn't commence work on his *Cello Concerto in E minor, Op.85,* until the summer of 1919. He worked with a new confidence and the premiere was scheduled for October. The soloist was Felix Salmond, appearing with the London Symphony Orchestra under their conductor, Alex Coates. It appears that Coates spent too much time rehearsing the rest of the programme at the expense of the concerto and the performance lacked any of the intensity and passion required. The critic for *The Observer* put the boot in, concluding in his review, 'There have been rumours about during the week of inadequate rehearsal. Whatever the explanation, the sad fact remains that never, in all possibility, has so great an orchestra made so lamentable an exhibition of itself...' How was it possible for a work to recover from such a drubbing? The ever-loyal Alice Elgar raged about Coates, 'That brutal, selfish, ill-mannered bounder'. Elgar was obviously distressed but apportioned no blame to the soloist. He was still convinced it was one of his finest works. He was not alone.

A recording of the concerto was made in 1920, with John Barbirolli as a member of the orchestra (cello). His connection to the work extended to the epic recording by Jacqueline du Pré, when he conducted the London Symphony Orchestra more than 40 years later. The work had been largely side-lined in the intervening years and it took the young 20-year-old du Pré to bring out all the longing, sadness, romance and almost orgiastic passion of the work. All of these emotions were subsequently amplified by du Pré's early death at the age 41 from multiple sclerosis. It had taken a beautiful young woman to unlock the power and emotion that Elgar doubtless intended. Maybe the searing melancholy of the work anticipated the death of Elgar's own loving wife, who died in 1920. Whatever the conflicting emotions he was experiencing at the time of the composition, the concerto finally found its true voice, one that has endured. Today it ranks as one of the most popular pieces of classical music in Britain.

Elgar was one of four British composers prominent at the end of the Great War, each deeply marked by its effects, not least as two of them were saddled with Germanic names. Fritz (later to be known as Frederick) Delius was born in Bradford to a wealthy German father who became a prominent wool merchant. Although constantly lionised as an English composer by the conductor Thomas Beecham, Delius was in effect an internationalist. He spent much of his life in America, France, Norway and Germany. His English roots were probably best illustrated only by his continuing love of cricket. His music has been likened to Marmite (you either love it or hate it).

Prior to the war Delius had been living in France with his wife. The hostilities forced him to return to England. Thomas Beecham had already championed Delius's work and, during a visit to London in 1913, had introduced him to the elite of British society with the help of his mistress, Lady Emerald Cunard. It was during this period that Delius completed work on his *North Country Sketches*. Here at least was a composition that owed its origins to his childhood memory of the Pennine Dales of the West Riding of Yorkshire. The conflicting influences during his life are illustrated by his opera *Fennimore and Gerda*. Often referred to as an orchestral opera, Delius wrote the libretto himself in German. The premiere was scheduled for the Cologne Opera House but the war intervened. Eventually its first performance took place at the Frankfurt Opera House in October 1919. No doubt the war was particularly painful for Delius, coming from his background. Some are convinced that he had no great love for the country of his birth, and certainly scarcely a note of his music was written in England.

Without Thomas Beecham, Delius and his work may well have disappeared into obscurity. Beecham constantly championed him and undoubtedly massaged and manipulated his reputation to make him appear more English than he really was. Frederick Delius died in France in 1934, where he was buried. He had, however, expressed a wish to be buried in the country of his birth. Beecham showed an ongoing commitment to Delius by helping to have his body exhumed and interred at St Peter's Church in Limpsfield, Surrey. The story doesn't end there. The ceremony was postponed due to Jelka, Delius's wife, being very ill. Beecham gave the graveyard oration, describing Delius as 'a great Englishman'. Two days later Jelka died and was buried alongside her husband. Beecham died in 1961 and some years later his body was also exhumed and buried in St Peter's churchyard, so that he too could remain close to the man he thought of as the greatest English composer. No doubt Beecham's efforts have been rewarded as Delius is constantly referred to on radio and in the media as English, and generally we are happy to accept him as such, as much of his music is truly beautiful.

Gustavus von Holst was not a great name to be burdened with just prior to the war so he shortened it to Gustav Holst. The son of a Swedish father and English mother, he was born in Cheltenham in 1874. Despite volunteering Holst was too old to serve in the war. Already a respected composer and teacher of music, his early choral works were followed by the *Planet Suite*, which he started in 1914 and completed two years later. The work commences with *Mars (The Bringer of War)*. Many presumed that this dramatic work acknowledged some premonition about the war that was shortly to engulf the world. Despite its ominous build-up to a frightening climax the composer always denied this inference. It certainly vividly illustrates the savagery and futility of war. *Mars* was followed by *Venus (The Bringer of Peace)*, *Mercury (The Winged Messenger)*, *Jupiter (The Bringer of Jollity)*, *Saturn (The Bringer of Old Age)*, *Uranus (The Magician)* and *Neptune (The Mystic)*.

In 1918 Holst was allowed to serve his country by working for the YMCA's education department in Salonica. He was still in Greece when Adrian Boult and the Queen's Hall Orchestra gave a private premiere performance of *The Planets* before an invited audience. In 1919 Boult introduced *The Planet Suite* to the wider British public and within a year it was being lauded in the United States. This rather shy, painfully thin, anaemic Englishman had found his musical voice. His work was more influenced by Stravinsky than Elgar, or his friend, Vaughan Williams. Although he had written very little during the war, its effects pursued him. On his return from Salonica in 1919 he composed what many consider to be one of the greatest choral works of all time, *Ode to Death*, based on a poem by the American, Walt Whitman, which reflected the quiet, sombre mood of the country. Despite his foreign-sounding name and the European influence on his work, Gustav Holst has rightly been placed at the forefront of British composers.

By 1919 Ralph Vaughan Williams was already an acknowledged composer of rare talent. His 1910 work, *Fantasia on a Theme by Thomas Tallis*, was performed for the first time that year at Gloucester Cathedral. It was in 1914 that he started composing what is now the most popular classical work in Britain. There is some dispute regarding the origins of *The Lark Ascending*. What is certain is that it was prompted by a poem by George Meredith.

> As up he wings the spiral stair,
> A song of light, and pierces air
> With fountain ardor, fountain play,
> To reach the shining tops of day,
> And drink in everything discern'd
> An ecstasy to music turn'd,

What is also certain is that *The Lark Ascending* is a war child. The lark's ascent can be interpreted as a journey toward death. According to the composer George Butterworth (who was killed in the war), Williams was already working on the piece early in 1914. An explanation more burdened with significance finds the composer on holiday in Margate on the very day of the outbreak of war. As he watched ships preparing to go out on exercises the idea came to him and he started jotting down thoughts on a notepad. Rumour has it that a vigilant schoolboy either completed a citizen's arrest or contacted the police, having convinced himself the composer was a spy. Whatever, the work was mothballed for the duration of the war.

Already in his 40s, Williams was old enough to avoid military service. Instead he volunteered to be an ambulance driver and stretcher-bearer at the front. He served in the Royal Army Medical Corps driving ambulances in France and Greece, ending up as a lieutenant in the RA. He lost comrades and friends. Exposure to the constant carnage, the dreadful injuries and deaths affected him deeply. This was apparent in some of his subsequent work. In 1919 he turned again to the embryonic *The Lark Ascending*. It was premiered as a piece for violin with piano accompaniment in 1920, before it emerged in its full orchestral form the following year. It was performed by the British Symphony Orchestra, conducted by Adrian Boult. A contemporary review stated, 'It showed serene disregard for the fashions of today or yesterday.' The war had been savage, but it prompted an extraordinary outpouring of creativity across all the arts.

Celebrity and stardom were normally the preserve of film stars or sports personalities but opera, in the considerable form of Dame Nelly Melba, was not about to be side-lined. This

Australian star continued to draw crowds and there was much anticipation when she was booked to appear in *La Bohème* to mark the reopening of Covent Garden in May 1919. She was the original demanding diva. She insisted that only she should have the key to her dressing room at Covent Garden. 'There are lots of duchesses, but only one Melba,' she declared. She mixed exclusively with the rich, famous and titled. After the war she found London drab and shabby. She was horrified to see brown tweed suits in the stalls rather than couture gowns and tiaras. Like a stately galleon she entered the stage under full sail, milking the applause. To many her voice was already in decline. It hardly seemed to matter. Opera had returned to London.

Influenza was not the only epidemic sweeping the country in 1919. Opera fans and concert buffs were welcome to their dreary evenings, the young wanted excitement, to throw off the gloom threatening to engulf the country. They wanted to dance. Not staid waltzes or foxtrots. Not even the twizzle or the shimmy. Ragtime was old hat, pushed aside by the arrival of jazz, or jass. Couples were invited to rock'n'roll, the meaning of which had respectable young ladies colouring, whilst their mothers reached for the smelling salts. Dancehalls across the country were filled to bursting. 'Jazzing' began with the arrival of the all-white Original Dixieland Jazz Band. They opened a UK tour at the London Hippodrome in April 1919 and were a sensation. White men playing black men's music was foot tapping and exciting, yet somehow quite acceptable. The band quickly moved on to a two-week stint at the Palladium, and was even invited to Buckingham Palace to perform for the King and his invited guests. Jazz was surely becoming respectable. Well, not quite!

American records were sold at inflated prices, allowing couples to practise their dance moves at home. British bands started offering cover versions but they tended to be stilted and lightweight compared to the power of the originals. Something in the British character, an emotional block, held the players back. It was jazz by numbers, neutered, emasculated. Jazz was Negro music. It tended to excite or alarm the girls, whilst British men were not sure what to make of it at all. Another drawback was that the jazz numbers were often difficult to dance to unless you lost all restraint and that surely wouldn't do. The Prince of Wales came to the rescue by giving jazz his blessing. Pale-faced upper crust members of society tried to lose their inhibitions as they jigged clumsily to the basic beat. By August a proper Negro band had arrived in the shape of the Southern Syncopated Orchestra. Aldus Huxley described it as 'Music more barbarous than any folk art for hundreds of years.' African-Americans were delighted that, as in France, they were treated far better in Britain than at home. A certain amount of fraternisation took place and the snide remark, 'I understand she is partial to a little chocolate' took hold, although inter-racial romance was considered a step too far by most.

The jazz craze spread throughout Britain, with Glasgow particularly noted for throwing off any Celtic reserve. In London's Bond Street, Martan's Club changed its name to The Dixie Club. Rector's in Tottenham Court Road and the Grafton Galleries in Piccadilly attracted the posh set. The opening of the vast Hammersmith Palais cemented the dance craze for the general public. In a smart move they booked Nick La Rocca's Original Dixieland Jazz Band for the opening night. The band received an ecstatic reception from the packed crowd of dancers. The former site of a tram depot had been transformed. Over 5,000 tickets were sold for the opening night and those attending were not to be disappointed. True, the dance floor was so crowded that it was extremely difficult to move, but who cared as they swayed under a Chinese sign welcoming them to 'A Grotto of Peerless Delight'. Everywhere was decorated in lavish Chinese style, the work of architect Bertie Crewe. There were brightly coloured, lacquered panels that contrasted with the huge, black, lacquered ceiling. A pagoda stretched to the ceiling, which was covered with lettering signifying good luck. The dance floor was vast and constructed of the finest Canadian maple. There were two bands, situated at each end of the dance floor. As one completed their session so the other started, offering the chance for non-stop dancing. The floor was never empty. Those arriving alone were catered for with a 'sixpenny partner' to help them to dance the night away. Small tables were dotted around the dance floor for those wanting, or needing, to rest after their exertions. No alcohol was available, but none was needed as couples danced to the point of exhaustion.

The press was full of advertisements for dance lessons, but none seemed necessary if you lost yourself in the frenzy of the jazz sensation. Not surprisingly, the Duke of Portland didn't approve. He hated 'the flat-footed negro antics', whilst the *Daily Mail* was appalled by 'the jungle elements of the dance and the primitive rituals of Negro orgies'. Once more the British suspicion and contempt for foreign influences was showing. Strangely, *The Tatler* was less stuffy. High society's favourite magazine reported: 'They say the nightclubs are opening up in droves and dressmakers say they're dizzy with the orders for dance frocks that keep on pourin' in and they just can't have enough niggers to play jazz music and I hear they are thinkin' of hirin' out squads of loonies to make the mad jazz noises till there are more ships available to bring the best New York jazz musicians over!'

The older generation was almost as vehement in condemning the new craze. Surely it reflected a worrying malaise and overreaction to the privations and troubles of the war? A society wag suggested that, 'brows were being worn very low this year.' This was not music but merely noise, a dangerous noise, appealing only to the basest instincts. Even the titles of the songs were demeaning. *The Alcoholic Blues, Blues My Naughty Sweetie Gives to Me* and *Jazz Baby* all sent a message of loose morals and declining standards. But the young weren't listening. They had just been witness to the launching of the Jazz Age, which was to define the 1920s.

Although there was an increasing number of people who owned gramophones, the driver of music in many homes was the piano. Those from wealthy backgrounds were sometimes entertained with recitals by friends or relatives after dinner. Even the most modest parlour often sported a 'sit-up' piano. Great emphasis was still placed on self-entertainment. Impromptu 'sing-songs' often formed the basis for this entertainment, belting out the popular songs of the day such as *I Wish I Could Shimmy like my Sister Kate* or *I Ain't Got Nobody*. The British particularly liked nostalgic songs like *Alice Blue Gown*, or those popularised by the music halls such as *Don't Dilly Dally on the Way*. 1919 also saw the creation of the song so dear to the supporters of West Ham United. *I'm Forever Blowing Bubbles* was soon being sung in pubs and whistled in the streets.

Although the sales of gramophones were growing steadily, it was still sheet music that created the greatest profits. Printing costs were low, even for small runs, and songs selling many thousands cost the publishers next to nothing to create. With home entertainment so widespread the demand for sheet music was enormous. Patriotic songs like *Pack up Your Troubles in*

Your Old Kit Bag continued to sell well, even after the end of the war. Sales of sheet music increased further if a photograph of the singer was featured on the front cover.

Musicians gathering in Archer Street in London's West End, waiting to be hired, constantly had to learn new numbers as the public's taste in popular music swung wildly from new novelty songs to jazz. It remained difficult for British players to replicate the basic power of jazz as it required improvisation, which was proving difficult for many British musicians, no matter how talented. These men on the bandstand, dressed in tails with their hair slicked back, were happier displaying jollity rather than raw emotion and improvisation. Old films show the dancers similarly self-conscious, the men dapper but still buttoned-up, whilst the ladies are either languid or embarrassingly unco-ordinated. Most seem to be refusing to be 'abandoned', and certainly showing no sign of intimacy or smooching. Perhaps that came later. Young people who had endured so much were nevertheless dancing in clouds of cigarette smoke, hopefully towards a better future. Whilst the young danced the night away their parents preferred a visit to the theatre or music hall.

18

YOU WERE WONDERFUL DARLING

For some, going to the theatre was more about being seen rather than any great interest in what was taking place on stage. It was a social event, a chance for the ladies to show off their latest slinky gowns purchased in Paris and to give the family jewellery an airing. Most of the chaps looked all right as well. All hair cream and white tie and tails, although some of the younger men were opting for dinner jackets. Musicals were fun but, oh those dreary plays! 'Look as if you are interested, or even vaguely understand Shakespeare, and under no account fall asleep.'

It was estimated that roughly only 7 per cent of the population went to the theatre each year, in spite of hundreds of repertory companies touring the country. There was scarcely a sizeable town or city that didn't boast at least one theatre. Of course, the signs of class and wealth were seldom absent from British life so for some it was important to be seen – in the stalls or preferably in a box of your own. Being served champagne in comfort at the interval was so much more enjoyable than having to deal with the scrum in the bar, all terrible din, perspiration and hoi polloi! Even those poor people stuck up in the gods made an effort. Best suits for the men and a nice cotton frock for their ladies. A good evening could be enjoyed by all, with the prospect of a cosy supper later at some intimate restaurant, or in the luxurious surroundings of a grand hotel.

A visit to the theatre was in stark contrast to the musical halls, whose origins dated back to the 17th-century pubs and taverns where regular singsongs were organised. By the 1830s supper rooms were opening where artists performed to a raucous background of singing, shouting and swearing. Food was served at long wooden tables and it was often thrown at performers failing to please. The stage was a raised platform within easy reach of the crowd. This reputation for unruly behaviour continued as purpose-built music hall theatres began appearing. The first of these was in Southwark but it was still relatively small. Whilst pubs like the famous Eagle on the City Road continued to provide musical entertainment, the potential for commercial music halls on a grand scale was now obvious. In 1852 the Canterbury Music Hall in Lambeth opened, with a seating capacity of over 700. Whilst the venue was larger and grander, the behaviour of the audiences didn't improve. The demand for, and potential of, music halls saw a rash of new venues opening across the provinces and in Scotland, where Glasgow soon obtained the reputation for being the most challenging place for artists to perform.

The clientele for music halls had always been predominantly male and, in an attempt to improve behaviour, special 'Ladies' Evenings' were organised. By the 1880s there were hundreds of venues in London alone. They mainly drew in the working class and a few young 'swells' who fancied a night out 'slumming it'.

Though most of the middle classes gave music halls a wide berth, owing to their reputation for vulgar and risqué material, the war years were a highpoint in their popularity. The coarse and rowdy behaviour of the audience could descend into violence. Alcohol was banned from the auditorium in 1914, which led to an improvement in audience behaviour. Booze was still available in bars at the theatres but only served in the intervals. The atmosphere remained charged and noisy, with acts not up to scratch getting 'the bird'.

The outbreak of war inevitably saw a surge in the popularity of patriotic songs. Songs like *Pack up Your Troubles in Your Old Kit Bag* and *It's a Long Way to Tipperary* were sung with such fervour that passers-by on the streets outside could hear the lyrics clearly. The proliferation of venues encouraged hundreds of new performers to 'take to the boards'. By constantly touring the country it was possible for an act to keep the same routine for months on end. It was unlikely an audience in Plymouth would have heard a joke told up in Leeds only weeks before, although a comedian's success was usually more down to delivery rather than content.

By 1919 the problems that were eventually to lead to the demise of music halls were beginning to appear. The main threat came from films. The young were going to picture houses in their droves. Suddenly music halls were old fashioned. Queues outside cinemas equalled empty seats in theatres. The rigid format of the music hall was being relaxed, with more emphasis on variety shows that offered a greater choice of acts. There was more trouble waiting in the wings with the introduction of radio, which encouraged people to stay at home for their entertainment. The 'talkies' posed an even greater threat, but music hall struggled on until the arrival of television finally killed it off.

1919 was a significant year for a number of music hall's greatest stars. Marie Lloyd was known as 'the queen of music hall'. She had learned her trade the hard way, appearing at the famous Eagle pub on City Road at the age of 15. It was a tough introduction but right from the start she carried audiences along with her. She was loud, extrovert and increasingly risqué. She gained a reputation for singing songs spiced with innuendo. *A Little of What You Fancy Does You Good* was a particular favourite and often had the audience on their feet joining in. My mother was taken to see Marie Lloyd at Collins Music Hall in Islington, on the understanding that she never told her father. Although she had been to the Metropolitan Theatre on Edgware Road, it was seeing Marie Lloyd that she often recalled. Outside the theatre there were whelk stalls and a man selling roasted chestnuts. Many of the audience were already in high spirits as they had spilled out from the pub next door to the theatre. There were a few cut glass accents, drowned out by the excited cockney babble. A good-humoured crowd was pushing across the rather grand entrance hall. Inside, they sat on plush velvet seats. Most of the ladies still wore their hats, making it difficult for my mother to see the whole stage. Her impression of the auditorium was one of rather faded grandeur. As the orchestra took its place in the pit, the audience noisily took their seats. For a time, the overture and opening acts were applauded politely, then someone in the balcony started throwing sweets down on those sitting in the stalls. There was a commotion, and the offender was ejected to a mixture of cheers and booing whilst the performers on stage carried on with their act. Despite real efforts to improve the behaviour of audiences, the unrestrained origins of the music hall refused to adapt to middle-class respectability. At the interval there was a mass exodus to the bars and by the time Marie Lloyd appeared on stage it was pandemonium, the atmosphere both exciting and rather frightening for a young girl.

Marie Lloyd was a controversial figure and not just for her suggestive songs. Her private life was a mess. She had three marriages and two divorces. Always outspoken, she became increasingly unreliable, often turning up late for performances or staggering into scenery because of her heavy drinking. Perhaps due to her feelings of insecurity she restricted her appearances mostly to London and the south of England. In 1919, just when it was thought that her career was in terminal decline, she came up with a song that instantly restored her popularity. Dressed in rags and wearing a battered old hat she sang *My Old Man Said Follow the Van*. The song describes a mother leaving home to avoid being pursued by the rent man. Timing is everything. The lyrics hit a nerve with so many suffering hardships after the war. Despite its success Lloyd was devastated not to be invited to appear at the Royal Variety Performance, held at the London Coliseum in July 1919. She had previously been turned down for the first Royal Variety Show in 1912 because of her dubious reputation. The 1919 Pageant of Peace was commanded by the King 'to show appreciation of the generous manner in which artists of the variety stage have helped the numerous forces funds connected with the war.' Lloyd felt she had contributed to the war effort by regularly visiting factories in an attempt to raise morale. This cut no ice with establishment figures who considered her to be an embarrassment and not at all suitable to appear in front of royalty.

As it turned out, the show could have done with her to liven up what appears to have been a rather dreary affair.

The audience was described as being cold and passive. This was later attributed to them being unsure of how to react in front of the royal party. An outpouring of emotion might have been considered unbecoming and a touch common. No one was prepared to run the risk of offending the famously undemonstrative King. The comedians George Robey and Harry Tate were used to feeding off the audience's responses. It must have been intimidating to be confronted by general silence and tepid applause. A full orchestra and choir, conducted by Edward Elgar, was greeted with rather more enthusiasm, but generally the British stiff upper lip remained firmly in place.

Vesta Tilley was six years older than Marie Lloyd and also heading towards the end of her career. She had been a male impersonator since the age of six. Her father had raised her in the theatre. He was an actor but often took on the important role of music hall chairman and master of ceremonies. Although contemporaries and rivals for the public's affection, Tilley and Marie Lloyd were total opposites, both in their private lives and in how they approached their work on stage. Lloyd had a tempestuous private life and was incisive and spontaneous. Tilley, by contrast, avoided scandal and her success as a male impersonator was due to detailed observation and endless practice of every spoken word and minute gesture. She used padding to create a convincing masculine figure. She never cut her hair short but braided it to be worn under a wig. Her favourite characters were the typical 'man about town', immaculately dressed and dapper. Her popular song, *Burlington Bertie*, describes a dandy who stays out all night partying. At the Royal Variety Show in 1912 she appeared as *Algy the Piccadilly Johnny*. It was reckoned that 'he' was the most perfectly dressed man in the house.

How strange it seems to us now that a male impersonator singing a few songs and reciting the odd monologue could become such a star. Perhaps it dates back to our love of pantomime and the theatrical tradition of cross-dressing. Tilley became one of Britain's highest paid performers, regularly pulling in £500 a week. She often created new characters in order to keep her act fresh. Hers was a constant learning process of observation. She very cleverly portrayed every nuance of the upper classes and as a consequence had a huge working class following, who loved her gentle mocking of those with wealth and influence. She was even more popular with women as she skewered men's pomposity and, although faithful in her impersonations, managed to make them seem rather ridiculous. Her gentle mockery was not entirely divorced from the work of the suffragettes and the struggle for the vote. In a small way Vesta Tilley became something of a symbol of independence for women in their march towards gender equality.

Tilley had married quietly in a registry office back in 1890. Her husband, Walter de Frece, also had a theatrical background. He was involved in theatrical management and by the end of the war had acquired over a dozen theatres nationwide, becoming a very wealthy man. It was this underlying wealth that allowed Vesta Tilley to enhance her reputation greatly during the war. She and her husband ran an enormously successful recruitment drive, to the extent that she became known as 'Britain's best recruiting sergeant'. She performed at concerts, singing patriotic songs like *Jolly Good Luck to the Girl Who Loves a Soldier*. She donated all the proceeds of these wartime concerts to local children's charities. In 1919 her husband was knighted for his services to the war effort. He later became an MP before the couple went off to live in Monte Carlo. She achieved the goal of many a humble hoofer by finding fame and fortune, together with a title, no less. Lady de Frece made a year-long farewell tour during 1919 and 1920, continuing to give the proceeds to local charities. Her final performance was at the London Coliseum in 1920. Almost two million people signed *The People's* tribute to an unlikely stage icon.

Although *Burlington Bertie* was one of Vesta Tilley's best-known songs, another male impersonator who sang the more memorable *Burlington Bertie From Bow* trumped it. Ella Shields may not be remembered today but her parody on Tilley's original song lives on:

> I'm Burlington Bertie, I rise at 10:30,
> And saunter along like a toff.
> I walk down the Strand, with my gloves in my hand,
> Then I walk down again with them off.
> I'm all airs and graces, correct easy paces,
> Without food so long I forget where my face is,
> I'm Bert, Bert, I haven't a shirt,
> But my people are well off you know,
> Nearly everyone knows me, from Smith to Lord Rosebery
> I'm Burlington Bertie from Bow.

Harry Lauder's catchy songs and lyrics made him a worldwide superstar. Although many of his songs had a strong Scottish theme it was sometimes felt that he had a stronger following in England and the US than the country of his birth. He was accused of ridiculing the Scottish people, although some of the criticism may have been fuelled by jealousy at his huge wealth and resentment that he spent most of his time away from his homeland. There is no doubt that his success was brought about by his own unique talent for creating songs that are easily identifiable and still remain popular today. It is ironic that some of his best known, like *I love A Lassie* and *Roaming in the Gloaming*, which are identified worldwide as great Scottish songs, should find so many detractors in Scotland. Popularity can obviously be a two-edged sword. Americans in particular couldn't get enough of Harry Lauder. He toured the States more than 20 times during his career. He also appeared in Canada, New Zealand and Australia. He was in Melbourne at the outbreak of the war and though he continued with his tour, on returning home he threw himself into helping recruitment. It is reckoned that he was responsible for thousands signing up. Winston Churchill referred to Lauder as 'Scotland's greatest ever ambassador'. By now Lauder was mixing in the highest social circles, which may have added to resentment at home about him denying his roots.

Despite upsetting some, there is no doubt that Harry Lauder was a real patriot. As well as staging recruitment concerts he made visits to the troops in the trenches, where he came under fire. He also launched the Harry Lauder Million Pound Fund, created to help injured Scottish servicemen to return to civilian life. During his time at the front he gave up to four concerts a day, accompanying himself on a mini piano that he'd had made especially for easy transportation. He was knighted by King George V in January 1919 for his contribution to the war effort, giving a concert at Buckingham Palace shortly afterwards.

A sad recurring theme is the number famous men whose sons were killed in the conflict. It illustrates how fame, status or noble birth was no protection once the young men entered the battlefields, and reflects the devastation inflicted on ordinary as well as extraordinary families. Harry Lauder was appearing in *Three Cheers* at the Shaftesbury Theatre in London when he received a telegram informing him of his son's death. It was January 1 1916 and yet three days later he was back on stage, upholding the tradition that the show must go on. Soon hurtful rumours were circulating concerning the manner of his son John's death.

Like many a successful man Lauder doted on his only son. He gave him the best possible education (though, significantly, not in Scotland). After attending the City of London School, John went up to Cambridge. He was essentially English yet Harry invested a chunk of his wealth to buy his son Glenbranter, a sizeable estate in Argyllshire. The tenants were none too impressed by the new young landlord. He had an unfortunate and arrogant manner and spoke with a posh English accent. He talked thoughtlessly of purchasing large quantities of sheep, which would impact on the earnings of his tenants. Not a good start. To his credit, John, who had been on tour with his father in Australia when war was declared, came home and enlisted with the Argyll and Sutherland Highlanders, with whom he had served before as a territorial officer. By 1914 he was already a captain, which some felt was due to his background and connections and was therefore resented. Many of the men under his command were his estate workers who were already prejudiced against him. Although generally acknowledged as a competent officer, his manner towards his soldiers continued to jar and irritate. There was a significant lull in the fighting near Pozières over Christmas in 1916 and, despite no action being reported in his sector, on December 29 it was announced that John had been killed. The regimental diary stated simply 'A+D companies in trenches. Captain J. C. Lauder killed.

One other rank injured.' A rumour took hold that John Lauder had been shot by one of his own men. Many such accusations were made following the deaths of unpopular officers but few, if any, were proven. Despite many crawling over the available evidence it seems far more likely that John Lauder was killed by an enemy sniper. Lurid tales of him executing captured Germans and dancing a victory jig in full view of the German lines also seem far-fetched. It's more likely that John was picked off by a sniper in an unguarded moment. The rumours circulated back in Britain to the distress of Harry Lauder who, to his credit, continued with his selfless war work. It was recognised that his subsequent huge hit *Keep Right on to the End of the Road* captured in words the sense of his loss.

British theatre was dominated by musicals after the war. The public wanted to be entertained, not depressed by gloomy plays. Shakespeare took refuge at the Memorial Theatre, Stratford-upon-Avon, with a production of *Richard III*. For those seeking a little artistic stimulation there was always a visit to the ballet. Duff Cooper went to a performance given by the Ballet Russes and was later entertained, along with the company, at a private dinner given at the Savoy. Ever on the lookout for a pretty girl, he confided in his diary that he was disappointed in the appearance of the ballerina, Lubov Tchernicheva. He had a chat in French with the ballet master, Léonide Massine, but 'didn't find him very forthcoming'. Ballet Russes pushed the boundaries and took ballet to a new level. Based in Paris, the company toured extensively across Europe. It featured the very best young Russian dancers and broke new ground by co-operating with leading composers like Prokofiev and Stravinsky. The costumes and stage sets, under the direction of Sergei Diaghilev, appealed to a new young audience. Ballet suddenly seemed thoroughly modern and exciting. The fashion designer, Coco Chanel, insisted that 'Diaghilev invented Russia for foreigners.' New ballets for 1919 included Manuel de Falla's *The Three-Cornered Hat*, *El sombrero de tres picos*, premiered at the Alhambra, London, in July, choreographed by Léonide Massine, sets and costumes by none other than Picasso. Unimpressed? How about in February 1920 Stravinsky's *Le chant du rossignol*, sets and costumes by Matisse?

Whilst the London stage was dominated by musical productions, none of them lived long in the memory. *The Eclipse*, showing at the Garrick Theatre, only ran for seventeen performances, surely missing a trick as earlier in May there had been a total solar eclipse, the longest since the 15th century. Perhaps the connection wasn't publicised enough or maybe the show was just dire. Productions such as *Baby Bunting* at the Shaftesbury and *The Girl for the Boy* at the Duke of York's fared rather better, but certainly didn't break any records. Meanwhile, there was a theatrical spat going on at the vast London Hippodrome in Leicester Square. The well-known comedian, George Robey, was working himself into a lather and threatening to resign. He was appearing in the review *Joy Bells* and objected to a spot being allocated to the Original Dixieland Jazz Band. They stole the show but stuffy old George eventually won and the band was transferred to other venues. Jazz and film were now making a twin assault on theatre attendance. It needed a huge hit to attract the audiences back again. Perhaps a show written by Ivor Novello would do the trick.

Novello was blessed with matinee idol looks and a precocious talent. In 1914, at the age of 21, he wrote *Keep the Home Fires Burning*. This tapped in perfectly to the patriotic sentiment of the time and sales of recordings and sheet music, both in Britain and America, brought fame and fortune to the composer. His war record failed to reach the same dizzy heights. He enlisted in 1916 and was posted to the training school of the Royal Naval Air Service. After crashing two planes it was thought safer for all concerned for him to be sent to the Air Ministry in London, where he stayed until the end of the war. Back in civvy street, Novello teamed up with Howard Talbot to write the music for *Who's Hooper*, a musical comedy staged at the Adelphi Theatre. The show was well received and played for 349 performances. Songs included *My London Town* and *There's an Angel Watching Over Me*.

Ivor Novello was just one of many new stars waiting to take the theatre by storm. In December 1919 a waif-like 12-year-old made her debut in *Bluebell in Fairyland*. Jessie Matthews was sensational and would become one of Britain's greatest stars, famous for her outrageous private life as much as the huge talent she displayed on stage and in film. Jack Buchanan had already made an impression, touring with the West End hit *Tonight's the Night*. He was tall and elegant and thought to represent the perfect Englishman, although he was actually Scottish. He could sing and dance with studied ease. He finally achieved stardom in 1921 in the review *A to Z*. A 20-year-old Noel Coward was waiting in the wings, about to be unleashed on the British public. Meanwhile *Kissing Time*, a musical farce set in France, written and adapted by P. G. Wodehouse and Guy Bolton, pulled in the crowds. It ran from May 1919 to July 1920, notching up 430 performances. The star cast of Yvonne Arnaud, Stanley Holloway and Leslie Henson no doubt helped, but the show, even with a lesser-known cast, went on a hugely successful tour of the country.

Despite their problems it was too early to write off the music halls. They offered a grand night out. A visit to the theatre could be memorable, but allowing yourself to be swept along by the audience participation at the music hall was more fun. If you'd had your fill of theatre and dance, the 'shopping experience' was being redefined to help you while away the hours.

19

A LITTLE RETAIL THERAPY

*It is not just modern society that is addicted to retail therapy.
It was probably Adam Smith in* Wealth of Nations *who first
referred to Britain as a 'nation of shopkeepers'. If the cap fits,
wear it. For some, shopping remained a necessary chore in
order to keep the household supplied with the essentials, like
food. For others it provided a pleasure all of its own. Even
window-shopping could provide distraction from the stresses
of everyday life, a chance to daydream. That gorgeous dress or
fashionable sofa might be too expensive now but maybe one
day... The grandest could leave their butler or cook to buy the
everyday provisions, but even they would occasionally venture
into a favourite store. For ladies there were regular visits to the
dressmaker, whilst the gentleman of the house made the odd
trip to his tailor (paying him months later, or taking his business
elsewhere if he was badgered with reminders). For some retailers
it seems as if securing the business of the grandest households
was second only to being awarded the Royal warrant: a
connection they could boast about to draw in more trade, which
made actually being paid a bonus.*

At the other end of the scale were the street markets, a live, vibrant and noisy theatre away from the main urban centres, which had thrived across the country since the Middle Ages. There were market towns from Sherborne in the south to Alnwick in the north of England, whilst Scotland could boast of around 40 historic market towns. They were also a major part of Welsh life, and in Northern Ireland Ballymena market dates back to the 17th century. Almost every village of any size supported its own shops. Farmers often doubled up as butchers, with whole carcasses hanging in the windows. The squeal of animals being slaughtered was commonplace. Bakers often served surrounding villages, making daily deliveries by horse and cart. Weekly visits to the local market town were a highlight. The main street would be closed and given over to sheep and cattle as they were driven into pens for sale. The cry of the auctioneer, the frightened noise of the cattle, gypsies telling fortunes, stallholders shouting their wares, shepherds still wearing old-fashioned smocks, all added to the excitement. A symbol of the old and new, tethered horses would shift nervously in their shafts as a car parked noisily alongside. Modernisation was elbowing its way into this oldest and most traditional area of British life.

The urban population of England and Wales surged from just over 10 million in 1800 to a staggering 40 million a hundred years later. This provided the impetus for the most ambitious retailers to transform their method of trading and by the mid-19th century an emerging middle class was ready to indulge its thirst for shopping. Whilst there were still tens of thousands of independent shops trading across Britain, they were coming under attack from all sides. Specialist retailers were horrified to find stores selling a huge variety of goods under one roof, which they considered to be unfair trading.

The expansion of the railway network led to a major breakthrough in distribution, making goods more readily available. The extension of the hugely successful drapery trade led, indirectly, to the forming of department stores, and a new and aggressive breed of retailers decided to expand the range of goods on offer to their customers. Retailers started to require that goods be paid for at the time of purchase, rather than offering extended credit and the increased cash flow allowed them to expand. Newcastle, rather than London, led the way towards the first fully fledged department store. Bainbridge's decided to expand their offering beyond drapery, to include associated products like gloves, handbags and stockings. Hot on their heels came Kendal, Milne and Faulkner (1835–1862) in Manchester who were more ambitious, introducing furniture and upholstery. The blueprint for success was set. Soon, forward-looking drapers across Britain were expanding their ranges. Availability of product was the only restraint. Howells in Cardiff was, by 1919, the destination for shoppers visiting the Welsh capital. Jenners in Edinburgh drew in the great and the good from Morningside and beyond. Whilst in Cheltenham, the retired brigadiers and their wives flocked to Cavendish House. (It's still there, as part of House of Fraser.)

London was not about to be left behind in this retail revolution and they soon became leaders rather than followers. Strangely, at the end of the 19th century, Oxford Street was still dominated by small independent shops, but their days were numbered. By the start of the 20th century Harrods was already London's most famous and successful store. Competition was increasingly fierce, with Barkers in neighbouring Kensington boasting over 60 separate departments. With this rapid expansion many stores struggled with unsuitable premises. Gamages, the value store in Holborn, traded from a warren of passages, hallways and flights of steps, making it difficult to be efficient. It was time for the architects and property developers to get involved.

Technical advances were now required to make shopping an enjoyable experience rather than a chore. A payment system, necessary to speed up transactions, was bought in from the US. It created a cash pathway that was still in use well into the 1940s, involving metal containers that were dispatched from a department to the central cash desk by way of a system of overhead tubes. The cash and sales invoice were placed in the container and any change and a receipt returned by the same method.

By 1919 department stores were an integral part of British life. They offered an escapist distraction from the ongoing effects of war. Now it was time for store owners to establish their own market niche and identify their potential clientele. The war had brought about a fundamental change in society. Women were becoming more independent. Some sniffy store owners complained that 'there is a new breed of ladies who want the most up-to-date fashions but at a very modest outlay!' Some retailers were forced to cut their profit margins and sell in greater quantities in order to gain the same return. Independent shopkeepers muttered darkly that the increased buying power of the stores enabled them to sell the same products at cheaper prices. In London's West End small retailers were under lethal attack and were soon to all but disappear. To a lesser extent the same was happening in the provinces. The choice of goods was ever larger as imports increased and goods arrived from around the world, including those from the still mighty empire.

Harrods was typical of a store emerging from very humble beginnings. It started life in a single room on its present site in 1851. The building we know today was completed in 1905, following a major fire a decade earlier. As the business became established Harrods announced that you could purchase virtually anything, no matter how obscure, and they would source it. The store also boasted the most luxurious and comprehensive food hall. It was possible to buy anything, from a bag of sugar to a haunch of venison. Harrods had already become a national institution, with a company slogan proclaiming 'Everything for Everybody.' Maybe they should have added 'at a price'.

Jenners, in Edinburgh, had much in common with its London cousin. It, too, started as a humble draper's shop. Frequently referred to as the 'Scottish Harrods', it suffered a catastrophic fire in 1895 and was rebuilt on the site that it still occupies today in Princes Street. The new building eventually included electric lighting and hydraulic lifts. It was granted the Royal warrant in 1911 and by 1919 was ready for a period of rapid increase in trade.

A further danger to small retailers was highlighted in 1919, with the takeover of Harvey Nichols by Debenhams. Takeovers and amalgamations were to become central to retailing during the 20th century. Huge buying blocks were created, forcing ever-cheaper prices from suppliers. The takeover of Harvey Nichols was significant as it was the only real competition for Harrods in Knightsbridge. Harrods had already taken over the Dickens & Jones store, situated on Regent Street, in 1914. Battle lines were being drawn for an increasingly competitive retail market.

Buyers in the London stores created their own fiefdoms. They were courted, wined and dined by suppliers anxious for their orders. They were so influential that queues of salesmen and directors waited patiently to be granted an interview. Provincial store buyers, whilst still powerful, enjoyed the odd trip away from their office, but the need to visit them at their store spawned a new form of salesman, known as commercial travellers. Some were supplied with company cars to help them reach their far-flung customers. Others travelled by train, taking their samples in wooden trunks that were transported to a local hotel where a temporary showroom was set up for the buyers to view and select from the latest ranges on offer. Most cities and large towns now had their own department stores. One of the largest was Lewis's in Liverpool, who also had stores in Birmingham and Manchester. As the stores grew in size and scope restaurants were included, and the Manchester store even had its own ballroom. Everything possible was provided in an attempt to pull in the customers. For most, entering a major department store was like experiencing an unreal world, one of luxury and temptation far removed from their lives: all expensive perfume, grand staircases and beautifully displayed stock. Each purchase was overseen by a shop assistant, who would carefully wrap it or arrange for it to be delivered. The customer was king or queen for that moment, and addressed politely as sir or madam. For the wealthy this was business as usual but for the developing middle class, unused to such deference, it was a brief moment of empowerment.

By 1919 London's Regent Street was undergoing a series of redevelopments that had been planned prior to the war. For Swan & Edgar at the northern end of the street it was a necessity as a Zeppelin had bombed its premises in 1917. Whilst the new, imposing store rose beside them, they traded from a number of adjoining buildings. The following year the store was acquired by Harrods, after unexpectedly poor trading. Across the street was a store advertising itself as 'Jay's Mourning Warehouse'. It occupied a strange niche in the market. Mourning was still strictly observed in 1919, at a time of so many bereaved. The store also sold ranges of clothes suitable for the 'mature lady'. Changes in fashions eventually led to the demise of the business, which had been trading since 1841.

Perhaps it was Liberty that had most success in establishing a reputation for selling unique, avant-garde goods. Before the mock Tudor store was completed in 1924 they had become famous for their huge range of exclusive fabrics and exotic goods, imported from the Far East and India. They had long been at the forefront of trend setting design. A great supporter of the arts and crafts movement, they were now promoting the attractions of art nouveau and art deco. Their 1919 catalogue announced 'The present difficulties of manufacturing do not prevent Liberty & Co from supplying their customers with a wide selection of their famous silks and silk velveteen etc.' It went on to explain that, apart from their Eastern imports, they always made their 'specialities' in Great Britain. Then, with the ongoing animosity to Germany, they concluded, 'The firm's historic hand prints from our works at Morton Abbey always enabled them to be absolutely independent of Alsatian and German printers.' The catalogue claimed 'the world-famous Liberty silks are particularly suitable for underclothing on account of their softness, graceful draping and durability.' The catalogue illustrated luxurious dresses, gowns and hats that typified emerging fashions.

An evening gown in silk velvet and hand-embroidered in pure silk was selling for a hefty 25 guineas.

Whilst Harrods was the most successful and profitable store in London, and Liberty by far the most stylish, it was Selfridges that kept raising the bar. Constantly introducing innovations, and backed by a huge advertising budget, the store was like a palace and was a real draw for Londoners and tourists alike. What is it about short men that gives them extra drive and determination to succeed? When Gordon 'Harry' Selfridge was rejected by the US military for being too short it lit a fuse of unbridled ambition in him. He overcame the height problem by wearing Cuban heels. He worked for more than 20 years at Marshall Field, a leading Chicago retailer, where he rose through the ranks learning all aspects of the trade. He didn't rush into marriage but when he did, at age 42, it was to Rosalie Buckingham, a hugely wealthy heiress. By 1904 Selfridge was ready to open his own store in Chicago, which he sold in short order at a considerable profit. On a visit to London with his wife in 1906, he was shocked at how unimaginative most British retailers were. Backed by their huge wealth, Selfridge decided to shake up the British retail trade that he was convinced lagged way behind American and even Parisian stores. He took a massive gamble by purchasing land at the unfashionable end of Oxford Street. He sensed a huge opportunity to apply some of his considerable retail expertise learned in the extremely competitive US market. The area surrounding his proposed new store was still populated with small stores, most of whose owners continued to live 'above the shop'. They were in for a terrible shock. Within two years of his arrival he had invested an estimated staggering £400,000. His motto, 'The customer is always right' struck a chord with the public. Edwardian conventions were cast aside. Now it was acceptable for ladies to walk out unaccompanied, he set about appealing to this newly emancipated market. In 1910 he opened the first ground floor beauty hall, an innovation that is still copied today: enter any department store and you will be confronted with displays brimming with perfumes and cosmetics. Ever the showman and a restless spirit, it is Selfridge who is reckoned to have made the first business flight, in 1919. He travelled to Hendon Aerodrome before boarding a De Havilland 9, which flew him to RAF Baldonnel, having touched down in Chester for refuelling. He was in Ireland to orchestrate the takeover of Brown Thomas in Grafton Street, which was, and still is, the leading Dublin store. The trip is typical of this retail showman.

Whilst he continued to modernise British retailing, there was a significant battle going on at the other end of Oxford Street: significant but unusual, as the battle was between father and son. The John Lewis ethos, that its entire staff should be partners in the business, had an extremely difficult birth, first emerging in 1919. The original founder, John Lewis, belonged to the old school. A Victorian figure with piercing eyes and a bushy white beard, he had a strained relationship with his son Spedan, whose revolutionary ideas he viewed with alarm. They had a fundamental disagreement on how the business should be run. The old man was very set in his ways and autocratic in his approach.

Spedan Lewis was only 28 when he took over managerial control of Peter Jones in Sloane Square in 1914. Previously he had worked in the Oxford Street store and, at the age of 21, he received a quarter share in the business from his father. Excused military service owing to a serious riding accident, he set about transforming the part of the empire under his control. By 1915 he had set up a system of staff committees to enable his employees to have a platform to raise concerns and make proposals. It was only open to non-management staff, so they had direct contact with their boss and could talk to him frankly. He had already published a fortnightly staff paper called *The Gazette*, where staff could also raise any concerns. Peter Jones had been performing poorly before he joined. Spedan was convinced this was because staff conditions were poor and the directors were taking too much in salaries and dividends, whilst the staff were undervalued and poorly paid. He extended the committee to include the growing number of managers and, in 1919, a full staff council met for the first time. Explaining his actions on 20 September in *The Gazette* he wrote, 'It is quite true that good governance is not a proper substitute for self-governance. Therefore the staff ought to be made self-governors as fast and completely as the actual facts of existing trade conditions allow.'

So, in 1919 the partnership scheme evolved. It contained three groups of contributors: the shareholders, who would provide capital, managers, and the managed. The only dividend-yielding shares available to the public would be debentures or preference shares. After all trading expenses and dividends were paid, the remaining profit would be divided amongst the staff in proportion to their pay. The profit distributed was called 'Partnership Benefit' and in future all those working at Peter Jones were to be known as partners. This was revolutionary but it had the desired effect in increasing trade, to the extent that the new partners were paid a bonus of 15 per cent of their salaries, equating to seven weeks extra pay. Spedan Lewis was one of Britain's greatest philanthropists, transferring over £1 million in shares for the benefit of all the partners. In return he received deferred bonds on which he waived all his claims to interest.

Cut now to John Lewis in Oxford Street and the contrast could hardly be greater. Despite the encouraging results from Peter Jones, set in his ways and autocratic in his approach to staff, old John Lewis remained convinced that his methods were best. The result was a strike in 1920. Whilst sales assistants at the store with three years' experience were paid £2 15s a week, they were charged 10/- a week for food and a further 10/- for board at the staff hostel. Their pay was considered to be low for central London, and another source of complaint was that they were not allowed to leave the shop during their lunch break. Two stores, only a few miles apart, belonging to the same organisation and yet so different in their approach to staff relations. The strike was scheduled to take place during a planned mammoth sale. John Lewis had no intention of being blackmailed by his workers. He closed every department, transferring the small number of staff not striking into the silk department. To his delight the entire stock was sold by 4 o'clock in the afternoon. The strike dragged on for weeks but the crabby 84-year-old had no intention of backing down. He issued a notice to 'Our young men and maidens. What is it that gives rise to this unwholesome atmosphere? It is the vapourings of the accursed trade unions!' He was quoted as saying of his striking staff: 'If I see them on their hands and knees I shall not take them back!' And he didn't. He had won. There were other people prepared to fill the vacant posts. This was an amazing and profound family rift. It was 1924 before the two men settled their differences. The old man lived on to be 92 but in 1928 Spedan acquired his father's interest in the Oxford Street shop and continued to widen the enlightened management methods he had initiated at Peter Jones.

The leading retailers appeared to throw up larger-than-life characters who shared a work ethic, ambition and dynamism. Some, like 'Harry' Selfridge, were showmen, whilst others shunned publicity. Some had a drive for self-interest and success that bordered on paranoia. The choice for consumers was constantly growing. To the thousands of small shops and department stores, a new player was now added. The multiple stores didn't offer the grandeur of their departmental cousins but concentrated on value and low price, often made possible by bulk buying. They were able to bring greater pressure to bear on suppliers, extracting an extra price benefit that they were able to pass on to the consumer. The founders of these new giants became grudgingly admired, but also feared by their staff and competitors. These were hard, self-made men, who were as tough and uncompromising as old John Lewis, but not stuck in the past. They employed modern methods of manufacturing and retailing to extract every last ounce of value and used every square foot of selling space available to maximise sales.

Montague Burton provided a template for impoverished immigrants. A Lithuanian Jew, he arrived in Britain unable to speak English. In 1901, at the age of 16, he started selling second-hand clothes door-to-door in Manchester. Within a couple of years he had opened his first shop in Chesterfield, selling ready-to-wear suits. By the outbreak of war his empire had expanded to 14 shops and a manufacturing facility in Leyland. By now his made-to-measure service was the largest in the world. The war provided the opportunity for rapid expansion as he transferred his production from suits to uniforms. Despite marrying in 1909 he had retained his own name of Mashe David Osinsky. By 1917 this was causing problems and he listed his name as Montague Burton on his son's birth certificate (the name of his first shop in Chesterfield). It was reckoned that Burton manufactured about a quarter of all British service uniforms during the war. The rise to riches was far from complete as the company moved to the Hudson Road factory in Leeds, where eventually he employed 10,000 people and produced over 30,000 suits a week. Like Spedan Lewis he was considered a good, yet autocratic, employer. The staff canteens were excellent, providing tasty food at a low cost. He even employed a staff dentist and an eye specialist, recognising the strain caused by focussed needlework. Burton was obviously a driven man, but also a role model for others to follow. He was knighted in 1971.

Just prior to the war there had been dozens of chain stores with 10 or more outlets and in 1919 the real advantages gained by the multiples began to crystallise. In addition to the increased buying power allowing them to obtain better prices, their corporate identity, company logo and uniform store layout offered the consumer a sense of familiarity and imbued trust. Staff training was introduced, although the speed of each transaction was considered more important than the 'fawning' attention encouraged in the department stores. For the multiple stores everything was designed to give value for money, rather than cosseting the customer.

W. H. Smith used the rapid growth of the railway network to expand their business. The first bookstall opened at Euston in 1848 and hundreds of others followed across the country. In 1905 the Great Western Railway, together with the London and North Western, imposed steep rental increases. W. H. Smith promptly set about opening hundreds of branches in streets leading to the stations. These were the forerunners of the high street newsagents and booksellers that are still around today.

By 1919 the company livery and store layout provided the consumers with a brand that they were familiar with and which could be trusted.

Whilst individual grocers continued to thrive, food was an obvious target for multiple stores. Immediately after the Great War the Home & Colonial Stores were the market leader, with several hundred outlets. It was a lead that was shortly to be overtaken by another great name in British retailing. John Sainsbury was described in the *Grocer's Gazette* as 'an unapologetic dictator', but it was his vision and drive that set the benchmark for food retailing in Britain and pointed the way towards the supermarkets we know today.

Sainsbury's celebrated their 50th anniversary in 1919, by which time they were operating from over 120 stores. An advertisement extended 'hearty thanks for the loyal support of our customers during the food control year just closed.' (Butter, margarine and lard remained rationed). It continued, 'We are most anxious to see a speedy return to the Sainsbury standards and quality and price, and customers may rely upon our making the greatest efforts to serve them in this direction.'

Sainsbury's was one of the first retail companies to give all their shops a standard corporate look. They were already embracing a managerial ethos popular in the US. By 1909 the company had published their first rulebook for branch managers. It defined opening hours and standards of staff dress and behaviour. In addition, it gave advice on store display, stock control and the monitoring of sales by identifying the fastest-selling and most profitable products. Each shop was laid out with marble-topped counters, behind which immaculately dressed assistants stood by, anxious to help. The bacon department alone employed several staff, each rasher was sliced to order. The butter and cheese were also sold in individual portions. There was a sense of theatre. The smart uniforms of the assistants, topped by crisp white aprons, were set against a background of white-tiled walls. The abiding memory was the smell. The wonderful aroma of coffee and tea competed with cured bacon. The coffee was ground and blended to each customer's requirements. There was still relatively little pre-packaged food. Most items had to be weighed and wrapped. There was always a large selection of teas available, most of which were measured direct from wooden tea chests. There was a set ritual and skill in the way each item was prepared, whilst the customer sat at the counter chatting to the assistant. Grocery shopping was still a social as much as an essential activity.

Marks & Spencer's can trace their origins back to Leeds market in the 1880s. The firm grew on the back of the slogan 'Don't ask, it's a penny.' By 1919 the penny bazaar format had been dropped and replaced by a new maximum price of five shillings. During the war the stores had concentrated on small haberdashery items like buttons and elastic, needles and thread, all necessary for mending clothes during a period of restricted supply. With the end of the war the larger stores now concentrated on supplying clothes and textiles. American trading methods were being instituted by Simon Marks, the dynamic son of the founder of the company. He was exploring the possibility of forming partnerships with his leading suppliers. Meanwhile, unlike most British shops, he displayed his goods on open trays for customers to inspect rather than tucking them away behind counters. Although the shops remained mostly based in the north of England, they now numbered around 150. Of these, 126 were turning over less than £5,000 per year, with even the most successful not breaking the £10,000 barrier.

Despite this, the multiple stores were on the march and in the process changing the face of British retailing. The shopper was now being offered an extraordinary choice, from the attention and service of the local shops to the grandeur and excitement of the department stores, but it was the multiple groups with their modern marketing and cheaper prices that were fuelling the British obsession with shopping. Some customers still travelled to the stores by bus or train, whilst others caused a stir in their gleaming new motor cars.

20

CUTTING A DASH

It is not just Britain that produces snobs. That American arbiter of taste, Lucius Beebe, declared, 'How you travel is who you are.' A whole new world of travel opportunities was opening up and, as ever, there was a section of British society keen to do it in style. The love affair Britain had with the car before the war accelerated in 1919 with a sales boom. The urge for freedom to roam, started by the humble pedal bicycle, had extended into motorcycle and car ownership. Horizons were widened, allowing people to travel hundreds of miles from their home, with the adventurous even venturing onto the Continent.

'What I want to do when peace comes,' Harold Nicholson wrote longingly towards the end of the war, 'is to motor in a two-seater through France and Spain.' He added, 'I have no wish at all to fit on a stand-up collar and go to a reception at Londonderry House.' He was not alone. There was a shared longing to get away across the country, away from the war and the restrictions it continued to impose.

The rise in car ownership was estimated at about 180,000, with another 280,000 motorcycles careering around the country. A speed limit of 25 mph was largely being ignored, despite safety not being a priority in car design. Statistics for road accidents were not compiled until 1926 but there were doubtless many accidents, particularly as there was no requirement to take a driving test before being let loose on the road. My father told the story of how his first ride on a motorcycle was hair-raising, and only ended when he ran out of petrol, having been unable to locate the brakes. Although the roads outside the major cities were largely deserted, traffic congestion soon became a problem, particularly in central London. Horse-drawn vehicles and carts still jostled for space in a chaotic and bad-tempered melee. Traffic jams were often the result of frequent breakdowns, with many cars being extremely unreliable.

Guests visiting a stately pile for the weekend now tended to arrive by car rather than horse-drawn carriage. A van containing all the clothes and sporting gear was frequently sent in advance, so everything would be in place by the time they arrived. More modest cars were also beginning to appear in less fashionable areas and in the suburbs there was much twitching of net curtains as a neighbour parked his new car ostentatiously outside his front door. There was already a healthy second-hand car market, and earnest young men spent hours tinkering under the bonnet of their newly acquired banger in preparation for a spin in the countryside with their girlfriend. Plain and boring men were suddenly transformed into desirable dates. Those who had avoided military service and done well out of the war were particularly reviled, but a smart car often overcame any prejudice.

One motor company dominated the British car market. Over 40 per cent of all cars sold were Fords. The first Ford car had been imported into Britain in 1903. It was priced at a hefty £750 and had a top speed of 28 mph. Initially production was a relatively drawn-out process. Cars were assembled to order by a small team of workers. By 1913 Ford had developed the basic techniques required for mass production, resulting in the world's first moving production line. This enabled a huge increase in the number of cars produced and in turn led to cheaper prices. There were now more than 20 Model T Fords being produced every hour. Suddenly, owning a car was not just for the wealthy.

Overseeing this commercial and social revolution was the brooding presence of the complex and controversial Henry Ford. A sparse, good-looking man, he possessed a restless desire for success and was something of an enigma. He paid his workers well and expected them to live sober and thrifty lives. He was a pacifist who gave much of the profits from his wartime production to the US government. He refused to deal with the unions but also had a deep distrust of Wall Street. It may have been his dealings there that led to his deep-seated anti-Semitism. Even in his business he could be dogmatic to his own detriment. He resisted the need to introduce a conventional gear stem for the Model T, preferring to stay with a method used on motorcycles. He was rigid in his diet, was known as a practical joker and an obsessive collector of Americana. A strange and difficult man.

In 1920 this generous, philanthropic, anti-Semite pacifist founded *The Dearborn Independent*, a newspaper reflecting his view that 'a vast Jewish conspiracy is infecting America.' A series of articles featured in the paper was published in four volumes titled *The International Jew*. In excess of 1 million copies were produced and distributed, in part through his massive dealership network. The book was also published in Germany, and Henry Ford had the dubious distinction of being the only American to be mentioned in Adolf Hitler's *Mein Kampf*. As the Model Ts continued to roll off the production line at Trafford Park in Manchester, it is doubtful that many British purchasers knew about Ford's racist views. They were just excited about owning their first car. Whilst there was a great number of manufacturers in Britain, most subsequently folded or became part of a corporate group.

In 1919 two leading British car brands were established, founded by men who achieved great success in their own lifetime. William Morris started his business career running a bicycle supply and repair shop. Realising the future lay in motor transport he sold the bicycle business and purchased a small garage. From these modest premises he repaired cars but also sold leading brands, including Humber and Singer. In 1913 he built his first Bullnose Morris, which sold for £145. By the following year he was producing a steady stream of cars, before the war intervened. During the hostilities he manufactured a range of munitions for the government, resuming car manufacture in 1919. He produced only 400 vehicles that year but by 1925 his Cowley factory was making over 50,000 cars. From bicycle shop owner to becoming Viscount Nuffield in a little over 30 years was some achievement.

Walter Owen Bentley was fascinated by speed from childhood. He left school at 16 to serve an exclusive five-year apprenticeship with the Great Northern Railway in Doncaster. He gained his engineering skills the hard way, through years of 'sweat and dirt'. He worked on the design and manufacture of locomotives in the foundry, together with the fitting and erecting workshops. Away from work he purchased his first motorcycle. In 1907 his passion for speed led him to enter the 400-mile London to Edinburgh race: quite a challenge in those days, but he achieved it within the allotted time, earning him a gold medal. With his background, and £2000 borrowed from his family, he became a director of the French car manufacturer DFP and also the concessionaire for their range in Britain. Taking further loans, he bought out his partners and, with his brother, formed Bentley and Bentley in 1912.

During the war Bentley was commissioned in the Royal Navy where he developed and improved a number of engines whilst working in an experimental department at Humber in Coventry. They were considered to be some of the most advanced aero-engines of their day. Discharged with a £2,000 gratuity in recognition of his wartime work, Bentley employed a number of his wartime colleagues to establish Bentley Motors Ltd in 1919. Bentley, together with Henry Varley, who had worked at Vauxhall, and Frank Burgess, from Humber, created an iconic brand of grand tourers produced at their factory in Cricklewood. Their mission was to produce cars of uncompromising luxury combined with outstanding performance. Doubtless the same principles apply today, although it is worth remembering when passing one of their imposing showrooms that their founder was someone prepared to get his hands dirty in pursuit of his dream; a reminder for those immaculately dressed showroom staff, perhaps. Not everyone was impressed by the relentless increase in engine capacity that characterised the Bentley marque. Rival Ettore Bugatti famously dismissed the Bentley as '*Le camion plus vite du monde*' – the world's fastest lorry.

A gleaming new Bentley was just a dream for most motorists. So too would have been a Vauxhall Interior Drive Cabriolet, advertised in *The Sphere* in July 1919 for £1,300. If the Ford T was also too expensive it was time, surely, to invest in a motorcycle? The AJS, made by A. J. Stevens and Co in Wolverhampton, was the ultimate in two-wheel transport. The quality was guaranteed by every part being made by hand. Cheaper alternatives were Triumph or Royal Enfield, both of which produced plenty of power and had a pillion for a long-suffering girlfriend. Improved technology was opening up a raft of opportunities for thousands of people to expand their world.

Whilst travelling by car or air was still a novel experience for most, it was, of course, the railways that had revolutionised 19th-century Britain. It was still exciting to take a long train journey. The crowded platform created an atmosphere of tension and anticipation. Porters heaved luggage aboard and waited, hand outstretched, for the expected tip. Sadness abounded as desolate lovers prepared to part. Passengers leant out from open windows to wave or watch the train prepare to leave. The guard's whistle marked the train's departure, against a background of belching smoke and soot, the great beast, snorting and snarling like an impatient horse being held at the tapes, would slowly gasp and groan as it pulled away. On board, each compartment was separated from the corridor by a sliding door. In first class the comfortably upholstered seats had armrests and antimacassars. Just under the luggage rack were colourful prints of places of interest and seaside towns, bathed in perpetual sunshine. The small sliding windows were kept firmly shut to avoid soot floating in and dirtying one's clothes. Gardens could be glimpsed alongside the platforms of smaller stations, each taking a pride in its pristine appearance, a feature marvelled at particularly by foreign travellers. Freshly prepared meals were available in the dining car, to be enjoyed whilst the constantly changing scenery went flashing by. Surprisingly good quality wine accompanied the food. On long-distance journeys down to Devon or Cornwall sleeper accommodation was available, as it was on the London to Edinburgh route, which could be completed in a little over seven hours. The perpetual motion of the train helped send you to sleep and before you knew it, a steward would be knocking on the door with an early morning cup of tea and a round of toast. Despite the changing face of travel a long journey by train could still evoke feelings of excitement and romance.

If you were looking for a combination of luxury and excitement a trip across the Atlantic in one of the great liners would fit the bill. Arriving by car in Southampton, passengers were escorted through the crowded departure lounge before climbing the gangplank and being welcomed by one of the ship's officers. There was only one snag. Great ocean liners like Cunard's *Aquitania* and *Mauritania*, together with White Star Line's *Olympic* had all been used during the war as troop carriers or served as hospital ships. Each ran what was termed an 'austerity' service towards the end of 1919, before being sent off to Tyneside or Belfast for a complete refit. Cunard did have some improvements for their 'austerity' passengers. The gunmetal grey used during the war was replaced with full Cunard livery, but the 1920s were the golden age of Atlantic travel. No doubt the 'austerity' service would have been considered quite acceptable by today's standards, but within months passengers would be offered comfort and cosseting not witnessed since. These ships were really 5-star floating hotels. The *Aquitania* had an Elizabethan grill and Louis XIV dining room, both furnished to replicate the period. There was a gentlemen's smoking room, a Palladian lounge and an Egyptian-themed swimming pool. 'B' deck was rather special. Reached by a number of fast-moving lifts, it was here that the most luxurious suites were found, each served by their own butler and with their own parlour and lounge. Named after artists such as Gainsborough, Reynolds and Van Dyke, they represented a world of sumptuous luxury. Throughout the rest of the ship, all areas in first and second class were panelled in the finest English timber. The furniture in both public rooms and in the cabins was made from walnut, and the chairs covered in petit point tapestry.

The *Aquitania* had 750 first class passengers, 600 in second and 2,000 crammed into third class. It was the *Aquitania's* captain, James Charles, who established the tradition of the captain's table, where he entertained important guests. Those travelling in first class were expected to wear full evening dress, complete with decorations. The ladies sported the latest gowns, whilst the family jewels were given an airing. The dining table groaned under the weight of the food on offer, ranging from roast oxen to grilled antelope, and reckoned to be better than any in a West End restaurant. It is doubtful if large numbers of people will ever travel in such comfort again. At the end of the voyage, with the sound of the ship's orchestra playing *Land of Hope and Glory*, the passengers ploughed into the hustle and razzmatazz that was New York.

Speed over comfort would eventually bring about the demise of the Transatlantic lines but, despite the heroics of Alcock and Brown, the competition from air travel appeared a long way off. Another less well-known Atlantic air crossing took place only a month after Alcock and Brown, in an airship. The R34 was originally commissioned by the government and developed to challenge German Zeppelins. By the time the giant airship was ready for service the war had ended. Built at an estimated cost of £250,000 and extending to the length of two football pitches, the R34 became the first airship to complete the return journey across the Atlantic and consolidated Britain's triumphs in aeronautics. After a series of test runs the R34 left East Fortune Aerodrome on 2 July 1919, under the command of Major G. H. Scott and a crew of thirty. Hammocks were erected between the walkway and a gramophone playing the latest jazz records provided the entertainment. To ease the payload some crew members had been left behind, but one was so disappointed that he hid between some girders and gasbags. The stowaway was discovered after he became nauseous. A second stowaway was Woopsie, the station cat. Undeterred, the R34 continued its journey, landing in Minneola Long Island on 6 July. Although they had started with almost 5000 gallons of fuel, by the time they landed they only had enough to last around another 40 minutes. Their outward journey had taken 108 hours and 12 minutes.

The airship stayed in America for three days before commencing the return trip. Huge crowds cheered as they set off at six minutes to midnight on Wednesday 10 July. One of the five engines was put out of action by a broken connection rod but the R34 continued at a sedate pace and completed the return journey in all the threes: three days, three hours and three minutes, and at an average speed of 43mph. Another trip into the unknown was successfully completed. This second aeronautical triumph within a month certainly raised spirits. The sky now really was the limit.

There appeared to be an opportunity for successful commercial airship flights. In August the first scheduled airship service was launched in Berlin, flying a Zeppelin LZ120. Germany had always been at the forefront of airship construction. Although flights continued for the next 20 years, progress was punctuated by well-publicised accidents, culminating in the Hindenburg disaster.

With a surplus of military aircraft coming onto the market it didn't take long for commercial airlines to appear. By March 1919 there was already an air service operating between Folkestone and Cologne. In May A. V. Roe opened Britain's first scheduled service from Manchester. In July Hounslow Heath became London's first commercial aerodrome, with Aircraft Transport & Travel (AT&T) flying a De Havilland DH9. Later in the year they started an international service to Le Bourget in Paris, incorporating the first scheduled air service, which made it, in effect, the world's first international service. By September Handley Page Transport Ltd was joining in the fun, flying converted wartime bombers from Cricklewood to Paris. Domestic flights were also viable propositions, and the British Aerial Transport Company started flights from London to Birmingham. There were also flights linking Leeds to Hounslow. Handley Page achieved a significant first by offering in-flight food at a cost of three shillings on their service to Brussels. It was from these modest beginnings that a giant aircraft industry developed.

In 1919 the aerodrome was renamed an airport. Based in Southampton, the Supermarine Company was fighting for survival. During the war they had developed a number of military flying boats. After buying them back, Supermarine converted and modified the flying boats for commercial use. It was hoped that lack of available airfields would boost their prospects, although they were never really practical as passenger planes. No matter, the press announced 'Southampton has become the world's first airport' and the name stuck.

The chance to fly to Paris attracted a number of affluent women to seek out Coco Chanel, a 36-year-old dress designer who was suddenly the talk of the fashion industry. She'd recently opened a sizeable boutique in the fashionable Rue Cambon. Starting from a small shop in Deauville she subsequently added a branch in Biarritz, which had maintained a neutral stance during the war. This enabled her to build up a wealthy clientele who were captivated by her ability to create clothes based, initially, on humble jersey fabric. Years later she said 'My fortune is built on that old jersey that I'd put on because it was cold in Deauville.'

An attractive woman, she took a succession of wealthy lovers who helped to finance her burgeoning career. Her expansion into Paris was partly bankrolled by a wealthy, well-connected, Englishman with whom she had been involved since 1910. In 1918 the dashing Boy Capel married the Honourable Diana Wyndham, whose first husband had been killed in 1914. This did not stop his affair with Coco, but 1919 turned out to be a bittersweet year for her. Despite the success of her new shop she was devastated by the death of her lover on 22 December in a motor accident, when he was supposedly on his way to spend Christmas with her. In a life of numerous affairs Chanel continued to claim that Boy Capel was the only true love of her life. She lamented, 'I have lost everything.' Her sense of loss was surely eased as her talent for designing clothes that had the 'luxury of simplicity' propelled her to international success. Within a few years she had branches in the world's most important capitals. Her association with the Nazis tarnished her legacy during the Second World War. Despite this she must rank as one of the most influential designers of the 20th century. Lady Diana Wyndham's response to her husband's death was no doubt complicated by her romantic association with Duff Cooper. The merry-go-round of affairs amongst the aristocracy was continuous. Too much time on their hands, perhaps?

A wide range of influences was beginning to dictate the fashion trends in department stores as well as couture houses. The flared skirt, generally retained during the war, was replaced by the 'barrel-line'. This created a tubular look. Whilst skirts were still long, designers were anxious to contain the female figure within the cylinder. It was the start of a boyish look that was to set the fashion tone in the 1920s. Young ladies with generous curves let fashion dictate that their busts had to be flattened. The waistline disappeared and was transferred to the hips in preparation for the 1920s flapper. The public mood was for escapism. The influence of jazz, film stars and the relaxation of convention were obvious. Having the vote encouraged women to expand their interests and take advantage of new opportunities that had previously been reserved for men. They couldn't wait to get behind the wheel of a car. Each new activity called for additions to their wardrobe. Despite most cars being closed in rather than exposed to the elements, the need arose for long driving coats. Alternatively, a leather jacket and huge driving gauntlets caused quite a stir.

Tennis parties were incredibly popular. It was too early for shorts to be acceptable so rallies were undertaken whilst wearing a jersey skirt, teamed with a blouse or sweater. Golf was increasing in popularity and female players might wear a chic beret to set off their tweed skirt and sturdy brogues. The thought of ladies wearing trousers on the links would have had members choking on their gin and tonics. Horsey ladies were already wearing baggy jodhpurs, and the one area where women could wear trousers without criticism was on the ski slopes. Burberry specialised in sportswear. Chunky knitted sweaters, wool scarves and fur-lined gloves were on offer, as well as brightly coloured ski suits and breeches. A trip to Switzerland in the winter was becoming a must for the *bon ton*.

For years it was thought that having a suntan was reserved for labourers and those working the land. The image of the pale English Rose was being undone with holiday trips by the wealthy to the south of France. Suddenly having a suntan indicated that you could afford to turn your back on the traditionally cold and damp British resorts. Sunbathing spawned a new industry, producing protective creams whilst swimwear designers were creating costumes that would have shocked previous generations. The old serge and wool swimwear made way for sleeveless designs in multi-coloured fabrics, still hardly revealing by modern standards but much more practical for swimming, and with not so much flesh on show as to inflame male viewers. The statutory rubber-swimming cap was something of a passion killer. Whilst the cosseted class bathed in the sunny Mediterranean, those staying at home braved the Channel and the North Sea, covered in goose pimples.

Foreign holidays and participating in exclusive sports were not options for most women. Dreaming is a form of escapism and the increased availability of ladies' fashion on show in department stores provided the opportunity. Window-shopping is free and the racks in the shops were bulging. The fashion and style column in the *Daily Mirror* reported,

There is a delightful gaiety about the shops in the West End. One is reminded at every turn that the war is really over and one may desire party frocks without any sense of guilt. The windows are a positive riot of attractive colourings, and those little vanities that are so dear to one's heart are back again.

The influence of art deco, jazz and folk art all jostled for attention in the stores and on the high street. There was a craze for far eastern design in dresses and fabrics. Liberty's helped promote an interest in design based on ancient Egypt. If foreign travel was out of the question, at least it was possible to transport yourself around the world through the clothes you wore. There was a gentle drift away from femininity towards the gamine look that dominated for large parts of the 1920s.

Whilst typists and domestic servants window-shopped, affluent women felt the need to change their clothes two or three times a day. A skirt and jumper in the morning, perhaps, suitable to instruct the housekeeper about the duties required of the staff that day. After a quick discussion with cook about the menu for dinner, another change for a ladies' lunch. Back home for yet another change into a brightly coloured frock to welcome the man of the house home, just in time for a swift cocktail before changing for dinner. Evening wear was an essential part of any lady's wardrobe and required constant visits to one's dressmaker for fittings, plus visits to favoured stores to keep abreast of the latest fashion trends.

The choice of dress depended on the importance of the occasion. Gowns were beautifully made, often with hand-finished embroidery or appliqué. They were usually calf- or ankle-length, often with a plunging low back. There were slinky silks or satins and sumptuous rich velvets in brilliant colours. The outfit might be rounded off with an intricately worked shawl or mantle and a small, tasselled brocade handbag. Soft leather shoes with two-inch heels would complete the look, creating what was hopefully a stunning impression. Men's evening dress was sedate by comparison. The long black tailcoat was worn with a white waistcoat, whilst the stiff, starched front of the dress shirt and winged collar was never comfortable to wear, particularly in hot weather or in a stuffy dining room. The white bow tie, and trousers with silk stripes to the sides and knife-edge creases, completed the outfit that was essential when attending formal events. The young much preferred the more relaxed dinner jacket or tuxedo, worn with white shirt and black tie. Some older men were also beginning to wear dinner jackets for private dinners, parties and less formal gatherings.

Whilst many had to make do with their demob suits, there was an attempt to break out from what was a very prescriptive dress code. Social etiquette was still considered important. Wearing brown shoes with a blue suit indicated a lack of breeding, whilst wearing grey shoes was the equivalent of walking into a crowded room with your fly buttons undone. Wearing an open neck shirt without a cravat would cause raised eyebrows. The list was endless, a constant trap awaiting the unwary. Standard daywear was a three-piece navy or grey suit. A black jacket with pinstripe trousers was favoured in the city and by bank managers and solicitors. At the weekend a well-cut tweed suit or a sports jacket worn with flannels was standard. 'Get a hat to get ahead' was popular advice and, because dress defined your social status, most men continued to wear hats. From the top hat and bowler to the ubiquitous cloth cap, each spoke volumes as to your background. The British (particularly the English) had a highly refined social radar that continued to influence every aspect of life. The 'old boy network' was at its height. Most placed more importance on where you came from rather than what you could do or where you were going, a code that was understood throughout society. Imposters were normally exposed, although exceptions were made for extreme wealth. It was an unhealthy background that blighted Britain's prospects within a changing world. Perhaps it was time to reflect.

21

TAKING STOCK

In the history of the world a year is just the blink of an eye, yet so much can happen: enough to change a life, a nation, or even the world. The year 1919 was a pause for breath in a world that was attempting to recover from a bout of madness. Britain was like a boxer who, despite being declared the winner, has been punched to the point of exhaustion.

After an initial flush of celebration, victory felt hollow and meaningless to most. This was illustrated at a huge gathering of recently discharged servicemen held in Hyde Park immediately after the Armistice. These were all men given an early release because of wounds or injuries sustained at the front. Dressed in civilian clothes but wearing a silver badge to indicate they had been honourably discharged they waited, lined up in mass ranks, to be inspected by their King. The authorities were worried about the effect the Russian revolution might have had on any 'hotheads' in the crowd. The reception given to the King astride his horse, accompanied by his two eldest sons, was certainly cool and sullen. Behind the King and his sons Queen Alexandra and Queen Mary travelled in a horse-drawn coach. There was little cheering, and a voice at the back of the crowd cried 'Where is this land fit for heroes?' The men were angry at the delay in the payment of their pensions. The future held out the prospect of prolonged unemployment, particularly for those severely injured. The crowd surged forward and broke ranks, surrounding the King's horse, and spooking those pulling the carriage of the Queen Alexandra and Queen Mary. The King was jostled but he remained calm, looking straight ahead. The crowd were not aggressive, but seemingly seeking the King's support. If he had been pulled from his horse the future of the country may well have been different. As it was, the popular Queen Alexandra continued to wave, the smile never leaving her face. Eventually the crowds parted and the royal party continued on its way to Buckingham Palace. A crisis had been averted but this was a warning of trouble to come as the New Year beckoned.

Perhaps it was hoped that the New Year would bring a change of mood, but it was as if the gods were conspiring to punish Britain for its victory. Scotland had contributed more than its fair share to the war effort, both in terms of losses of men and victories won. This certainly applied to the men from the Isle of Lewis. This outpost of Britain had lost about 1,000 men in the hostilities. On New Year's Eve the quayside at the Kyle of Lochalsh was crowded with servicemen looking forward to welcoming in the New Year in style. The regular ferry to Stornaway, the *SS Sheila*, was already full to capacity and the navy ordered *HMY Iolaire* to cross the Minch to pick up the remaining men. Before the war the *Iolaire* had been a luxury yacht, but during the previous four years it had been used by the Royal Navy as a patrol boat.

Arriving from Stornoway the *Iolaire* (Gaelic for 'sea eagle') was delayed as worries about her passenger capacity and safety implications were discussed. There were only two lifeboats and 80 lifejackets available. It also transpired that she had never previously sailed into the tricky Stornoway harbour at night. Matters were bought to a head when two trains arrived, packed with naval reservists. The pressure to take part in the New Year celebrations led to 284 men being allowed on the ship. She left at 9:30pm and it wasn't long before the wind increased and waves crashed onto the deck. This didn't dampen the spirits of the men, who were unaware of the dangers lying ahead. Gale-force winds whipped up huge waves but there was no alarm as the captain was familiar with the waters approaching Stornoway, although previously this had always been during the hours of daylight. He carried on in the darkness, with sleet further hampering visibility. Although they were within hailing distance of land, the ship overshot the harbour before smashing into 'The Beasts of Holm', a group of jagged rocks that were illuminated only by a flickering warning light. There remains doubt about what led to this catastrophic lack of judgment. A rumour concerning drunkenness among the crew has never been silenced or proved. On impact with the 'Beasts' the *Iolaire* went over instantly, throwing many passengers overboard into the freezing sea. The tragedy was that she was only about 20 yards from land. Some men who hadn't been thrown into the raging sea jumped in anyway, confident they could swim ashore. Most were dashed against the rocks. By 3 o'clock the ship's back broke and she went down.

John McLeod managed to swim ashore and then threw ropes to other survivors flailing about in the water. He managed to pull 25 ashore in an act of strength and bravery still remembered today. For those relatives and friends waiting to welcome their loved ones it was a ghastly start to the New Year. Over 200 of those on board the *Iolaire* perished that night. As news of the disaster filtered out it only added to the general feeling of disenchantment felt across the country. With the Spanish 'flu epidemic still taking its toll, it was as if fate was conspiring to punish the country. Coupled with unemployment and lack of housing, perhaps victory had been achieved at too great a cost. But the human spirit rarely remains subdued for long.

The young represented the future. The importance of the next generation in filling the gap left by the huge loss of young men was obvious. Education could provide the answer and yet it was the difference in opportunities available between those attending private and state schools that created an ongoing problem, an automatic and early establishment of social division. They did at least have one thing in common. Attending school was tough and sometimes barbaric. Pupils in inner city or village schools were frequently taught by one teacher, who covered the entire syllabus. Lack of books saw many learn to write on slates with chalk. Discipline was fierce and, if thought necessary, facts were literally beaten into the youngsters. It sort of worked in one way, as it is noticeable that letters sent home by soldiers at the front were almost invariably written in a neat hand and with correct spelling. Of course there were children who struggled, but overall it was a generation that was encouraged to become inquisitive and knowledgeable through extensive reading.

Life at Britain's most exclusive public schools was, if anything, even tougher than the state sector. Shipped off, often at the age of seven, young boys were subject to bullying by masters wearing gowns and ruling like gods. It has often been noted that men from private school backgrounds who fall foul of the law take prison in their stride. Lack of privacy, harsh discipline and foul food is nothing that they haven't already experienced.

The segregation of the education system created a gap that in a socially conscious society remained with most throughout their lives. For the public schoolboys it engendered a tribal sense of belonging to a protected club that underlined the social pecking order. For some, including the priggish 16-year-old Evelyn Waugh, it provided an unwarranted sense of superiority. A homosexual scandal at Sherborne School involving his elder brother Alec saw Evelyn being sent to Lancing College, presumably to distance him as far as possible from the source of the shame. Lancing, whilst not in the top league of private schools, had a reputation for inculcating High Church principles. The young Waugh declared his first day at Lancing to be 'generally damnable'. A month later he seemed to be getting used to his new surroundings. The entry in his diary for October 24 describes an exam he was taking with the school's Combined Cadet Corps. An address, made by the officer in charge, 'gave us to expect the most fearful flood of the guards-major type for the inspection. When we got down there we found the most blatantly man from the ranks I've ever seen. He was not even a temporary gentleman but a permanent oik.' In later life Waugh did admit he was appalled by the 'consistent caddishness' expressed in his youthful diaries. It does emphasise the class divide and the sense of superiority felt by some of those from a relatively privileged background. It was a peculiarly British custom to judge people on their accent and family background.

Despite the continuing social divisions, it was the perceived fall in moral standards that was causing wider concern. There had been a huge increase in illegitimate births during the war. This was compounded by a massive rise in the number of reported cases of venereal diseases. All those visits to French and Belgian brothels were bearing poisonous fruit at home. It was considered by many to be a national disgrace. Young girls had been put under increasing pressure to 'throw their hat over the haystack' by young men going off to war or home on leave. It was often the most gullible and innocent girls who fell pregnant. There was so much ignorance about sex that many girls didn't even understand what was happening to them as their waistline expanded. It is difficult for us to appreciate this total lack of knowledge, but sex was seldom discussed openly. Some believed that even kissing was likely to produce a baby. It is obvious that many young girls did succumb and had to live with the consequences. Having a child out of wedlock was considered to bring shame on the entire family. The term 'bastard' was not just a swear word but a burden to be carried through life. To avoid gossip, girls were sent off to distant aunts. The stigma was even worse in Catholic Ireland where young women were consigned to the mercy of sanctimonious nuns and work in the convent laundry. It is estimated that about 10,000 women, or rather girls, passed through the infamous Magdalene Laundries from 1922 to the almost unbelievably recent date of 1996.

Giving birth was still a dangerous business. Any well-to-do young lady who fell for the charms of a groom or someone from a lower social standing and became pregnant was dispatched abroad in the hope that a suitable home could be found for the baby. Then, hopefully, the young lady could return home to society with her reputation unblemished. Marriage amongst the upper crust was often more to do with furthering family fortunes than love. It was hoped that a son and heir, plus a spare, would ensure the family line before a more liberal approach to marriage could be undertaken, providing, of course, discretion was exercised. Hypocrisy was alive and well in Britain. The discretion shown by the gilded few was mirrored by the rest of the population, with no one wanting to 'wash dirty linen' in public. On the surface all must appear well ordered and respectable, meanwhile the streets of Britain's leading towns and cities continued to be lined with prostitutes, many of whom were under age.

It was against this background that a young Scottish woman emerged to change Britain's perceptions about sex and birth control. Marie Stopes was born in Edinburgh in 1880. A former suffragist with an academic background, she qualified as a paleobotanist before marrying Reginald Gates in 1911. The marriage was never consummated, which obviously led to tensions and the eventual breakdown of the relationship. It is unclear whether her husband was impotent or a homosexual. She avoided the stigma attached to divorce with the marriage being annulled in 1914. Despite her own lack of experience, she wrote a book emphasising the importance of sexual love. Initially, publishers shied away from such a controversial subject. In 1918 she remarried. Humphrey Roe was a wealthy industrialist and it was with his financial backing that a publisher was found. Her book *Married Love* was published in the same year as her marriage and it caused a mighty stir. It was condemned by the Church, whilst the Royal Society of Medicine described it as being 'deleterious and dangerous'. Thousands of copies were sold within weeks of publication. Her dramatic advice to women was to be 'neither simply maternal nor unashamedly loose'. A taboo had been broached; suddenly women were being advised to enjoy sex without feeling wanton or sinful.

An even more important part of Stopes's message was to use contraception rather than relying on the rhythm method or the 'hope for the best' approach. She set out to cut the number of unwanted pregnancies, particularly amongst the poorest in society. Anaesthetic was only available to those who could afford it. A further book, *Wise Parenthood*, was published in 1919. Continuing with her theme she appealed to men to 'remember each act of union must be tenderly wooed for and won.' Probably a forlorn hope, but Stopes had been successful in opening up a national debate, albeit one normally only discussed in the privacy of the bedroom. Her views also gave rise to a raft of jokes that Marie certainly would not have approved of. However, the importance of her views was underlined by the author Arnold Bennett in his introduction to *Wise Parenthood*: 'The wise progress of the idea of birth regulation is one of the outstanding social phenomena of the times. But it cannot astonish the thoughtful, for the idea appeals almost irresistibly to the common sense and the conscience of civilised beings, and nothing save superstition and ignorance can impair or impede its triumph.' He was right.

It is strange that two women who were to have such an effect on the slow march to equality should have been born within 15 months of each other. Nancy Astor was born into a poor family in Virginia in 1879. The family's fortunes improved vastly when her father moved in to the construction business and she was packed off to finishing school to enable her to mix comfortably in high society. The money was obviously well spent as she managed to net Robert Gould Shaw II, a leading socialite. A teenage bride, she duly produced a son in 1898, but the marriage was already in trouble and they finally divorced in 1903. Undeterred, Nancy set off for England with her sister, Phyllis. Wealthy American 'belles' had a great track record in wowing, and ultimately marrying, British aristocrats. Being divorced and having a child would surely be a real handicap in storming the gates of buttoned-up British high society? Not for Nancy. Attractive, lively and witty, she was soon the centre of attention. She was introduced to Waldorf Astor, the son of the fabulously wealthy industrialist and philanthropist, Lord Astor. Already a member of parliament, Waldorf found he had much in common with Nancy. To start with they had both been born on the same day in 1879. Originally from New York, his father brought the family to England in 1903 and they became British citizens in 1909. It was a romance that was meant to be and they duly married. They were given the beautiful Cliveden Estate in Buckinghamshire as a wedding present from the noble Lord, and they also lived in one of London's finest houses in St James's Square when staying in the capital. A glittering social whirl awaited them when suddenly Nancy's father-in-law was struck down with a massive heart attack. With the death of his father Waldorf inherited the title but had to vacate his Parliamentary seat.

It is difficult to imagine a less likely candidate to become the first woman to take her seat in the House of Commons than Nancy Astor, but she was up for the fight. How could a twice-married American divorcee, living in the lap of luxury, ever hope to connect with the electorate? But she did. Winston Churchill, the Minister for War, was appalled. Never a great supporter of female suffrage, Nancy irritated him further with her strong views on teetotalism. She pointed out, 'I want to know when I have a good time.'

As she toured the Plymouth constituency she found she was getting huge support, particularly from women. People were won over by her informal, unstuffy style. She didn't avoid the most deprived parts of Plymouth, and she became adept at dealing with hecklers by diffusing the situation with a winning sense of humour. She wasn't standoffish, but approachable and down-to-earth. She became something of a symbol of hope for women, a new more assertive breed that she represented despite her background. Only a year earlier, another woman had made history in the 'Coupon' election after the war. Countess Markievicz had become the first woman to be elected to parliament when she was returned for the constituency of St Patrick's, Dublin. She insisted she was 'being imprisoned by a foreign enemy' and refused to take a seat. She went on to be one of Nancy Astor's fiercest critics, insisting that Nancy was so privileged that she was totally out of touch with the problems of ordinary people. Despite this, Astor was elected on 28 November as member for Plymouth, with a majority of 5,000. Along with Marie Stopes, Nancy Astor was laying down a marker for future generations of women to follow. Despite this we cannot ignore Stopes's enthusiasm for eugenics. She attended the inaugural congress of the Eugenics Society in 1912 and became a fellow in 1921. Her championing of birth control was indivisible from her elitist views on human perfectibility. In the following year she sent a round robin to the parliamentary candidates in the upcoming election:

I agree with the present position of breeding chiefly from the C3 population and burdening and discouraging the A1 is nationally deplorable [sic], and if I am elected to Parliament, I will press the

Ministry of Health to give such scientific information through the Ante-natal Clinics, Welfare Centres and other institutions in its control as will curtail the C3 and increase the A1.

Whilst some women were celebrating, homosexual men had to live secret lives. Homosexuality was known as the 'abominable crime' and subject to widespread opprobrium. Sexual activity between men was a crime and punishable by a lengthy spell in jail. Clubs and pubs known to be the haunts of 'queers' were subject to regular raids by the police. Well-known figures in the world of ballet and theatre were sometimes shielded by their celebrity or by bribes to the police. Many gay men chose marriage as a smokescreen. Lesbians were not subject to prosecution but were rather a subject of fascination that prompted much gossip and ribald jokes. It appeared the loucheness of Berlin had migrated to London, in the form of women with shorn hair, wearing dinner jackets and cavorting quite openly in clubs and restaurants. An aspiring 18-year-old actor called Noel Coward spent the night after the Victory Ball in the back of a Rolls-Royce with the opium-addicted bisexual, Antonio Candarillas. This slowly more open engagement with the topic of sexuality was illustrated by the screening of the first openly homosexual film in 1919. *Different from Others* was marketed as an educational film and was an instant hit at the box office. Made in Germany, it endorsed the general feeling in Britain that the Germans were both evil and dissolute.

Added to ongoing worries about moral decline was the prevalence of drug taking, particularly amongst the wealthy young. *The Tatler* reported quite openly on fashionable 'dope parties'. *The Daily Express* sent a reporter to investigate London's drug culture. What he discovered was a world of decadence. He wrote about a visit he made to a drugs party in Piccadilly. Getting slightly carried away, he referred to 'sensual curtains and hangings. Low-shaded purple lights and a wanton atmosphere of lassitude'. The host 'lisped like a woman, had a nervous, jerky movement of his hands and reeked overwhelmingly of perfume'. His hand was 'limp and clammy to touch. He had dull, heavy eyes, a languorous manner and a silent, almost cat-like gait.' One guest confided in the reporter that 'Doping is quite a hobby among society women in Paris.' Another told him, with typical British understatement, 'I knew a girl who used dope a lot. Her description of the sensation was most interesting!' Duff Cooper was worried about his wife's dependence on drugs. She did at least indulge in style, with her cocaine bought to her each morning in silver salt cellars. As the year drew to a close his worries increased. He reported in his diary that Diana had declined to have lunch as she was unwell.

> I thought she was looking very bad, obviously suffering from a debauch of morphine. When we got to bed I charged Diana with her naughtiness. At first she denied it but eventually confessed. I told her how ugly it made her look. Fear of ugliness is, I think, the best preventative!

Christmas offered a chance to throw off collective depression. The stores along Oxford Street and throughout the country were bulging with tempting gifts. Several fashion editors were suggesting that garments with feather trimmings were it. They continued with this theme by recommending a feather fan as a most acceptable present. There were examples that contained just one plume or, as an alternative, several feathers fitted into a long tortoiseshell handle. Charming little shoulder capes trimmed with ostrich feathers appeared – perfect for a Christmas party – whilst evening cloaks were much in vogue. For the men Moss Bros still used the phrase 'From khaki to mufti' in their advertising for a selection of town and country wear. The Savoy Hotel even offered their guests a personal shopper to help purchase their Christmas gifts. Turkeys, chickens and rabbits hung from butcher's hooks for those who could afford them. The staff on country estates and in grand old town houses worked endlessly to prepare for the guests due to arrive for the celebrations.

In contrast, young Bob Foskett, living in the village of Lubenham, near Market Harborough, joined his school friends to go carol singing. They ended up at Hothorpe Hall. When they had finished singing they were invited into the main hall where maids distributed mince pies from silver dishes and glasses of hot punch for the adults. Then it was back home to the small family cottage. With the house full of visiting relatives, the excited children were put to bed, sleeping head to toe. Whilst they slept, a relative went out with a billhook and returned with the biggest branch they could find. This was placed in a bucket and decorated with tinsel and lighted candles. When the children awoke in the morning the cottage had been transformed with holly and paper chains. For even the poorest homes it was a time for celebration. For those living in the country, next morning it was off to watch the local hunt gather for the traditional Boxing Day meet. Whilst so much in Britain was changing, centuries-old traditions lived on.

As the New Year approached it was time to reflect. It had been a difficult year, despite the sense of hope and excitement experienced with the ending of the war. A constant tussle of conflicting emotions where sadness and grief collided with the need to look to the future. Huge crowds gathered in Trafalgar Square and at St Paul's Cathedral on New Year's Eve. They sang *Land of Hope and Glory* and on the stroke of midnight joined hands to bellow out *Auld Lang Syne*. There was hardly a military uniform to be seen. The pause for breath after the greatest conflict the world had ever witnessed was over. A new decade beckoned.

SELECT BIBLIOGRAPHY

Berry, Claude *The Racehorse in Twentieth Century Art* (The Sportsman's Press, 1989).

Blum, Daniel *Silent Screen* (Spring Books, 1953).

Cox, Edward *In Our Own Fashion* (Harley Publishing, 1956).

Cannadine, David *George V: The Unexpected King* (Allen Lane, 2014).

Chambers, James *The English House* (Methuen, 1985).

Cooper, Duff *The Duff Cooper Diaries* (Weidenfeld & Nicolson, 2005).

Coward, Noel *The Letters of Noel Coward* (Alfred Knopf, 2007).

Dasent, Arthur *Piccadilly: In Three Centuries* (Nonsuch Publishing, 2007).

Davis, John *A History of Britain* (Macmillan Press, 1999).

De Courcy, Anne *The Fishing Fleet* (Phoenix, 2012).

Donaldson, Francis *Edward IV* (Weidenfeld & Nicolson, 1974).

English, Alan *The Sunday Times Sporting Century*.

Ereira, Alan *The People's England* (Routledge & Kegan, 1981).

Fowler, Edward *British Dance Bands* (Gramophone Publications, 1985).

Fox, Caroline *Stanhope Forbes and the Newlyn School* (David & Charles, 1993).

Grimes, Dorothy *Like Dew Before the Sun* (Dorothy Grimes, 1991).

Hopwood, Beverley *Green and Pleasant Land* (Macmillan, 1999).

Heron, Roy *The Story of a Sporting Artist* (Webb & Bower, 1983).

Huggins, Mike *Horseracing and the British* (Manchester University Press, 2003).

Jackson, Alan *London's Metroland* (Capital Transport Publishing, 2006).

Jackson, Stanley *The Savoy* (F. Muller, 1979).

Laver, James *Costume and Fashion* (Thames & Hudson Ltd, 1969).

Lethbridge, Lucy *Servants: A Downstairs View of Twentieth Century Britain* (Bloomsbury, 2013).

Linnane, Fergus *London Crime & Vice* (Sutton Publishing, 2005).

Masset, Claire *Department Stores* (Shire Library, 2012).

Massingberd, Hugh Watkin, David *The London Ritz: A Social and Architectural History* (Aurum Press, 1980).

Moynahan, Brian *The British Century* (Random House, 1997).

Nicolson, Juliet *The Great Silence* (John Murray, 2009).

Walter, Rose *Good Neighbours* (Cambridge University Press, 1942).

Wilson, Elizabeth, Yaylor, Louise *Through the Looking Glass: A History of Dress from 1860 to the Present Day* (BBC Books, 1989).

Winder, Robert *Bloody Foreigners: The Story of Immigration to Britain* (Abacus, 2004).

Yass, Marion *Britain Between the Wars* (Wayland, 1975).

INDEX